the

POWER

of

UNITY

the POWER *of* UNITY

OVERCOMING RACIAL DIVISIONS, REBUILDING AMERICA

COMPILED BY
BONNIE J. TAYLOR

WITH A FOREWORD BY
ROBERT C. HENDERSON

BAHÁ'Í
PUBLISHING

WILMETTE, ILLINOIS

Bahá'í Publishing
401 Greenleaf Avenue, Wilmette, Illinois 60091

22 21 20   4 3 2

Library of Congress Cataloging-in-Publication Data
Names: Taylor, Bonnie J., compiler.
Title: The power of unity : overcoming racial divisions, rebuilding America
/
    compiled by Bonnie J. Taylor.
Description: Wilmette, Illinois : Bahá'í Publishing, 2019. | Includes
    bibliographical references.
Identifiers: LCCN 2019003812 | ISBN 9781618511447 (alk. paper)
Subjects: LCSH: Bahai Faith. | Race relations—Religious aspects—Bahai
    Faith. | United States—Race relations. | Reconciliation—Religious
    Aspects—Bahai Faith. | Concord—Religious aspects—Bahai Faith.
Classification: LCC BP388.R44 P69 2019 | DDC 297.9/3176284—dc23
LC record available at https://lccn.loc.gov/2019003812

Cover design by Jamie Hanrahan
Book design by Patrick Falso

CONTENTS

FOREWORD

O Children of Men!

Know ye not why We created you all from the same dust? That no one should exalt himself over the other. Ponder at all times in your hearts how ye were created. Since We have created you all from one same substance it is incumbent on you to be even as one soul, to walk with the same feet, eat with the same mouth and dwell in the same land, that from your inmost being, by your deeds and actions, the signs of oneness and the essence of detachment may be made manifest. Such is My counsel to you, O concourse of light! Heed ye this counsel that ye may obtain the fruit of holiness from the tree of wondrous glory.

—Bahá'u'lláh, the Hidden Words, Arabic, no. 68

This book is about unity—what unity is, how unity works, and the work that unity does. Its contents are drawn from the Bahá'í writings and expatiate on the central organizing principle of the Bahá'í Faith, the oneness of humankind.

From its inception in 1863 the Bahá'í community was dedicated to the principle of the unity of all peoples. Bahá'u'lláh, Prophet-Founder of the Bahá'í Faith, established the oneness of humankind as the Faith's organizing principle. His teachings specifically forbade slave trading, made eliminating racial prejudice a spiritual law of the Faith, encouraged interracial marriage, and explained that the unity of the races is a precondition to the establishment of everlasting social justice and peace within and among nations.

In the practice of the Bahá'í teachings,

Bahá'ís rely upon faith in God, daily prayer, meditation, and study of the sacred texts to effect the transformation of character necessary for personal growth and maturity; however, their aim is to create a world civilization that will in turn react upon the character of the individual.

. . .

Guided and inspired by such principles, the Bahá'í community has accumulated more than a century of experience in creating models of unity that transcend race, culture, nationality, class, and the differences of sex and religion, providing empirical evidence that humanity in all its diversity can live as a unified global society. Bahá'ís see unity as the law of life; consequently, all prejudices are perceived as diseases that threaten life.[1]

The Bahá'í teachings state clearly that prejudices of all kinds are destructive of the "divine foundations" of God's purpose for creation. They emphasize that all of the warfare and bloodshed in human history has been the outcome of prejudice of some kind, whether it is of race, religion, nationality, or ethnicity.[2]

Moreover, Bahá'ís believe that diversity is an indispensable element of unity. That the full beauty, power, and potential of individual human beings—the families they establish; the communities in which they reside; and, the nations from which they hail—become manifest as they build bonds and ties that are stronger than blood among people of diverse backgrounds.

While the Bahá'í teachings are global in scope and application, they also speak specifically to America and to the imperative of eliminating racial prejudice as a necessary prerequisite to the achievement of world peace in which, Bahá'ís believe, America is destined to play a leading role. The Bahá'í writings express the confident hope that the *"American democracy be the first*

---

1. National Spiritual Assembly of the Bahá'ís of the United States, *The Vision of Race Unity: America's Most Challenging Issue*, pp. 11–12.
2. 'Abdu'l-Bahá, *The Promulgation of Universal Peace*, p. 401.

nation to establish the foundation of international agreement," "the first nation to proclaim the universality of mankind," and "the first to upraise the Standard of the Most Great Peace."[3]

The Bahá'í teachings establish the urgency and priority of the struggle to build unity among the races and links them directly to the refinement of spirit and character among individual Bahá'ís, the development of the Bahá'í community itself, and the transformation of the American nation and of global civilization. Bahá'ís believe that the "transformation of the nation as a whole begins with the initiative and change of character of the individuals who compose it."[4]

In the light of the Bahá'í Faith's mission of race unity, it is hardly surprising that Thornton Chase, the first American Bahá'í (1894) and a white man, was a distinguished captain of black troops in the Civil War. After the war, Chase taught in a school for black children.

As if by an act of providence, the American Bahá'í community was thus seeded by a man who had committed his life to the emancipation of slaves and the education and development of black people in order to promote the advancement of racial equality and social justice in the newly salvaged American nation.

In 1912, early in the American Bahá'í community's development, when 'Abdul-Bahá, the son and appointed successor of Bahá'u'lláh, came to the United States, His emphasis on the importance of race unity was so clear and consistent that the *New York Times* described His mission as being "to do away with prejudices . . . prejudice of nationality, of race, or religion." They quoted Him as saying, "The time has come for humanity to hoist the standard of the oneness of the human world, so that dogmatic formulas and superstitions may end."[5]

---

3. Ibid., p. 49.

4. National Spiritual Assembly of the Bahá'ís of the United States, *The Vision of Race Unity: America's Most Challenging Issue*, p. 11.

5. "A Message from 'Abdu'l-Bahá, Head of the Bahá'ís," *New York Times*, April 21, 1912; see *Star of the West*, vol. 9, p. 360.

During His 239-day tour of the United States, 'Abdul-Bahá demonstrated by word and deed the primacy of the principle of race unity. He poured attention on black children, calling them black roses. He insisted on the integration of a dinner party among white well-to-do Bahá'ís by refusing to be seated until a black guest, Mr. Louis Gregory, could be retrieved and seated next to Him. He lavished special praise on interracial gatherings, which he addressed, consistently expressing his special happiness to see the races gathered together. He spoke at Howard University and the Annual Conference of the National Association for the Advancement of Colored People, explaining the social and spiritual importance of race unity and social justice. And, He warned audiences that because race unity was a prerequisite to peace, failure to make progress would cause the streets to "run with blood."[6]

'Abdul-Bahá blazed the trail of race unity and social justice at a time in American history when the "Jim Crow" segregation laws had gained impetus from the 1885 Supreme Court ruling that the 14th Amendment to the U.S. Constitution did not protect any black person from discrimination by private businesses and individuals, but only from discrimination by states. The ruling strengthened a racial caste system that was "reinforced from the pulpits of many of America's churches, and pronounced as evident truth by scientists who claimed that persons of color were innately inferior both intellectually and culturally to whites."[7]

During the "Red Summer" of 1919, when the blood of racial warfare ran in the streets of Chicago, St. Louis, Cincinnati, the District of Columbia, and thirty-seven other cities throughout the United States, 'Abdul-Bahá instructed American Bahá'ís to convene a race amity conference, the first ever held in the history of the country.

A few years later, Shoghi Effendi, then the Guardian and Head of the Bahá'í Faith, reminded the American Bahá'ís of the example of 'Abdul-Bahá, explaining that the growth and social influence of the Bahá'í Faith would

---

6. 'Abdu'l-Bahá, quoted in Shoghi Effendi, *Citadel of Faith*, p. 126.
7. "Race Unity in America: An Active Movement Since 1912." https://ohiobahai.org/race-unity-in-america-an-active-movement-since-1912/

depend, to a large degree, on the progress of their efforts to foster unity among the races. He emphasized that freedom from racial prejudice was the "supreme injunction" of the Faith of Bahá'u'lláh and the "hallmark of a true Bahá'í character." And, he explained that while conferences and banquets are important, the mission of the Bahá'í Faith is to bring about a complete transformation in the spirit and character of the individual in order to establish spiritual unity and social justice in the greater community and in the nation as a whole.[8]

He called upon Bahá'ís to search their hearts and rid them of any trace of bias, saying: "Let every believer, desirous to witness the swift and healthy progress of the Cause of God, realize the twofold nature of his task. Let him first turn his eyes inwardly and search his own heart and satisfy himself that in his relations with his fellow-believers, irrespective of color and class, he is proving himself increasingly loyal to the spirit of his beloved Faith and to the example of ['Abdul-Bahá]."[9]

He further instructed the Bahá'ís on a new course of community building, social action, and discourse, which has been sustained and reinforced for a century and continues to this day as core elements of the Five Year Plan currently underway among Bahá'ís throughout the world.

He wrote, "In their relations amongst themselves as fellow-believers, let them not be content with the mere exchange of cold and empty formalities often connected with the organizing of banquets, receptions, consultative assemblies, and lecture-halls."[10]

He went on to call for a pattern of community life characterized by intimate social relations among the races that would foster deep and lasting spirits of friendship and brotherhood.

He specified that in order to advance this mission, Bahá'ís must integrate every aspect of their lives, saying, "In their homes, in their hours of relax-

---

8. Shoghi Effendi, *Bahá'í Administration*, p. 130; ibid., quoted in *The Bahá'í World*, Vol. II, p. 23.

9. Shoghi Effendi, *Bahá'í Administration*, p. 130.

10. Ibid.

ation and leisure, in the daily conduct of business transactions, in the association of their children, whether in their study-classes, their playgrounds, and club-rooms, in short under all possible circumstances, however insignificant they appear, the community of the followers of Bahá'u'lláh should satisfy themselves that in the eyes of the world at large and in the sight of their vigilant Master ('Abdul-Bahá) they are the living witnesses of those truths which He fondly cherished and tirelessly championed to the very end of His days."[11]

Over a decade later, in 1938, Shoghi Effendi reinforced the urgency of this mission, saying, "As to racial prejudice, the corrosion of which, for well-nigh a century, has bitten into the fiber, and attacked the whole social structure of American society, it should be regarded as constituting the most vital and challenging issue confronting the Bahá'í community at the present stage of its evolution." He went on to explain the stringent demands of the Bahá'í mission, "the ceaseless exertions which this issue of paramount importance calls for, the sacrifices it must impose, the care and vigilance it demands, the moral courage and fortitude it requires, the tact and sympathy it necessitates, invest this problem, which the American believers are still far from having satisfactorily resolved, with an urgency and importance that cannot be overestimated."[12]

For over a century, American Bahá'ís have worked diligently to champion social justice and to build communities based on Bahá'í teachings and principles. They were active in the Civil Rights Movement and continue to this day to work with people and groups committed to interracial cooperation. They published books and documents, including a statement on race titled *The Vision of Race Unity: America's Most Challenging Issue*, conducted numerous studies in *Models of Unity: Racial, Religious, and Ethnic*, initiated thousands of race unity projects (2000 projects this year alone), and carried out a series of global plans aimed at adapting a community building process to the unique challenges of our contentious age.

---

11. Ibid.
12. Shoghi Effendi, *The Advent of Divine Justice*, ¶51.

This book is but one example. Originally published in 1986 under the title *The Power of Unity: Beyond Racial Prejudice*, the current edition is refreshed and expanded with guidance from the Universal House of Justice, the international governing body of the Bahá'í Faith, and the National Spiritual Assembly of the Bahá'ís of the United States, the governing body for American Bahá'ís.

The current edition includes recent letters from the Universal House of Justice guiding Bahá'ís to broaden their efforts to eliminate racial prejudice in light of the complexity of modern social reality. In the context of the growing diversity and the "multifaceted" and often "less blatant" but "more intractable" lingering expressions of racial prejudice so prevalent in today's world, the guidance of the Universal House of Justice provides a social and spiritual framework—encompassing community building, social action, and social discourse—designed to exert a shaping influence on ourselves, our neighborhoods, and on society as a whole.[13]

During His visit to the United States, 'Abdul-Bahá stressed that racial prejudice is, in essence, a spiritual problem that must be overcome by a superior power that will "overshadow the effect of all other forces at work in human conditions." "That irresistible power," He explained, "is the love of God."[14]

The guidance contained in this book rests on that unshakable conviction. And it goes further. It promises that if we take care to ingrain the spiritual imperative of unity in our habits of thought, our habits of the heart, and in our habits of behavior; and if we master the disciplines of community building, then, guided by the principle of oneness, we can transform ourselves and change the spiritual and material condition of our nation.

Robert C. Henderson

January 2019

---

13. The Universal House of Justice, letter dated 10 April 2011, to an individual believer.

14. 'Abdu'l-Bahá, *The Promulgation of Universal Peace*, p. 94.

ONENESS: OUR HUMAN REALITY

One Human Species

There is none other God but Him—He Who hath created you from a single soul, . . . (The Báb, *Selections from the Writings of the Báb,* no. 2:38:2)

The incomparable Creator hath created all men from one same substance, and hath exalted their reality above the rest of His creatures. (Bahá'u'lláh, *Gleanings from the Writings of Bahá'u'lláh,* no. 34.8)

Ye are all the leaves of one tree and the drops of one ocean. (Bahá'u'lláh, *Tablets of Bahá'u'lláh,* p. 129)

Verily God is fully capable of causing all names to appear in one name, and all souls in one soul. (Bahá'u'lláh, *Tablets of Bahá'u'lláh,* p. 183)

In like manner, when thou strippest the wrappings of illusion from off thine heart, the lights of oneness will be made manifest. (Bahá'u'lláh, *The Seven Valleys,* p. 38)

The children of men are all brothers, and the prerequisites of brotherhood are manifold. Among them is that one should wish for one's brother that which one wisheth for oneself. (Bahá'u'lláh, *The Tabernacle of Unity,* p. 41)

O CHILDREN OF MEN! Know ye not why We created you all from the same dust? That no one should exalt himself over the other. Ponder at all times in your hearts how ye were created. Since We have created you all from one same substance it is incumbent on you to be even as one soul, to walk with

3

the same feet, eat with the same mouth and dwell in the same land, that from your inmost being, by your deeds and actions, the signs of oneness and the essence of detachment may be made manifest. Such is My counsel to you, O concourse of light! Heed ye this counsel that ye may obtain the fruit of holiness from the tree of wondrous glory. (Bahá'u'lláh, The Hidden Words, Arabic, no. 68)

The gift of God to this enlightened age is the knowledge of the oneness of mankind and of the fundamental oneness of religion. War shall cease between nations, and by the will of God the Most Great Peace shall come; the world will be seen as a new world, and all men will live as brothers. ('Abdu'l-Bahá, 'Abdu'l-Bahá in London, pp. 19–20)

God, the Almighty, has created all mankind from the dust of earth. He has fashioned them all from the same elements; they are descended from the same race and live upon the same globe. He has created them to dwell beneath the one heaven. As members of the human family and His children He has endowed them with equal susceptibilities. He maintains, protects and is kind to all. He has made no distinction in mercies and graces among His children. ('Abdu'l-Bahá, The Promulgation of Universal Peace, p. 413)

He has said, and has guarded His statement by rational proofs from the Holy Books, that the world of humanity is one race, the surface of the earth one place of residence and that these imaginary racial barriers and political boundaries are without right or foundation. ('Abdu'l-Bahá, The Promulgation of Universal Peace, p. 324)

Prejudices of all kinds—whether religious, racial, patriotic or political—are destructive of divine foundations in man. All the warfare and bloodshed in human history have been the outcome of prejudice. This earth is one home and native land. God has created mankind with equal endowment and right to live upon the earth. As a city is the home of all its inhabitants although each may have his individual place of residence therein, so the earth's surface is one wide native land or home for all races of humankind. ('Abdu'l-Bahá, *The Promulgation of Universal Peace*, p. 401)

Reality is one and indivisible. Therefore, the prejudices and bigotries which exist today among the religions are not justifiable, inasmuch as they are opposed to reality. All prejudices are against the will and plan of God. Consider, for instance, racial distinction and enmity. All humanity are the children of God; they belong to the same family, to the same original race. There can be no multiplicity of races, since all are the descendants of Adam. This signifies that racial assumption and distinction are nothing but superstition. In the estimate of God there are no English, French, Germans, Turkish or Persians. All these in the presence of God are equal; they are of one race and creation; God did not make these divisions. These distinctions have had their origin in man himself. Therefore, as they are against the plan and purpose of reality, they are false and imaginary. We are of one physical race, even as we are of one physical plan of material body—each endowed with two eyes, two ears, one head, two feet. ('Abdu'l-Bahá, *The Promulgation of Universal Peace*, p. 416)

Bahá'u'lláh, addressing all humanity, said that Adam, the parent of mankind, may be likened to the tree of nativity upon which you are the leaves and blossoms. Inasmuch as your origin was one, you must now be united and agreed; you must consort with each other in joy and fragrance. He pronounced prejudice—whether religious, racial, patriotic, political—the destroyer of the body politic. He said that man must recognize the oneness of humanity, for all in origin belong to the same household, and all are servants of the same God. Therefore, mankind must continue in the state of fellowship and love, emulating the institutions of God and turning away from satanic promptings, for the divine bestowals bring forth unity and agreement, whereas satanic leadings induce hatred and war. ('Abdu'l-Bahá, *The Promulgation of Universal Peace*, p. 172)

In the human kingdom itself there are points of contact, properties common to all mankind; likewise, there are points of distinction which separate race from race, individual from individual. If the points of contact, which are the common properties of humanity, overcome the peculiar points of distinction, unity is assured. On the other hand, if the points of differentiation overcome the points of agreement, disunion and weakness result. One of the important questions which affect the unity and the solidarity of mankind is the fellowship and equality of the white and colored* races. Between these two races certain points of agreement and points of distinction exist which warrant just and mutual consideration. The points of contact are many; for in the material or physical plane of being, both are constituted alike and exist under the same law of growth and bodily development. Furthermore, both live and move in the plane of the senses and are endowed with human intelligence. There are many other mutual qualifications. In this country, the United States of America, patriotism is common to both races; all have equal rights to citizenship, speak one language, receive the blessings of the same civilization, and follow the precepts of the same religion. In fact numerous points of partnership and agreement exist between the two races; whereas the one point of distinction is that of color. Shall this, the least of all distinctions, be allowed to separate you as races and individuals? In physical bodies, in the law of growth, in sense endowment, intelligence, patriotism, language, citizenship, civilization and religion you are one and the same. A single point of distinction exists—that of racial color. God is not pleased with—neither should any reasonable or intelligent man be willing to recognize—inequality in the races because of this distinction. ('Abdu'l-Bahá, *The Promulgation of Universal Peace*, pp. 93–94)

"Throughout the animal kingdom," He ['Abdu'l-Bahá] explains, "we do not find the creatures separated because of color. They recognize unity of species

---

* The Central Figures of the Bahá'í Faith and Shoghi Effendi, in their talks, tablets, and letters, used terminology that was common and acceptable at the time.

and oneness of kind. If we do not find color distinction drawn in a kingdom of lower intelligence and reason, how can it be justified among human beings, especially when we know that all have come from the same source and belong to the same household? In origin and intention of creation mankind is one. Distinctions of race and color have arisen afterward." (Shoghi Effendi, *The Advent of Divine Justice*, ¶56)

In this wondrous Age, at this time when the Ancient Beauty, the Most Great Name, bearing unnumbered gifts, hath risen above the horizon of the world, the Word of God hath infused such awesome power into the inmost essence of humankind that He hath stripped men's human qualities of all effect, and hath, with His all-conquering might, unified the peoples in a vast sea of oneness.

Now is the time for the lovers of God to raise high the banners of unity, to intone, in the assemblages of the world, the verses of friendship and love and to demonstrate to all that the grace of God is one. Thus will the tabernacles of holiness be upraised on the summits of the earth, gathering all peoples into the protective shadow of the Word of Oneness. ('Abdu'l-Bahá, *Selections from the Writings of 'Abdu'l-Bahá*, no. 7.2–3)

We belong to an organic unit and when one part of the organism suffers all the rest of the body will feel its consequence. This is in fact the reason why Bahá'u'lláh calls our attention to the unity of mankind. . . . (On behalf of Shoghi Effendi, letter dated 14 April 1932, to a Bahá'í family, in *Lights of Guidance*, no. 446)

World order can be founded only on an unshakeable consciousness of the oneness of mankind, a spiritual truth which all the human sciences confirm. Anthropology, physiology, psychology, recognize only one human species, albeit infinitely varied in the secondary aspects of life. Recognition of this truth requires abandonment of prejudice—prejudice of every kind—race, class, colour, creed, nation, sex, degree of material civilization, everything which enables people to consider themselves superior to others. (The Universal House of Justice, *The Promise of World Peace*, ¶39)

The Divine Criterion for the Measurement of Humanity

All praise and glory be to God Who, through the power of His might, hath delivered His creation from the nakedness of nonexistence, and clothed it with the mantle of life. From among all created things He hath singled out for His special favor the pure, the gem-like reality of man, and invested it with a unique capacity of knowing Him and of reflecting the greatness of His glory. This twofold distinction conferred upon him hath cleansed away from his heart the rust of every vain desire, and made him worthy of the vesture with which his Creator hath deigned to clothe him. It hath served to rescue his soul from the wretchedness of ignorance.

This robe with which the body and soul of man hath been adorned is the very foundation of his well-being and development. Oh, how blessed the day when, aided by the grace and might of the one true God, man will have freed himself from the bondage and corruption of the world and all that is therein, and will have attained unto true and abiding rest beneath the shadow of the Tree of Knowledge! (Bahá'u'lláh, *Gleanings from the Writings of Bahá'u'lláh*, no. 34.1–2)

A good character is, verily, the best mantle for men from God. With it He adorneth the temples of His loved ones. By My life! The light of a good character surpasseth the light of the sun and the radiance thereof. Whoso attaineth unto it is accounted as a jewel among men. The glory and the upliftment of the world must needs depend upon it. A goodly character is a means whereby men are guided to the Straight Path and are led to the Great Announcement. Well is it with him who is adorned with the saintly attributes and character of the Concourse on High. (Bahá'u'lláh, *Tablets of Bahá'u'lláh*, p. 36)

This span of earth is but one homeland and one habitation. It behoveth you to abandon vainglory which causeth alienation and to set your hearts on whatever will ensure harmony. In the estimation of the people of Bahá man's glory lieth in his knowledge, his upright conduct, his praiseworthy character, his wisdom, and not in his nationality or rank. (Bahá'u'lláh, *Tablets of Bahá'u'lláh*, p. 67)

Then it is clear that the honour and exaltation of man cannot reside solely in material delights and earthly benefits. This material felicity is wholly secondary, while the exaltation of man resides primarily in such virtues and attainments as are the adornments of the human reality. These consist in divine blessings, heavenly bounties, heartfelt emotions, the love and knowledge of God, the education of the people, the perceptions of the mind, and the discoveries of science. They consist in justice and equity, truthfulness and benevolence, inner courage and innate humanity, safeguarding the rights of others and preserving the sanctity of covenants and agreements. They consist in rectitude of conduct under all circumstances, love of truth under all conditions, self-abnegation for the good of all people, kindness and compassion for all nations, obedience to the teachings of God, service to the heavenly Kingdom, guidance for all mankind, and education for all races and nations. This is the felicity of the human world! This is the exaltation of man in the contingent realm! This is eternal life and heavenly honor! ('Abdu'l-Bahá, *Some Answered Questions*, no. 15.7)

A good character is in the sight of God and His chosen ones and the possessors of insight, the most excellent and praiseworthy of all things, but always on condition that its center of emanation should be reason and knowledge and its base should be true moderation. ('Abdu'l-Bahá, *The Secret of Divine Civilization*, ¶108)

Thus man is a perfect mirror facing the Sun of Truth and is the seat of its reflection. The splendour of all the divine perfections is manifest in the reality of man, and it is for this reason that he is the vicegerent and apostle of God. ('Abdu'l-Bahá, *Some Answered Questions*, no. 50.4)

Let us now discover more specifically how he is the image and likeness of God and what is the standard or criterion by which he can be measured and estimated. This standard can be no other than the divine virtues which are revealed in him. Therefore, every man imbued with divine qualities, who reflects heavenly moralities and perfections, who is the expression of ideal and

9

praiseworthy attributes, is, verily, in the image and likeness of God. If a man possesses wealth, can we call him an image and likeness of God? Or is human honor and notoriety the criterion of divine nearness? Can we apply the test of racial color and say that man of a certain hue—white, black, brown, yellow, red—is the true image of his Creator? We must conclude that color is not the standard and estimate of judgment and that it is of no importance, for color is accidental in nature. The spirit and intelligence of man is essential, and that is the manifestation of divine virtues, the merciful bestowals of God, the eternal life and baptism through the Holy Spirit. Therefore, be it known that color or race is of no importance. He who is the image and likeness of God, who is the manifestation of the bestowals of God, is acceptable at the threshold of God—whether his color be white, black or brown; it matters not. Man is not man simply because of bodily attributes. The standard of divine measure and judgment is his intelligence and spirit.

Therefore, let this be the only criterion and estimate, for this is the image and likeness of God. A man's heart may be pure and white though his outer skin be black; or his heart be dark and sinful though his racial color is white. The character and purity of the heart is of all importance. The heart illumined by the light of God is nearest and dearest to God, and inasmuch as God has endowed man with such favor that he is called the image of God, this is truly a supreme perfection of attainment, a divine station which is not to be sacrificed by the mere accident of color. ('Abdu'l-Bahá, *The Promulgation of Universal Peace*, pp. 96–97)

If no fruits of the Kingdom appear in the garden of his soul, man is not in the image and likeness of God, but if those fruits are forthcoming, he becomes the recipient of ideal bestowals and is enkindled with the fire of the love of God. If his morals become spiritual in character, his aspirations heavenly and his actions conformable to the will of God, man has attained the image and likeness of his Creator; otherwise, he is the image and likeness of Satan. Therefore, Christ hath said, "Ye shall know them by their fruits." ('Abdu'l-Bahá, *The Promulgation of Universal Peace*, p. 475)

Then it is evident that excellence does not depend upon color. Character is the true criterion of humanity. Anyone who possesses a good character, who has faith in God and is firm, whose actions are good, whose speech is good—that one is accepted at the threshold of God no matter what color he may be. ('Abdu'l-Bahá, *The Promulgation of Universal Peace*, p. 602)

In the Kingdom of God no distinction is made as to the color of the skin, whether it be black or white; nay, rather the heart and soul are considered. If the spirit is pure, the face is illumined, although it be black. If the heart is stained, the face is dark and depressed, although it may be of the utmost beauty. The colour of the pupils of the eye is black, yet they are the fountains of light.

Although the white colour is apparent, yet in it is hidden and concealed seven colours. Therefore whiteness and blackness have no importance; nay, rather the circle of distinction is based upon soul and heart. ('Abdu'l-Bahá, quoted in *Star of the West*, vol. 7, no. 5, p. 106)

Bahá'u'lláh once compared the coloured people to the black pupil of the eye surrounded by the white. In this black pupil you see the reflection of that which is before it, and through it the light of the Spirit shines forth.

In the sight of God colour makes no difference at all, He looks at the hearts of men. That which God desires from men is the heart. A black man with a good character is far superior to a white man with a character that is less good. ('Abdu'l-Bahá, *'Abdu'l-Bahá in London*, p. 68)

. . . you all are the servants of one God and, therefore, brothers, sisters, mothers and fathers. In the sight of God there is no distinction between whites and blacks; all are as one. Anyone whose heart is pure is dear to God—whether white or black, red or yellow. ('Abdu'l-Bahá, *The Promulgation of Universal Peace*, p. 600)

Today I am most happy, for I see here a gathering of the servants of God. I see white and black sitting together. There are no whites and blacks before

God. All colors are one, and that is the color of servitude to God. Scent and color are not important. The heart is important. If the heart is pure, white or black or any color makes no difference. God does not look at colors; He looks at the hearts. He whose heart is pure is better. He whose character is better is more pleasing. He who turns more to the Abhá Kingdom is more advanced. ('Abdu'l-Bahá, *The Promulgation of Universal Peace*, p. 60)

He ['Abdu'l-Bahá] again affirms, "there is no distinction of color; all are one in the color and beauty of servitude to Him. Color is not important; the heart is all-important. It mattereth not what the exterior may be if the heart is pure and white within. God doth not behold differences of hue and complexion. He looketh at the hearts. He whose morals and virtues are praiseworthy is preferred in the presence of God; he who is devoted to the Kingdom is most beloved. In the realm of genesis and creation the question of color is of least importance." (Shoghi Effendi, *The Advent of Divine Justice*, ¶56)

Intense is the hatred, in America, between black and white, but my hope is that the power of the Kingdom will bind these two in friendship, and serve them as a healing balm.

Let them look not upon a man's color but upon his heart. If the heart be filled with light, that man is nigh unto the threshold of his Lord; but if not, that man is careless of his Lord, be he white or be he black. ('Abdu'l-Bahá, *Selections from the Writings of 'Abdu'l-Bahá*, no. 76.2–3)

The only difference lies in the degree of faithfulness, of obedience to the laws of God. There are some who are as lighted torches, there are others who shine as stars in the sky of humanity. The lovers of mankind, these are the superior men, of whatever nation, creed, or color they may be. For it is they to whom God will say these blessed words, "Well done, My good and faithful servants." ('Abdu'l-Bahá, *Paris Talks*, no. 45.13)

I desire distinction for you. The Bahá'ís must be distinguished from others of humanity. But this distinction must not depend upon wealth—that they should become more affluent than other people. I do not desire for you financial distinction. It is not an ordinary distinction I desire; not scientific, commercial, industrial distinction. For you I desire spiritual distinction—that is, you must become eminent and distinguished in morals. In the love of God you must become distinguished from all else. You must become distinguished for loving humanity, for unity and accord, for love and justice. In brief, you must become distinguished in all the virtues of the human world—for faithfulness and sincerity, for justice and fidelity, for firmness and steadfastness, for philanthropic deeds and service to the human world, for love toward every human being, for unity and accord with all people, for removing prejudices and promoting international peace. Finally, you must become distinguished for heavenly illumination and for acquiring the bestowals of God. I desire this distinction for you. This must be the point of distinction among you. ('Abdu'l-Bahá, *The Promulgation of Universal Peace*, pp. 265–66)

Indeed, man is noble, inasmuch as each one is a repository of the sign of God. Nevertheless, to regard oneself as superior in knowledge, learning or virtue, or to exalt oneself or seek preference, is a grievous transgression. Great is the blessedness of those who are adorned with the ornament of this unity and have been graciously confirmed by God. (On behalf of The Universal House of Justice, letter dated 27 March 1978, to all National Spiritual Assemblies)

Humanity's Common Bonds

We have created you from one tree and have caused you to be as the leaves and fruit of the same tree, that haply ye may become a source of comfort to one another. Regard ye not others save as ye regard your own selves, that no feeling of aversion may prevail amongst you. (The Báb, *Selections from the Writings of the Báb*, no. 5:1:1)

Illumine and hallow your hearts; let them not be profaned by the thorns of hate or the thistles of malice. Ye dwell in one world, and have been created through the operation of one Will. Blessed is he who mingleth with all men in a spirit of utmost kindliness and love." (Bahá'u'lláh, *Gleanings from the Writings of Bahá'u'lláh*, no. 156.1)

It is not for him to pride himself who loveth his own country, but rather for him who loveth the whole world. The earth is but one country, and mankind its citizens. (Bahá'u'lláh, *Gleanings from the Writings of Bahá'u'lláh*, no. 117.1)

Be ye aware that the children of men are sheep of God and He their loving Shepherd, that He careth tenderly for all His sheep and maketh them to feed in His own green pastures of grace and giveth them to drink from the wellspring of life. Such is the way of the Lord. Such are His bestowals. Such, from among His teachings, is His precept of the oneness of mankind. ('Abdu'l-Bahá, *Selections from the Writings of 'Abdu'l-Bahá*, no. 17.4)

Human brotherhood is, likewise, as clear and evident as the sun, for all are servants of one God, belong to one humankind, inhabit the same globe, are sheltered beneath the overshadowing dome of heaven and submerged in the sea of divine mercy. Human brotherhood and dependence exist because mutual helpfulness and cooperation are the two necessary principles underlying human welfare. This is the physical relationship of mankind. ('Abdu'l-Bahá, *The Promulgation of Universal Peace*, p. 208)

Indeed, the world of humanity is like one kindred and one family. Because of the climatic differences of the zones, through the passing of ages colors have become different. In the torrid zone, on account of the intensity of the effect of the sun throughout the ages the black race appeared. In the frigid zone, on account of the severity of the cold and the ineffectiveness of the heat of the sun throughout the ages the white race appeared. In the temperate zone, the yellow, brown and red races came into existence. But in reality mankind is one race. Because it is of one race unquestionably there must be unity and harmony and no separation or discord. ('Abdu'l-Bahá, quoted in *Star of the West*, vol. 13, no. 11, p. 307)

Humanity shares in common the intellectual and spiritual faculties of a created endowment. All are equally subject to the various exigencies of human life and are similarly occupied in acquiring the means of earthly subsistence. From the viewpoint of creation human beings stand upon the same footing in every respect, subject to the same requirements and seeking the enjoyment and comfort of earthly conditions. Therefore, the things humanity shares in common are numerous and manifest. This equal participation in the physical, intellectual and spiritual problems of human existence is a valid basis for the unification of mankind. ('Abdu'l-Bahá, *The Promulgation of Universal Peace*, p. 320)

All the powers and attributes of man are human and hereditary in origin—outcomes of nature's processes—except the intellect, which is supernatural. ('Abdu'l-Bahá, *The Promulgation of Universal Peace*, p. 67)

There is perfect brotherhood underlying humanity, for all are servants of one God and belong to one family under the protection of divine providence. The bond of fraternity exists in humanity because all are intelligent beings created in the realm of evolutionary growth. There is brotherhood potential in humanity because all inhabit this earthly globe under the one canopy of heaven. There is brotherhood natal in mankind because all are elements of one human society subject to the necessity of agreement and cooperation. There is brotherhood intended in humanity because all are waves of one sea, leaves and fruit of one tree. This is physical fellowship which ensures material happiness in the human world. The stronger it becomes, the more will mankind advance and the circle of materiality be enlarged.

The real brotherhood is spiritual, for physical brotherhood is subject to separation. The wars of the outer world of existence separate humankind, but in the eternal world of spiritual brotherhood separation is unknown. Material or physical association is based upon earthly interests, but divine fellowship owes its existence to the breaths of the Holy Spirit. Spiritual brotherhood may be likened to the light, while the souls of humankind are as lanterns. The incandescent lamps here are many, yet the light is one. ('Abdu'l-Bahá, *The Promulgation of Universal Peace*, p. 179)

What is real unity? When we observe the human world, we find various collective expressions of unity therein. For instance, man is distinguished from the animal by his degree, or kingdom. This comprehensive distinction includes all the posterity of Adam and constitutes one great household or human family, which may be considered the fundamental or physical unity of mankind. Furthermore, a distinction exists between various groups of humankind according to lineage, each group forming a racial unity separate from the others. There is also the unity of tongue among those who use the same language as a means of communication; national unity where various peoples live under one form of government such as French, German, British, etc.; and political unity, which conserves the civil rights of parties or factions of the same government. All these unities are imaginary and without real foundation, for no real result proceeds from them. The purpose of true unity is real and divine outcomes. From these limited unities mentioned only limited outcomes proceed, whereas unlimited unity produces unlimited result. For instance, from the limited unity of race or nationality the results at most are limited. It is like a family living alone and solitary; there are no unlimited or universal outcomes from it.

The unity which is productive of unlimited results is first a unity of mankind which recognizes that all are sheltered beneath the overshadowing glory of the All-Glorious, that all are servants of one God; for all breathe the same atmosphere, live upon the same earth, move beneath the same heavens, receive effulgence from the same sun and are under the protection of one God. This is the most great unity, and its results are lasting if humanity adheres to it; but mankind has hitherto violated it, adhering to sectarian or other limited unities such as racial, patriotic or unity of self-interests; therefore, no great results have been forthcoming. Nevertheless, it is certain that the radiance and favors of God are encompassing, minds have developed, perceptions have become acute, sciences and arts are widespread, and capacity exists for the proclamation and promulgation of the real and ultimate

16

unity of mankind, which will bring forth marvelous results. It will reconcile all religions, make warring nations loving, cause hostile kings to become friendly and bring peace and happiness to the human world. It will cement together the Orient and Occident, remove forever the foundations of war and upraise the ensign of the Most Great Peace. These limited unities are, therefore, signs of that great unity which will make all the human family one by being productive of the attractions of conscience in mankind. ('Abdu'l-Bahá, *The Promulgation of Universal Peace*, pp. 266–68)

Another unity is the spiritual unity which emanates from the breaths of the Holy Spirit. This is greater than the unity of mankind. Human unity or solidarity may be likened to the body, whereas unity from the breaths of the Holy Spirit is the spirit animating the body. This is a perfect unity. It creates such a condition in mankind that each one will make sacrifices for the other, and the utmost desire will be to forfeit life and all that pertains to it in behalf of another's good. This is the unity which existed among the disciples of Jesus Christ and bound together the Prophets and holy Souls of the past. It is the unity which through the influence of the divine spirit is permeating the Bahá'ís so that each offers his life for the other and strives with all sincerity to attain his good pleasure. This is the unity which caused twenty thousand people in Persia to give their lives in love and devotion to it. It made the Báb the target of a thousand arrows and caused Bahá'u'lláh to suffer exile and imprisonment forty years. This unity is the very spirit of the body of the world. It is impossible for the body of the world to become quickened with life without its vivification. ('Abdu'l-Bahá, *The Promulgation of Universal Peace*, p. 268)

THE PROCESS OF UNITY

Spiritual Transformation

UNITY—THE COMMANDMENT

God hath verily purposed to bring the hearts of men together, though it require every means on earth and in the heavens. (Bahá'u'lláh, in *Bahá'í Meetings: The Nineteen Day Feast*, p. 17)

The first utterance of Him Who is the All-Wise is this: O children of dust! Turn your faces from the darkness of estrangement to the effulgent light of the daystar of unity. This is that which above all else will benefit the peoples of the earth. O friend! Upon the tree of utterance there hath never been, nor shall there ever be, a fairer leaf, and beneath the ocean of knowledge no pearl more wondrous can ever be found. (Bahá'u'lláh, *The Tabernacle of Unity*, p. 7)

O humankind! Verily, ye are all the leaves and fruits of one tree; ye are all one. Therefore, associate in friendship; love one another; abandon prejudices of race; dispel forever this gloomy darkness of human ignorance, for the century of light, the Sun of Reality hath appeared. Now is the time for affiliation, and now is the period of unity and concord. For thousands of years ye have been contending in warfare and strife. It is enough. Now is the time for unity. Lay aside all self-purposes, and know for a certainty that all men are the servants of one God Who will bind them together in love and agreement. (Bahá'u'lláh, quoted by 'Abdu'l-Bahá, *The Promulgation of Universal Peace*, pp. 458–59)

21

Today the one overriding need is unity and harmony among the beloved of the Lord, for they should have among them but one heart and soul and should, so far as in them lieth, unitedly withstand the hostility of all the peoples of the world; they must bring to an end the benighted prejudices of all nations and religions and must make known to every member of the human race that all are the leaves of one branch, the fruits of one bough. ('Abdu'l-Bahá, *Selections from the Writings of 'Abdu'l-Bahá*, no. 221.4)

In every dispensation, there hath been the commandment of fellowship and love, but it was a commandment limited to the community of those in mutual agreement, not to the dissident foe. In this wondrous age, however, praised be God, the commandments of God are not delimited, not restricted to any one group of people, rather have all the friends been commanded to show forth fellowship and love, consideration and generosity and loving-kindness to every community on earth. Now must the lovers of God arise to carry out these instructions of His: let them be kindly fathers to the children of the human race, and compassionate brothers to the youth, and self-denying offspring to those bent with years. The meaning of this is that ye must show forth tenderness and love to every human being, even to your enemies, and welcome them all with unalloyed friendship, good cheer, and loving-kindness. ('Abdu'l-Bahá, *Selections from the Writings of 'Abdu'l-Bahá*, no. 7.4)

The Bahá'ís are commanded to establish the oneness of mankind; if they cannot unite around one point how will they be able to bring about the unity of mankind? ('Abdu'l-Bahá, *Selections from the Writings of 'Abdu'l-Bahá*, no. 7.4)

God desires unity and love; He commands harmony and fellowship. Enmity is human disobedience; God Himself is love. ('Abdu'l-Bahá, *The Promulgation of Universal Peace*, p. 417)

You must . . . look toward each other and then toward mankind with the utmost love and kindness. You have no excuse to bring before God if you fail to live according to His command, for you are informed of that which constitutes the good pleasure of God. You have heard His commandments and precepts. You must, therefore, be kind to all men; you must even treat your enemies as your friends. You must consider your evil-wishers as your well-wishers. Those who are not agreeable toward you must be regarded as those who are congenial and pleasant so that, perchance, this darkness of disagreement and conflict may disappear from amongst men and the light of the divine may shine forth, so that the Orient may be illumined and the Occident filled with fragrance, nay, so that the East and West may embrace each other in love and deal with one another in sympathy and affection. Until man reaches this high station, the world of humanity shall not find rest, and eternal felicity shall not be attained. But if man lives up to these divine commandments, this world of earth shall be transformed into the world of heaven, and this material sphere shall be converted into a paradise of glory. It is my hope that you may become successful in this high calling so that like brilliant lamps you may cast light upon the world of humanity and quicken and stir the body of existence like unto a spirit of life. This is eternal glory. This is everlasting felicity. This is immortal life. This is heavenly attainment. This is being created in the image and likeness of God. And unto this I call you, praying to God to strengthen and bless you. ('Abdu'l-Bahá, *The Promulgation of Universal Peace*, p. 663)

As preordained by the Fountainhead of Creation, the temple of the world hath been fashioned after the image and likeness of the human body. In fact each mirroreth forth the image of the other, wert thou but to observe with discerning eyes. By this is meant that even as the human body in this world which is outwardly composed of different limbs and organs, is in reality a closely integrated, coherent entity, similarly the structure of the physical world is like unto a single being whose limbs and members are inseparably linked together.

Were one to observe with an eye that discovereth the realities of all things, it would become clear that the greatest relationship that bindeth the world of being together lieth in the range of created things themselves, and that cooperation, mutual aid and reciprocity are essential characteristics in the unified body of the world of being, inasmuch as all created things are closely related together and each is influenced by the other or deriveth benefit therefrom, either directly or indirectly.

Consider for instance how one group of created things constituteth the vegetable kingdom, and another the animal kingdom. Each of these two maketh use of certain elements in the air on which its own life dependeth, while each increaseth the quantity of such elements as are essential for the life of the other. In other words, the growth and development of the vegetable world is impossible without the existence of the animal kingdom, and the maintenance of animal life is inconceivable without the co-operation of the vegetable kingdom. Of like kind are the relationships that exist among all created things. Hence it was stated that cooperation and reciprocity are essential properties which are inherent in the unified system of the world of existence, and without which the entire creation would be reduced to nothingness.

In surveying the vast range of creation thou shalt perceive that the higher a kingdom of created things is on the arc of ascent, the more conspicuous are the signs and evidences of the truth that cooperation and reciprocity at the level of a higher order are greater than those that exist at the level of a lower order. For example the evident signs of this fundamental reality are more discernible in the vegetable kingdom than in the mineral, and still more manifest in the animal world than in the vegetable.

And thus when contemplating the human world thou beholdest this wondrous phenomenon shining resplendent from all sides with the utmost perfection, inasmuch as in this station acts of cooperation, mutual assistance and reciprocity are not confined to the body and to things that pertain to the material world, but for all conditions, whether physical or spiritual, such as those related to minds, thoughts, opinions, manners, customs, attitudes, understandings, feelings or other human susceptibilities. In all these thou shouldst find these binding relationships securely established. The more this interrelationship is strengthened and expanded, the more will human society advance in progress and prosperity. Indeed without these vital ties it would be wholly impossible for the world of humanity to attain true felicity and success.

Now consider, if among the people who are merely the manifestations of the world of being this significant matter is of such importance, how much greater must be the spirit of cooperation and mutual assistance among those who are the essences of the world of creation, who have sought the sheltering shadow of the heavenly Tree, and are favoured by the manifestations of divine grace; and how the evidences of this spirit should, through their earnest endeavour, their fellowship and concord, become manifest in every sphere of their inner and outer lives, in the realm of the spirit and divine mysteries and in all things related to this world and the next. Thus there can be no doubt that they must be willing even to offer up their lives for each other. ('Abdu'l-Bahá, in *Ḥuqúqu'lláh: The Right of God*, no. 61)

The earth has one surface. God has not divided this surface by boundaries and barriers to separate races and peoples. Man has set up and established these imaginary lines, giving to each restricted area a name and the limitation of a native land or nationhood. By this division and separation into groups and branches of mankind, prejudice is engendered which becomes a fruitful source of war and strife. Impelled by this prejudice, races and nations declare war against each other; the blood of the innocent is poured out, and the earth torn by violence. Therefore, it has been decreed by God in this day that these prejudices and differences shall be laid aside. All are commanded to seek the good pleasure of the Lord of unity, to follow His command and obey His will; in this way the world of humanity shall become illumined with the reality of love and reconciliation. ('Abdu'l-Bahá, *The Promulgation of Universal Peace*, pp. 449–50)

For the principle of the Oneness of Mankind, the cornerstone of Bahá'u'lláh's world-embracing dominion, implies nothing more nor less than the enforcement of His scheme for the unification of the world—the scheme to which we have already referred. "In every Dispensation," writes 'Abdu'l-Bahá, "the light of Divine Guidance has been focused upon one central theme. . . . In this wondrous Revelation, this glorious century, the foundation of the Faith of God and the distinguishing feature of His Law is the consciousness of the Oneness of Mankind." (Shoghi Effendi, *The World Order of Bahá'u'lláh*, p. 36)

Let there be no mistake. The principle of the Oneness of Mankind—the pivot round which all the teachings of Bahá'u'lláh revolve—is no mere outburst of ignorant emotionalism or an expression of vague and pious hope. Its appeal is not to be merely identified with a reawakening of the spirit of brotherhood and good-will among men, nor does it aim solely at the fostering of harmonious cooperation among individual peoples and nations. Its implications are deeper, its claims greater than any which the Prophets of old were allowed to advance. Its message is applicable not only to the individual, but concerns itself primarily with the nature of those essential relationships that must bind all the states and nations as members of one human family. It does not constitute merely the enunciation of an ideal, but stands inseparably associated with an institution adequate to embody its truth, demonstrate its validity, and perpetuate its influence. It implies an organic change in the structure of present-day society, a change such as the world has not yet experienced. It constitutes a challenge, at once bold and universal, to outworn shibboleths of national creeds—creeds that have had their day and which must, in the ordinary course of events as shaped and controlled by Providence, give way to a new gospel, fundamentally different from, and infinitely superior to, what the world has already conceived. It calls for no less than the reconstruction and the demilitarization of the whole civilized world—a world organically unified in all the essential aspects of its life, its political machinery, its spiritual aspiration, its trade and finance, its script and language, and yet infinite in the diversity of the national characteristics of its federated units.

It represents the consummation of human evolution—an evolution that has had its earliest beginnings in the birth of family life, its subsequent development in the achievement of tribal solidarity, leading in turn to the constitution of the city-state, and expanding later into the institution of independent and sovereign nations.

26

The principle of the Oneness of Mankind, as proclaimed by Bahá'u'lláh, carries with it no more and no less than a solemn assertion that attainment to this final stage in this stupendous evolution is not only necessary but inevitable, that its realization is fast approaching, and that nothing short of a power that is born of God can succeed in establishing it. (Shoghi Effendi, *The World Order of Bahá'u'lláh,* pp. 42–43)

The Bahá'í Faith upholds the unity of God, recognizes the unity of His Prophets, and inculcates the principle of the oneness and wholeness of the entire human race. It proclaims the necessity and the inevitability of the unification of mankind, asserts that it is gradually approaching, and claims that nothing short of the transmuting spirit of God, working through His chosen Mouthpiece in this day, can ultimately succeed in bringing it about. It, moreover, enjoins upon its followers the primary duty of an unfettered search after truth, condemns all manner of prejudice and superstition, declares the purpose of religion to be the promotion of amity and concord, proclaims its essential harmony with science, and recognizes it as the foremost agency for the pacification and the orderly progress of human society. . . . (Shoghi Effendi, *The Promised Day is Come,* ¶iii)

The proclamation of the Oneness of Mankind—the head corner-stone of Bahá'u'lláh's all-embracing dominion—can under no circumstances be compared with such expressions of pious hope as have been uttered in the past. His is not merely a call which He raised, alone and unaided, in the face of the relentless and combined opposition of two of the most powerful Oriental potentates of His day—while Himself an exile and prisoner in their hands. It implies at once a warning and a promise—a warning that in it lies the sole means for the salvation of a greatly suffering world, a promise that its realization is at hand.

Uttered at a time when its possibility had not yet been seriously envisaged in any part of the world, it has, by virtue of that celestial potency which the Spirit of Bahá'u'lláh has breathed into it, come at last to be regarded, by an increasing number of thoughtful men, not only as an approaching possibility, but as the necessary outcome of the forces now operating in the world. (Shoghi Effendi, *The World Order of Bahá'u'lláh*, p. 47)

Of the principles enshrined in these Tablets the most vital of them all is the principle of the oneness and wholeness of the human race, which may well be regarded as the hallmark of Bahá'u'lláh's Revelation and the pivot of His teachings. Of such cardinal importance is this principle of unity that it is expressly referred to in the Book of His Covenant, and He unreservedly proclaims it as the central purpose of His Faith. "We, verily," He declares, "have come to unite and weld together all that dwell on earth." "So potent is the light of unity," He further states, "that it can illuminate the whole earth." "At one time," He has written with reference to this central theme of His Revelation, "We spoke in the language of the lawgiver; at another in that of the truth seeker and the mystic, and yet Our supreme purpose and highest wish hath always been to disclose the glory and sublimity of this station." Unity, He states, is the goal that "excelleth every goal" and an aspiration which is "the monarch of all aspirations." "The world," He proclaims, "is but one country, and mankind its citizens." He further affirms that the unification of mankind, the last stage in the evolution of humanity towards maturity is inevitable, that "soon will the present day order be rolled up, and a new one spread out in its stead," that "the whole earth is now in a state of pregnancy," that "the day is approaching when it will have yielded its noblest fruits, when from it will have sprung forth the loftiest trees, the most enchanting blossoms, the most heavenly blessings." (Shoghi Effendi, *God Passes By*, pp. 343–44)

In the midst of the storm and stress of the battles of selfish interests being waged about them, stand the followers of the Most Great Name, their sight attracted to the rising Sun of God's Holy Cause, their hearts welded together in a bond of true unity with all the children of men, and their voices raised in a universal song of praise to the Glory of God and the oneness of mankind, calling on their fellowmen to forget and forgo their differences and join them in obedience and service to God's Holy Command in this Day. (The Universal House of Justice, *Messages, 1963–1986*, no. 77.2)

LOVE—THE SOURCE OF UNITY

Deal ye one with another with the utmost love and harmony, with friendliness and fellowship. He Who is the Daystar of Truth beareth Me witness! So powerful is the light of unity that it can illuminate the whole earth. The One true God, He Who knoweth all things, Himself testifieth to the truth of these words.

Exert yourselves that ye may attain this transcendent and most sublime station, the station that can insure the protection and security of all mankind. This goal excelleth every other goal, and this aspiration is the monarch of all aspirations. (Bahá'u'lláh, *Epistle to the Son of the Wolf,* p. 14)

Know thou of a certainty that Love is the secret of God's holy Dispensation, the manifestation of the All-Merciful, the fountain of spiritual outpourings. Love is heaven's kindly light, the Holy Spirit's eternal breath that vivifieth the human soul. Love is the cause of God's revelation unto man, the vital bond inherent, in accordance with the divine creation, in the realities of things. Love is the one means that ensureth true felicity both in this world and the next. Love is the light that guideth in darkness, the living link that uniteth God with man, that assureth the progress of every illumined soul. Love is the most great law that ruleth this mighty and heavenly cycle, the unique power that bindeth together the divers elements of this material world, the supreme magnetic force that directeth the movements of the spheres in the celestial realms. Love revealeth with unfailing and limitless power the mysteries latent in the universe. Love is the spirit of life unto the adorned body of mankind, the establisher of true civilization in this mortal world, and the shedder of imperishable glory upon every high-aiming race and nation.

Whatsoever people is graciously favored therewith by God, its name shall surely be magnified and extolled by the Concourse from on high, by the company of angels, and the denizens of the Abhá Kingdom. And whatsoever people turneth its heart away from this Divine Love—the revelation of the Merciful—shall err grievously, shall fall into despair, and be utterly destroyed. That people shall be denied all refuge, shall become even as the vilest creatures of the earth, victims of degradation and shame.

O ye beloved of the Lord! Strive to become the manifestations of the love of God, the lamps of divine guidance shining amongst the kindreds of the earth with the light of love and concord. ('Abdu'l-Bahá, *Selections from the Writings of 'Abdu'l-Bahá*, no. 12.1–3)

And in truth the fruit of human existence is the love of God, which is the spirit of life and grace everlasting. Were it not for the love of God, the contingent world would be plunged in darkness. Were it not for the love of God, the hearts of men would be bereft of life and deprived of the stirrings of conscience. Were it not for the love of God, the perfections of the human world would entirely vanish. Were it not for the love of God, no real connection could exist between human hearts. Were it not for the love of God, spiritual union would be lost. Were it not for the love of God, the light of the oneness of mankind would be extinguished. Were it not for the love of God, the East and the West would not embrace as two lovers. Were it not for the love of God, discord and division would not be transmuted into fellowship. Were it not for the love of God, estrangement would not give way to unity. Were it not for the love of God, the stranger would not become the friend. Indeed, love in the human world is a ray of the love of God and a reflection of the grace of His bounty. ('Abdu'l-Bahá, *Some Answered Questions,* no. 84.3)

We declare that love is the cause of the existence of all phenomena and that the absence of love is the cause of disintegration or nonexistence. Love is the conscious bestowal of God, the bond of affiliation in all phenomena. We will first consider the proof of this through sense perception. As we look upon the universe, we observe that all composite beings or existing phenomena are made up primarily of single elements bound together by a power of attraction. Through this power of attraction cohesion has become manifest between atoms of these composing elements. The resultant being is a phenomenon of the lower contingent type. The power of cohesion expressed in the mineral kingdom is in reality love or affinity manifested in a low degree according to the exigencies of the mineral world. We take a step higher into the vegetable kingdom where we find an increased power of attraction has become manifest among the composing elements which form phenomena. Through this degree of attraction a cellular admixture is produced among these elements which make up the body of a plant. Therefore, in the degree of the vegetable kingdom there is love. We enter the animal kingdom and find the attractive power binding together single elements as in the mineral, plus the cellular admixture as in the vegetable, plus the phenomena of feelings or susceptibilities. We observe that the animals are susceptible to certain affiliation and fellowship and that they exercise natural selection. This elemental attraction, this admixture and selective affinity is love manifest in the degree of the animal kingdom.

Finally, we come to the kingdom of man. As this is the superior kingdom, the light of love is more resplendent. In man we find the power of attraction among the elements which compose his material body, plus the attraction which produces cellular admixture or augmentative power, plus the attraction which characterizes the sensibilities of the animal kingdom, but still beyond and above all these lower powers we discover in the being of man the attraction of heart, the susceptibilities and affinities which bind men together, enabling them to live and associate in friendship and solidarity. It is, therefore, evident that in the world of humanity the greatest king and sovereign is love. If love were extinguished, the power of attraction dispelled, the affinity of human hearts destroyed, the phenomena of human life would disappear. ('Abdu'l-Bahá, *The Promulgation of Universal Peace*, pp. 356–57)

There are many ways of expressing the love principle; there is love for the family, for the country, for the race, there is political enthusiasm, there is also the love of community of interest in service. These are all ways and means of showing the power of love. Without any such means, love would be unseen, unheard, unfelt—altogether unexpressed, unmanifested! Water shows its power in various ways, in quenching thirst, causing seed to grow, etc. Coal expresses one of its principles in gas-light, while one of the powers of electricity is shown in the electric light. If there were neither gas nor electricity, the nights of the world would be darkness! So, it is necessary to have an instrument, a motive for love's manifestation, an object, a mode of expression.

We must find a way of spreading love among the sons of humanity.

Love is unlimited, boundless, infinite! Material things are limited, circumscribed, finite. You cannot adequately express infinite love by limited means.

The perfect love needs an unselfish instrument, absolutely freed from fetters of every kind. The love of family is limited; the tie of blood relationship is not the strongest bond. Frequently members of the same family disagree, and even hate each other.

Patriotic love is finite; the love of one's country causing hatred of all others, is not perfect love! Compatriots also are not free from quarrels amongst themselves.

The love of race is limited; there is some union here, but that is insufficient. Love must be free from boundaries!

To love our own race may mean hatred of all others, and even people of the same race often dislike each other.

Political love also is much bound up with hatred of one party for another; this love is very limited and uncertain.

The love of community of interest in service is likewise fluctuating; frequently competitions arise, which lead to jealousy, and at length hatred replaces love.

A few years ago, Turkey and Italy had a friendly political understanding; now they are at war!

All these ties of love are imperfect. It is clear that limited material ties are insufficient to adequately express the universal love.

The great unselfish love for humanity is bounded by none of these imperfect, semi-selfish bonds; this is the one perfect love, possible to all mankind, and can only be achieved by the power of the Divine Spirit. No worldly power can accomplish the universal love.

Let all be united in this Divine power of love! Let all strive to grow in the light of the Sun of Truth, and reflecting this luminous love on all men, may their hearts become so united that they may dwell evermore in the radiance of the limitless love. ('Abdu'l-Bahá, *Paris Talks*, no. 9.3–15)

When man's soul is rarified and cleansed, spiritual links are established, and from these bonds sensations felt by the heart are produced. The human heart resembleth a mirror. When this is purified human hearts are attuned and reflect one another, and thus spiritual emotions are generated. ('Abdu'l-Bahá, *Selections from the Writings of 'Abdu'l-Bahá*, no. 70.5)

The most important thing is to polish the mirrors of hearts in order that they may become illumined and receptive of the divine light. One heart may possess the capacity of the polished mirror; another, be covered and obscured by the dust and dross of this world. Although the same Sun is shining upon both, in the mirror which is polished, pure and sanctified you may behold the Sun in all its fullness, glory and power, revealing its majesty and effulgence; but in the mirror which is rusted and obscured there is no capacity for reflection, although so far as the Sun itself is concerned it is shining thereon and is neither lessened nor deprived. Therefore, our duty lies in seeking to polish the mirrors of our hearts in order that we shall become reflectors of that light and recipients of the divine bounties which may be fully revealed through them.

This means the oneness of the world of humanity. That is to say, when this human body politic reaches a state of absolute unity, the effulgence of the eternal Sun will make its fullest light and heat manifest. Therefore, we must not make distinctions between individual members of the human family. We must not consider any soul as barren or deprived. Our duty lies in educating souls so that the Sun of the bestowals of God shall become resplendent in them, and this is possible through the power of the oneness of humanity. The more love is expressed among mankind and the stronger the power of unity, the greater will be this reflection and revelation, for the greatest bestowal of God is love. Love is the source of all the bestowals of God. Until love takes possession of the heart, no other divine bounty can be revealed in it. ('Abdu'l-Bahá, *The Promulgation of Universal Peace*, pp. 19–20)

The love which exists between the hearts of believers is prompted by the ideal of the unity of spirits. This love is attained through the knowledge of God, so that men see the Divine Love reflected in the heart. Each sees in the other the Beauty of God reflected in the soul, and finding this point of similarity, they are attracted to one another in love. This love will make all men the waves of one sea, this love will make them all the stars of one heaven and the fruits of one tree. This love will bring the realization of true accord, the foundation of real unity. ('Abdu'l-Bahá, *Paris Talks*, no. 58.7)

In the same way, when any souls grow to be true believers, they will attain a spiritual relationship with one another, and show forth a tenderness which is not of this world. They will, all of them, become elated from a draught of divine love, and that union of theirs, that connection, will also abide for-ever. Souls, that is, who will consign their own selves to oblivion, strip from themselves the defects of humankind, and unchain themselves from human bondage, will beyond any doubt be illumined with the heavenly splendors of oneness, and will all attain unto real union in the world that dieth not. ('Abdu'l-Bahá, *Selections from the Writings of 'Abdu'l-Bahá*, no. 84.5)

But there is need of a superior power to overcome human prejudices, a power which nothing in the world of mankind can withstand and which will overshadow the effect of all other forces at work in human conditions. That irresistible power is the love of God. It is my hope and prayer that it may destroy the prejudice of this one point of distinction between you and unite you all permanently under its hallowed protection. ('Abdu'l-Bahá, *The Promulgation of Universal Peace*, p. 94)

Not until the dynamic love we cherish for Him is sufficiently reflected in its power and purity in all our dealings with our fellow-men, however remotely connected and humble in origin, can we hope to exalt in the eyes of a self-seeking world the genuineness of the all-conquering love of God. Not until we live ourselves the life of a true Bahá'í can we hope to demonstrate the creative and transforming potency of the Faith we profess. Nothing but the abundance of our actions, nothing but the purity of our lives and the integrity of our characters, can in the last resort establish our claim that the Bahá'í spirit is in this day the sole agency that can translate a long-cherished ideal into an enduring achievement. (Shoghi Effendi, letter dated 24 November 1924, to the National Spiritual Assembly of the United States, in *Bahá'í Administration,* p. 68)

Humanity, torn with dissension and burning with hate, is crying at this hour for a fuller measure of that love which is born of God, that love which in the last resort will prove the one solvent of its incalculable difficulties and problems. Is it not incumbent upon us, whose hearts are aglow with love for Him, to make still greater effort, to manifest that love in all its purity and power in our dealings with our fellow-men? May our love of our beloved Master, so ardent, so disinterested in all its aspects, find its true expression in love for our fellow-brethren and sisters in the faith as well as for all mankind. I assure you, dear friends, that progress in such matters as these is limitless and infinite, and that upon the extent of our achievements along this line will ultimately depend the success of our mission in life. (Shoghi Effendi, *Bahá'í Administration,* p. 61)

This love amongst the believers is the magnet which will, above all else, attract the hearts and bring new souls into the Cause. Because obviously the teachings—however wonderful—cannot change the world unless the Spirit of Bahá'u'lláh's love is mirrored in the Bahá'í Communities. (On behalf of Shoghi Effendi, letter dated 27 October 1944, to an individual believer, in *The Compilation of Compilations,* vol. II, no. 1302)

Regarding your question about the need for greater unity among the friends, there is no doubt that this is so, and the Guardian feels that one of the chief instruments for promoting it is to teach the Bahá'ís themselves, in classes and through precepts, that love of God, and consequently of men, is the essential foundation of every religion, our own included. A greater degree of love will produce a greater unity, because it enables people to bear with each other, to be patient and forgiving. (On behalf of Shoghi Effendi, letter dated 7 July 1944, to an individual believer, quoted in *Bahá'í News*, no. 173, p. 3)

Most important of all is that love and unity should prevail in the Bahá'í Community, as this is what people are most longing for in the present dark state of the world. Words without the living example will never be sufficient to breathe hope into the hearts of a disillusioned and often cynical generation. (On behalf of Shoghi Effendi, letter dated 20 October 1945, to an individual believer, in *The Compilation of Compilations*, vol. II, no. 1307)

Unless and until the believers really come to realize they are one spiritual family, knit together by a bond more lasting than mere physical ties can ever be, they will not be able to create that warm community atmosphere which alone can attract the hearts of humanity, frozen for lack of real love and feeling. (On behalf of Shoghi Effendi, in *The Individual and Teaching: Raising the Divine Call*, pp. 25–26)

We must love God, and in this state, a general love for all men becomes possible. We cannot love each human being for himself but our feeling towards humanity should be motivated by our love for the Father who created all men. (On behalf of Shoghi Effendi, letter dated 4 October 1950, to an individual believer, in *Lights of Guidance*, no. 1341)

RELIGION—THE PERFECT MEANS FOR ENGENDERING UNITY

The Faith of God hath in this day been made manifest. He Who is the Lord of the world is come and hath shown the way. His faith is the faith of benevolence and His religion is the religion of forbearance. This faith bestoweth eternal life and this religion enableth mankind to dispense with all else. It verily embraceth all faiths and all religions. Take hold thereof and guard it well. (Bahá'u'lláh, *The Tabernacle of Unity*, p. 59)

That which the Lord hath ordained as the sovereign remedy and mightiest instrument for the healing of all the world is the union of all its peoples in one universal Cause, one common Faith. (Bahá'u'lláh, *Gleanings from the Writings of Bahá'u'lláh*, no. 120.3)

The purpose of religion as revealed from the heaven of God's holy Will is to establish unity and concord amongst the peoples of the world; make it not the cause of dissension and strife. The religion of God and His divine law are the most potent instruments and the surest of all means for the dawning of the light of unity amongst men. The progress of the world, the development of nations, the tranquility of peoples, and the peace of all who dwell on earth are among the principles and ordinances of God. (Bahá'u'lláh, *Tablets of Bahá'u'lláh*, p. 129)

Naught but the celestial potency of the Word of God, which ruleth and transcendeth the realities of all things, is capable of harmonizing the divergent thoughts, sentiments, ideas, and convictions of the children of men. Verily, it is the penetrating power in all things, the mover of souls and the binder and regulator in the world of humanity. ('Abdu'l-Bahá, *Selections from the Writings of 'Abdu'l-Bahá*, no. 225.25)

As to the most great characteristic of the revelation of Bahá'u'lláh, a specific teaching not given by any of the Prophets of the past: It is the ordination and appointment of the Center of the Covenant ['Abdu'l-Bahá]. By this appointment and provision He has safeguarded and protected the religion of God against differences and schisms, making it impossible for anyone to create a new sect or faction of belief. To ensure unity and agreement He has entered into a Covenant with all the people of the world, including the interpreter and explainer of His teachings, so that no one may interpret or explain the religion of God according to his own view or opinion and thus create a sect founded upon his individual understanding of the divine Words. The Book of the Covenant or Testament of Bahá'u'lláh is the means of preventing such a possibility, for whosoever shall speak from the authority of himself alone shall be degraded. Be ye informed and cognizant of this. ('Abdu'l-Bahá, *The Promulgation of Universal Peace*, p. 642)

The purpose of the Blessed Beauty in entering into this Covenant and Testament was to gather all existent beings around one point so that the thoughtless souls, who in every cycle and generation have been the cause of dissension, may not undermine the Cause. He hath, therefore, commanded that whatever emanateth from the Centre of the Covenant is right and is under His protection and favor, while all else is error. ('Abdu'l-Bahá, *Selections from the Writings of 'Abdu'l-Bahá*, no. 183.3)

The essential purpose of the religion of God is to establish unity among mankind. The divine Manifestations were Founders of the means of fellowship and love. They did not come to create discord, strife and hatred in the world. The religion of God is the cause of love, but if it is made to be the source of enmity and bloodshed, surely its absence is preferable to its existence; for then it becomes satanic, detrimental and an obstacle to the human world. ('Abdu'l-Bahá, *The Promulgation of Universal Peace*, p. 282)

. . . religion must be the mainspring and source of love in the world, for religion is the revelation of the will of God, the divine fundamental of which is love. Therefore, if religion should prove to be the cause of enmity and hatred instead of love, its absence is preferable to its existence. ('Abdu'l-Bahá, *The Promulgation of Universal Peace*, p. 448)

True religion is the source of love and agreement amongst men, the cause of the development of praiseworthy qualities, but the people are holding to the counterfeit and imitation, negligent of the reality which unifies, so they are bereft and deprived of the radiance of religion. ('Abdu'l-Bahá, *The Promulgation of Universal Peace,* p. 249)

The disease which afflicts the body politic is lack of love and absence of altruism. In the hearts of men no real love is found, and the condition is such that, unless their susceptibilities are quickened by some power so that unity, love and accord may develop within them, there can be no healing, no agreement among mankind. Love and unity are the needs of the body politic today. Without these there can be no progress or prosperity attained. Therefore, the friends of God must adhere to the power which will create this love and unity in the hearts of the sons of men. Science cannot cure the illness of the body politic. Science cannot create amity and fellowship in human hearts. Neither can patriotism nor racial allegiance effect a remedy. It must be accomplished solely through the divine bounties and spiritual bestowals which have descended from God in this day for that purpose. This is an exigency of the times, and the divine remedy has been provided. The spiritual teachings of the religion of God can alone create this love, unity and accord in human hearts. ('Abdu'l-Bahá, *The Promulgation of Universal Peace,* p. 237)

It is certain that the greatest of instrumentalities for achieving the advancement and the glory of man, the supreme agency for the enlightenment and the redemption of the world, is love and fellowship and unity among all the members of the human race. Nothing can be effected in the world, not even conceivably, without unity and agreement, and the perfect means for engendering fellowship and union is true religion. "Hadst Thou spent all the riches of the earth, Thou couldst not have united their hearts; but God hath united them . . ."*

With the advent of the Prophets of God, their power of creating a real union, one which is both external and of the heart, draws together malev-

---

* Qur'an 8:64

olent peoples who have been thirsting for one another's blood, into the one shelter of the Word of God. Then a hundred thousand souls become as one soul, and unnumbered individuals emerge as one body. ('Abdu'l-Bahá, *The Secret of Divine Civilization*, ¶135–36)

The source of perfect unity and love in the world of existence is the bond and oneness of reality. When the divine and fundamental reality enters human hearts and lives, it conserves and protects all states and conditions of mankind, establishing that intrinsic oneness of the world of humanity which can only come into being through the efficacy of the Holy Spirit. For the Holy Spirit is like unto the life in the human body, which blends all differences of parts and members in unity and agreement. Consider how numerous are these parts and members, but the oneness of the animating spirit of life unites them all in perfect combination. It establishes such a unity in the bodily organism that if any part is subjected to injury or becomes diseased, all the other parts and functions sympathetically respond and suffer, owing to the perfect oneness existing. Just as the human spirit of life is the cause of coordination among the various parts of the human organism, the Holy Spirit is the controlling cause of the unity and coordination of mankind. That is to say, the bond or oneness of humanity cannot be effectively established save through the power of the Holy Spirit, for the world of humanity is a composite body, and the Holy Spirit is the animating principle of its life. ('Abdu'l-Bahá, *The Promulgation of Universal Peace*, pp. 456–57)

Bahá'u'lláh teaches that the world of humanity is in need of the breath of the Holy Spirit, for in spiritual quickening and enlightenment true oneness is attained with God and man. The Most Great Peace cannot be assured through racial force and effort; it cannot be established by patriotic devotion and sacrifice; for nations differ widely and local patriotism has limitations. Furthermore, it is evident that political power and diplomatic ability are not conducive to universal agreement, for the interests of governments are varied and selfish; nor will international harmony and reconciliation be an outcome of human opinions concentrated upon it, for opinions are faulty and intrinsically diverse. Universal peace is an impossibility through human and material agencies; it must be through spiritual power. There is need of a universal impelling force which will establish the oneness of humanity and destroy the foundations of war and strife. None other than the divine power can do this; therefore, it will be accomplished through the breath of the Holy Spirit. ('Abdu'l-Bahá, *The Promulgation of Universal Peace*, pp. 150–51)

Sincerity is the foundation-stone of faith. That is, a religious individual must disregard his personal desires and seek in whatever way he can wholeheartedly to serve the public interest; and it is impossible for a human being to turn aside from his own selfish advantages and sacrifice his own good for the good of the community except through true religious faith. For self-love is kneaded into the very clay of man, and it is not possible that, without any hope of a substantial reward, he should neglect his own present material good. That individual, however, who puts his faith in God and believes in the words of God—because he is promised and certain of a plentiful reward in the next life, and because worldly benefits as compared to the abiding joy and glory of future planes of existence are nothing to him—will for the sake of God abandon his own peace and profit and will freely consecrate his heart and soul to the common good. ('Abdu'l-Bahá, *The Secret of Divine Civilization*, ¶170)

The Faith of Bahá'u'lláh has assimilated, by virtue of its creative, its regulative and ennobling energies, the varied races, nationalities, creeds and classes that have sought its shadow, and have pledged unswerving fealty to its cause. It has changed the hearts of its adherents, burned away their prejudices, stilled their passions, exalted their conceptions, ennobled their motives, coordinated their efforts, and transformed their outlook. While preserving their patriotism and safeguarding their lesser loyalties, it has made them lovers of mankind, and the determined upholders of its best and truest interests. While maintaining intact their belief in the Divine origin of their respective religions, it has enabled them to visualize the underlying purpose of these religions, to discover their merits, to recognize their sequence, their interdependence, their wholeness and unity, and to acknowledge the bond that vitally links them to itself. This universal, this transcending love which the followers of the Bahá'í Faith feel for their fellow-men, of whatever race, creed, class or nation, is neither mysterious nor can it be said to have been artificially stimulated. It is both spontaneous and genuine. They whose hearts are warmed by the energizing influence of God's creative love cherish His creatures for His sake, and recognize in every human face a sign of His reflected glory. (Shoghi Effendi, *The World Order of Bahá'u'lláh,* pp. 197–98)

The teaching that we should treat others as we ourselves would wish to be treated, an ethic variously repeated in all the great religions, . . . sums up the moral attitude, the peace-inducing aspect, extending through these religions irrespective of their place or time of origin; it also signifies an aspect of unity which is their essential virtue, a virtue mankind in its disjointed view of history has failed to appreciate.

Had humanity seen the Educators of its collective childhood in their true character, as agents of one civilizing process, it would no doubt have reaped incalculably greater benefits from the cumulative effects of their successive missions. This, alas, it failed to do. (The Universal House of Justice, *The Promise of World Peace,* ¶17)

UNDERSTANDING THE BASES OF PREJUDICES AND DISUNITY

The accumulations of vain fancy have obstructed men's ears and stopped them from hearing the Voice of God, and the veils of human learning and false imaginings have prevented their eyes from beholding the splendor of the light of His countenance. (Bahá'u'lláh, *Tablets of Bahá'u'lláh,* p. 240)

Beware lest the desires of the flesh and of a corrupt inclination provoke divisions among you. Be ye as the fingers of one hand, the members of one body. Thus counselleth you the Pen of Revelation, if ye be of them that believe. (Bahá'u'lláh, *Gleanings from the Writings of Bahá'u'lláh,* no. 72.4)

42

Consider how men for generations have been blindly imitating their fathers, and have been trained according to such ways and manners as have been laid down by the dictates of their Faith. (Bahá'u'lláh, *Gleanings from the Writings of Bahá'u'lláh*, no. 13.11)

O heedless people! Ye repeat what your fathers, in a bygone age, have said. Whatever fruits they have gathered from the tree of their faithlessness, the same shall ye gather also. (Bahá'u'lláh, The Kitáb-i-Íqán, ¶229)

. . . man must independently investigate reality, for the disagreements and dissensions which afflict and affect humanity primarily proceed from imitations of ancestral beliefs and adherences to hereditary forms of worship. These imitations are accidental and without sanction in the Holy Books. They are the outcomes of human interpretations and teachings which have arisen, gradually obscuring the real light of divine meaning and causing men to differ and dissent. The reality proclaimed in the heavenly Books and divine teachings is ever conducive to love, unity and fellowship. ('Abdu'l-Bahá, *The Promulgation of Universal Peace*, p. 447)

Now the people of religion have lost sight of the essential reality of the spiritual springtime. They have held tenaciously to ancestral forms and imitations, and because of this there is variance, strife and altercation among them. Therefore, we must now abandon these imitations and seek the foundation of the divine teachings; and inasmuch as the foundation is one reality, the divergent religionists must agree in it so that love and unity will be established among all people and denominations. ('Abdu'l-Bahá, *The Promulgation of Universal Peace*, pp. 175–76)

Reality or truth is one, yet there are many religious beliefs, denominations, creeds and differing opinions in the world today. Why should these differences exist? Because they do not investigate and examine the fundamental unity, which is one and unchangeable. If they seek reality itself, they will agree and be united; for reality is indivisible and not multiple. It is evident, therefore, that there is nothing of greater importance to mankind than the investigation of truth. ('Abdu'l-Bahá, *The Promulgation of Universal Peace*, p. 85)

Ye observe how the world is divided against itself, how many a land is red with blood and its very dust is caked with human gore. The fires of conflict have blazed so high that never in early times, not in the Middle Ages, not in recent centuries hath there ever been such a hideous war, a war that is even as millstones, taking for grain the skulls of men. Nay, even worse, for flourishing countries have been reduced to rubble, cities have been levelled with the ground, and many a once prosperous village hath been turned into ruin. Fathers have lost their sons, and sons their fathers. Mothers have wept away their hearts over dead children. Children have been orphaned, women left to wander, vagrants without a home. From every aspect, humankind hath sunken low. Loud are the piercing cries of fatherless children; loud the mothers' anguished voices, reaching to the skies.

And the breeding-ground of all these tragedies is prejudice: prejudice of race and nation, of religion, of political opinion; and the root cause of prejudice is blind imitation of the past—imitation in religion, in racial attitudes, in national bias, in politics. So long as this aping of the past persisteth, just so long will the foundations of the social order be blown to the four winds, just so long will humanity be continually exposed to direst peril. ('Abdu'l-Bahá, *Selections from the Writings of 'Abdu'l-Bahá*, no. 202.2–3)

In order to find truth we must give up our prejudices, our own small trivial notions; an open receptive mind is essential. If our chalice is full of self, there is no room in it for the water of life. The fact that we imagine ourselves to be right and everybody else wrong is the greatest of all obstacles in the path towards unity, and unity is necessary if we would reach truth, for truth is one.

Therefore it is imperative that we should renounce our own particular prejudices and superstitions if we earnestly desire to seek the truth. Unless we make a distinction in our minds between dogma, superstition and prejudice on the one hand, and truth on the other, we cannot succeed. When we are in earnest in our search for anything we look for it everywhere. This principle we must carry out in our search for truth. ('Abdu'l-Bahá, *Paris Talks*, no. 41.7)

Rivalry between the different races of mankind was first caused by the struggle for existence among the wild animals. This struggle is no longer necessary: nay, rather interdependence and co-operation are seen to produce the highest welfare in nations. The struggle that now continues is caused by prejudice and bigotry. ('Abdu'l-Bahá, letter dated 20 August 1911, addressed to the First Universal Races Conference, quoted in *Star of the West*, vol. 2, no. 9, p. 5)

I shall ask you a question: Did God create us for love or for enmity? Did He create us for peace or discord? Surely He has created us for love; therefore, we should live in accordance with His will. Do not listen to anything that is prejudiced, for self-interest prompts men to be prejudiced. They are thoughtful only of their own will and purposes. They live and move in darkness. ('Abdu'l-Bahá, *The Promulgation of Universal Peace*, p. 57)

Whatsoever is conducive to unity is merciful and from the divine bounty itself. Every universal affair is divine. Everything which conduces to separation and estrangement is satanic because it emanates from the purposes of self. ('Abdu'l-Bahá, *The Promulgation of Universal Peace*, p. 289)

Concerning the prejudice of race: it is an illusion, a superstition pure and simple! For God created us all of one race. There were no differences in the beginning, for we are all descendants of Adam. In the beginning, also, there were no limits and boundaries between the different lands; no part of the earth belonged more to one people than to another. In the sight of God there is no difference between the various races. Why should man invent such a prejudice? How can we uphold war caused by an illusion?

God has not created men that they should destroy one another. All races, tribes, sects and classes share equally in the Bounty of their Heavenly Father. ('Abdu'l-Bahá, *Paris Talks*, no. 45.11–12)

We are all human, all servants of God and all come from Mr. Adam's family. Why, then, all these fallacious national and racial distinctions? These boundary lines and artificial barriers have been created by despots and conquerors who sought to attain dominion over mankind, thereby engendering patriotic feeling and rousing selfish devotion to merely local standards of government. As a rule they themselves enjoyed luxuries in palaces, surrounded by conditions of ease and affluence, while armies of soldiers, civilians and tillers of the soil fought and died at their command upon the field of battle, shedding their innocent blood for a delusion such as "we are Germans," "our enemies are French," etc., when, in reality, all are humankind, all belong to the one family and posterity of Adam, the original father. This prejudice or limited patriotism is prevalent throughout the world, while man is blind to patriotism in the larger sense which includes all races and native lands. From every real standpoint there must and should be peace among all nations. ('Abdu'l-Bahá, *The Promulgation of Universal Peace*, p. 501)

The earth is one earth, and the same atmosphere surrounds it. No difference or preference has been made by God for its human inhabitants; but man has laid the foundation of prejudice, hatred and discord with his fellowman by considering nationalities separate in importance and races different in rights and privileges. ('Abdu'l-Bahá, *The Promulgation of Universal Peace*, pp. 324–25)

Is it not imagination and ignorance which impels man to violate the divine intention and make the very bounties of God the cause of war, bloodshed and destruction? Therefore, all prejudices between man and man are falsehoods and violations of the will of God. ('Abdu'l-Bahá, *The Promulgation of Universal Peace*, p. 417)

The fifth principle of Bahá'u'lláh is: Prejudices of Religion, Race or Sect destroy the foundation of Humanity.

All the divisions in the world, hatred, war and bloodshed, are caused by one or other of these prejudices.

The whole world must be looked upon as one single country, all the nations as one nation, all men as belonging to one race. Religions, races, and nations are all divisions of man's making only, and are necessary only in his thought; before God there are neither Persians, Arabs, French nor English; God is God for all, and to Him all creation is one. We must obey God, and strive to follow Him by leaving all our prejudices and bringing about peace on earth. ('Abdu'l-Bahá, *Paris Talks*, no. 40.19–21)

One of the great reasons of separation is colour. Look how this prejudice has power in America, for instance. See how they hate one another! Animals do not quarrel because of their colour! Surely man who is so much higher in creation, should not be lower than the animals. Think over this. What ignorance exists! White doves do not quarrel with blue doves because of their colour, but white men fight with dark-coloured men. This racial prejudice is the worst of all. ('Abdu'l-Bahá, *'Abdu'l-Bahá in London*, p. 55)

"God," 'Abdu'l-Bahá Himself declares, "maketh no distinction between the white and the black. If the hearts are pure both are acceptable unto Him. God is no respecter of persons on account of either color or race. All colors are acceptable unto Him, be they white, black, or yellow. Inasmuch as all were created in the image of God, we must bring ourselves to realize that all embody divine possibilities." "In the estimation of God," He states, "all men are equal. There is no distinction or preference for any soul, in the realm of His justice and equity." "God did not make these divisions," He affirms; "these divisions have had their origin in man himself. Therefore, as they are against the plan and purpose of God they are false and imaginary." (Shoghi Effendi, *The Advent of Divine Justice*, ¶56)

Both sides [whites and blacks] have prejudices to overcome; one, the prejudice which is built up in the minds of a people who have conquered and imposed their will, and the other the reactionary prejudice of those who have been conquered and sorely put upon. (On behalf of Shoghi Effendi, letter dated 27 May 1957, to Bahá'í Inter-racial Teaching Committee, in *To Move the World*, p. 294)

The cause of universal education, which has already enlisted in its service an army of dedicated people from every faith and nation, deserves the utmost support that the governments of the world can lend it. For ignorance is indisputably the principal reason for the decline and fall of peoples and the perpetuation of prejudice. (The Universal House of Justice, *The Promise of World Peace*, ¶34)

The continuing problem of racism remains, . . . an issue of fundamental importance for the American people. Given that the problem has been created and reinforced over a period of several hundred years, it is reasonable to suppose that its remediation will occupy the Bahá'í community and the nation of which it is a part for some generations to come.

Many of your questions relate to the relative seriousness of the race issue as compared to other issues. You ask, for example, whether the building of harmony between the races is still "the most vital and challenging issue facing the American Bahá'í community." What is more important to understand is that the achievement of race unity is far from complete. There is little to be gained by trying to invent a precise way of ranking various complex problems such as racism or by attempting to resolve these problems on a piecemeal basis. The piecemeal efforts of those outside of the Bahá'í community who are concerned with the many grievous ills facing humanity have had little lasting success. Their well-meaning endeavours have suffered from a lack of appreciation of the spiritual origin of these illnesses and a lack of understanding that the only lasting solution lies in acceptance of the remedies of the Divine Physician.

You have also inquired as to the appropriate response when one feels offended by the comments of others during the discussion of matters pertaining to race. Owing to the legacy of victimization and also the sense of guilt which many feel in relation to this issue, the race-unity work can often arouse strong emotions. Thus, it is inevitable that there will be exaggerated expressions on the subject from time to time. Consultation, as you know, should be courteous and loving, but it should also be frank. In this area, as in others, the friends should be guided by the spirit of the teachings and strive for the golden mean. (On behalf of the Universal House of Justice, letter dated 24 March 1998, in *Most Challenging Issue*)

As to the need for scholarly works that will interpret the meaning of the issues created by the cruelties of slavery, it is not an empty hope that souls illumined by the Teachings of Bahá'u'lláh and equipped with trained minds will arise to author the kinds of treatises and books you rightly feel will promote understanding. But for those who have turned towards Him, the vision of human purpose given by the Divine Word illumines the way forward for all peoples. The legacy of pain passed down from the global history of man's cruelty to man so burdens and confuses peoples of various climes that there can be no more immediate necessity than to spread knowledge of that Word far and wide. Has it not conveyed the vital truth that "the Ancient Beauty hath consented to be bound with chains that mankind may be released from its bondage, and hath accepted to be made a prisoner within this most mighty Stronghold that the whole world may attain unto true liberty?" Surely, for any believer knowing this, the foremost act, the most important duty, is to present the Bahá'í message to all who will receive it now.

Regarding the question of slavery, its horrifying aftermath in America and the abetment of Christians, you are no doubt aware that enslaving other human beings and otherwise discriminating against them were not unique to members of this religious community. Centuries before the African slave trade was introduced to the West, it was practiced by Muslims in the East. In fact this act of enforced, uncompensated labor and the humiliation it imposed have been a common part of mankind's history stretching back to ancient times; Africans have themselves imposed slavery on different tribes residing among them. It is a sobering fact that this form of oppression has injured the lives of human groups across the planet. Erasing the scars so deeply etched on human consciousness requires a monumental remedy that only a Revelation of the global magnitude of the Bahá'í Faith can ensure. All so afflicted can now find relief in Bahá'u'lláh's assertion that, as the Divine Physician, He has prescribed the remedy for all that ails the world of humanity.

. . . Appreciating the uniqueness of this Day of Days ushered in by the Blessed Beauty surpasses by far the effect, however valuable, of any scholarly effort to provide interpretations of the dreadful acts and consequences of slavery; for with the vision of the future unveiled by His Word all things become new and memories of a horrific past fade in the brilliance of the new Light. This vision assumes a special luminosity when considered in the sense of Bahá'u'lláh's characterization of the first Riḍván, the time of His great announcement in Baghdad, as the Day whereon "all created things were immersed in the sea of purification," whereon "the breezes of forgiveness were wafted over the entire creation." How clearly, then, He created a new beginning, separating the past from the present and beckoning the entire human race to the path leading towards realization of the ultimate and most glorious purpose for which it was created. In this same context, valuable understanding can as well be gained from a statement by Shoghi Effendi on the social evolution of humanity in face of the current challenge of the Bahá'í message. He wrote:

The long ages of infancy and of childhood, through which the human race had to pass, have receded into the background. Humanity is now experiencing the commotions invariably associated with the most turbulent stage of its evolution, the stage of adolescence, when the impetuosity of youth and its vehemence reach their climax, and must gradually be superseded by the calmness, the wisdom, and the maturity that characterize the stage of manhood. Then will the human race reach that stature of ripeness which will enable it to acquire all the powers and capacities upon which its ultimate development must depend.

The summons of Bahá'u'lláh to so outright a departure from the past moves us away from ancient models of activity, such as the experience of the Hebrews at the time of Moses—the prospects of our community do not fit into the framework of the recorded wanderings of that people. For Bahá'u'lláh, in vowing to create a new race, has provided the instruments by which the processes of the social transformation of those composing it are to be guided. He has given us the prescription for a new World Order, declaring that "mankind's ordered life hath been revolutionized through the agency of this unique, this wondrous System—the like of which mortal eyes have never witnessed." As His followers strive to raise up this System, which comprises the institutions of His administration at the local, national and global levels, the spiritual and practical powers of its world-shaping capacity will gradually increase. But we need dedicated souls in great numbers to accomplish what has to be done, and it is for this reason that the House of Justice has set forth a Five Year Plan that calls upon us all to make efforts to advance the process of entry by troops. As you are no doubt aware, this Plan represents the current stage in the operation of the charter of teaching outlined by 'Abdu'l-Bahá in the Tablets of the Divine Plan He addressed to the North American believers. (On behalf of The Universal House of Justice, in a letter dated 3 June 2007, to an individual believer)

ABOLISHING PREJUDICES AND RACISM

"O ye discerning ones!" Bahá'u'lláh has written, "Verily, the words which have descended from the heaven of the Will of God are the source of unity and harmony for the world. Close your eyes to racial differences, and welcome all with the light of oneness." (Shoghi Effendi, *The Advent of Divine Justice*, ¶55)

Behold the disturbances which, for many a long year, have afflicted the earth, and the perturbation that hath seized its peoples. It hath either been ravaged by war, or tormented by sudden and unforeseen calamities. Though the world is encompassed with misery and distress, yet no man hath paused to reflect what the cause or source of that may be. Whenever the True Counsellor uttered a word in admonishment, lo, they all denounced Him as a mover of mischief and rejected His claim. How bewildering, how confusing is such behavior! No two men can be found who may be said to be outwardly and inwardly united. The evidences of discord and malice are apparent everywhere, though all were made for harmony and union. (Bahá'u'lláh, *Tablets of Bahá'u'lláh*, p. 163)

How long will humanity persist in its waywardness? How long will injustice continue? How long is chaos and confusion to reign amongst men? How long will discord agitate the face of society?

This humble servant is filled with wonder, inasmuch as all men are endowed with the capacity to see and hear, yet we find them deprived of the privilege of using these faculties. This servant hath been prompted to pen these lines by virtue of the tender love he cherisheth for thee. The winds of despair are, alas, blowing from every direction, and the strife that divideth and afflicteth the human race is daily increasing. The signs of impending convulsions and chaos can now be discerned, inasmuch as the prevailing order appeareth to be lamentably defective. (Bahá'u'lláh, *Tablets of Bahá'u'lláh*, p. 171)

Ye who are servants of the human race, strive ye with all your heart to deliver mankind out of this darkness and these prejudices that belong to the human condition and the world of nature, so that humanity may find its way into the light of the world of God.

. . . Strive ye, therefore, with the help of God, with illumined minds and hearts and a strength born of heaven, to become a bestowal from God to man, and to call into being for all humankind, comfort and peace. ('Abdu'l-Bahá, *Selections from the Writings of 'Abdu'l-Bahá*, no. 202.13)

Strive with heart and soul in order to bring about union and harmony among the white and the black and prove thereby the unity of the Bahá'í world

52

wherein distinction of color findeth no place, but where hearts only are considered. Praise be to God, the hearts of the friends are united and linked together, whether they be from the east or the west, from north or from south, whether they be German, French, Japanese, American, and whether they pertain to the white, the black, the red, the yellow or the brown race. Variations of color, of land and of race are of no importance in the Bahá'í Faith; on the contrary, Bahá'í unity overcometh them all and doeth away with all these fancies and imaginations. ('Abdu'l-Bahá, *Selections from the Writings of 'Abdu'l-Bahá*, no. 75.1)

Therefore strive earnestly and put forth your greatest endeavor toward the accomplishment of this fellowship and the cementing of this bond of brotherhood between you. Such an attainment is not possible without will and effort on the part of each; from one, expressions of gratitude and appreciation; from the other kindliness and recognition of equality. Each one should endeavor to develop and assist the other toward mutual advancement. This is possible only by conjoining of effort and inclination. Love and unity will be fostered between you, thereby bringing about the oneness of mankind. For the accomplishment of unity between the colored and whites will be an assurance of the world's peace. Then racial prejudice, national prejudice, limited patriotism and religious bias will pass away and remain no longer. I am pleased to see you at this gathering, white and dark, and I praise God that I have had this opportunity of seeing you loving each other, for this is the means of the glory of humanity. This is the means of the good-pleasure of God and of eternal bliss in His kingdom. Therefore I pray in your behalf that you may attain to the fullest degree of love and that the day may come when all differences between you may disappear. ('Abdu'l-Bahá, quoted in Shoghi Effendi, *The Advent of Divine Justice*, ¶56)

As to racial prejudice, the corrosion of which, for well-nigh a century, has bitten into the fiber, and attacked the whole social structure of American society, it should be regarded as constituting the most vital and challenging issue confronting the Bahá'í community at the present stage of its evolution.

The ceaseless exertions which this issue of paramount importance calls for, the sacrifices it must impose, the care and vigilance it demands, the moral courage and fortitude it requires, the tact and sympathy it necessitates, invest this problem, which the American believers are still far from having satisfactorily resolved, with an urgency and importance that cannot be overestimated. White and Negro, high and low, young and old, whether newly converted to the Faith or not, all who stand identified with it must participate in, and lend their assistance, each according to his or her capacity, experience and opportunities to the common task of fulfilling the instructions, realizing the hopes, and following the example of ʻAbduʼl-Bahá. Whether colored or noncolored, neither race has the right or can conscientiously claim to be regarded as absolved from such an example. A long and thorny road, beset with pitfalls still remains untraveled, both by the white and the negro exponents of the redeeming Faith of Baháʼuʼlláh. On the distance they cover, and the manner in which they travel that road, must depend, to an extent which few among them can imagine, the operation of those intangible influences which are indispensable to the spiritual triumph of the American believers and the material success of their newly launched enterprise.

Let them call to mind, fearlessly and determinedly, the example and conduct of ʻAbduʼl-Bahá while in their midst. Let them remember His courage, His genuine love, His informal and indiscriminating fellowship, His contempt for and impatience of criticism, tempered by His tact and wisdom. Let them revive and perpetuate the memory of those unforgettable and historic episodes and occasions on which He so strikingly demonstrated His keen sense of justice, His spontaneous sympathy for the downtrodden, His ever-abiding sense of the oneness of the human race, His overflowing love for its members, and His displeasure with those who dared to flout His wishes, to deride His methods, to challenge His principles, or to nullify His acts. (Shoghi Effendi, *The Advent of Divine Justice*, ¶51–52)

Freedom from racial prejudice, in any of its forms, should, at such a time as this when an increasingly large section of the human race is falling a victim to its devastating ferocity, be adopted as the watchword of the entire body of the American believers, in whichever state they reside, in whatever circles they move, whatever their age, traditions, tastes, and habits. It should be consistently demonstrated in every phase of their activity and life, whether in the Bahá'í community or outside it, in public or in private, formally as well as informally, individually as well as in their official capacity as organized groups, committees and Assemblies. It should be deliberately cultivated through the various and everyday opportunities, no matter how insignificant, that present themselves, whether in their homes, their business offices, their schools and colleges, their social parties and recreation grounds, their Bahá'í meetings, conferences, conventions, summer schools and Assemblies. (Shoghi Effendi, *The Advent of Divine Justice*, ¶54)

As this problem, in the inevitable course of events, grows in acuteness and complexity, and as the number of the faithful from both races multiplies, it will become increasingly evident that the future growth and prestige of the Cause are bound to be influenced to a very considerable degree by the manner in which the adherents of the Bahá'í Faith carry out, first among themselves and in their relations with their fellow-men, those high standards of inter-racial amity so widely proclaimed and so fearlessly exemplified to the American people by our Master 'Abdu'l-Bahá.

I direct my appeal with all the earnestness and urgency that this pressing problem calls for to every conscientious upholder of the universal principles of Bahá'u'lláh to face this extremely delicate situation with the boldness, the decisiveness and wisdom it demands. I cannot believe that those whose hearts have been touched by the regenerating influence of God's creative Faith in His day will find it difficult to cleanse their souls from every lingering trace of racial animosity so subversive of the Faith they profess. How can hearts that throb with the love of God fail to respond to all the implications of this supreme injunction of Bahá'u'lláh, the unreserved acceptance of which, under the circumstances now prevailing in America, constitutes the hallmark of a true Bahá'í character?

Let every believer, desirous to witness the swift and healthy progress of the Cause of God, realize the twofold nature of his task. Let him first turn his eyes inwardly and search his own heart and satisfy himself that in his relations with his fellow-believers, irrespective of color and class, he is proving himself increasingly loyal to the spirit of his beloved Faith. Assured and content that he is exerting his utmost in a conscious effort to approach nearer every day the lofty station to which his gracious Master summons him, let him turn to his second task, and, with befitting confidence and vigor, assail the devastating power of those forces which in his own heart he has already succeeded in subduing. Fully alive to the unfailing efficacy of the power of Bahá'u'lláh, and armed with the essential weapons of wise restraint and inflexible resolve, let him wage a constant fight against the inherited tendencies, the corruptive instincts, the fluctuating fashions, the false pretences of the society in which he lives and moves.

In their relations amongst themselves as fellow-believers, let them not be content with the mere exchange of cold and empty formalities often connected with the organizing of banquets, receptions, consultative assemblies, and lecture-halls. Let them rather, as equal co-sharers in the spiritual benefits conferred upon them by Bahá'u'lláh, arise and, with the aid and counsel of their local and national representatives, supplement these official functions with those opportunities which only a close and intimate social intercourse can adequately provide. In their homes, in their hours of relaxation and leisure, in the daily contact of business transactions, in the association of their children, whether in their study-classes, their playgrounds, and club-rooms, in short under all possible circumstances, however insignificant they appear, the community of the followers of Bahá'u'lláh should satisfy themselves that in the eyes of the world at large and in the sight of their vigilant Master they are the living witnesses of those truths which He fondly cherished and tirelessly championed to the very end of His days. If we relax in our purpose, if we falter in our faith, if we neglect the varied opportunities given us from time to time by an all-wise and gracious Master, we are not merely failing in what is our most vital and conspicuous obligation, but are thereby insensibly retarding the flow of those quickening energies which can alone insure the vigorous and speedy development of God's struggling Faith. (Shoghi Effendi, letter dated 12 April 1927, to the National Spiritual Assembly of the United States and Canada, in *Bahá'í Administration*, pp. 129–30)

Let the white make a supreme effort in their resolve to contribute their share to the solution of this problem, to abandon once for all their usually inherent and at times subconscious sense of superiority, to correct their tendency towards revealing a patronizing attitude towards the members of the other race, to persuade them through their intimate, spontaneous and informal association with them of the genuineness of their friendship and the sincerity of their intentions, and to master their impatience of any lack of responsiveness on the part of a people who have received, for so long a period, such grievous and slow-healing wounds. Let the Negroes, through a corresponding effort on their part, show by every means in their power the warmth of their response, their readiness to forget the past, and their ability to wipe out every trace of suspicion that may still linger in their hearts and minds. Let neither think that the solution of so vast a problem is a matter that exclusively concerns the other. Let neither think that such a problem can either easily or immediately be resolved. Let neither think that they can wait confidently for the solution of this problem until the initiative has been taken, and the favorable circumstances created, by agencies that stand outside the orbit of their Faith. Let neither think that anything short of genuine love, extreme patience, true humility, consummate tact, sound initiative, mature wisdom, and deliberate, persistent, and prayerful effort, can succeed in blotting out the stain which this patent evil has left on the fair name of their common country. Let them rather believe, and be firmly convinced, that on their mutual understanding, their amity, and sustained cooperation, must depend, more than on any other force or organization operating outside the circle of their Faith, the deflection of that dangerous course so greatly feared by 'Abdu'l-Bahá, and the materialization of the hopes He cherished for their joint contribution to the fulfillment of that country's glorious destiny. (Shoghi Effendi, *The Advent of Divine Justice*, ¶58)

[Complete freedom from prejudice] should be the immediate, the universal, and the chief concern of all and sundry members of the Bahá'í community, of whatever age, rank, experience, class, or color, as all, with no exception, must face its challenging implications, and none can claim, however much he may have progressed along this line, to have completely discharged the stern responsibilities which it inculcates. (Shoghi Effendi, *The Advent of Divine Justice*, ¶37)

A tremendous effort is required by both races if their outlook, their manners, and conduct are to reflect, in this darkened age, the spirit and teachings of the Faith of Bahá'u'lláh. Casting away the fallacious doctrine of racial superiority, with all its attendant evils, confusion, and miseries, and welcoming and encouraging the intermixture of races, and tearing down the barriers that now divide them, they should each endeavor, day and night, to fulfill their particular responsibilities in the common task which so urgently faces them. Let them, while each is attempting to contribute its share to the solution of this perplexing problem, call to mind the warnings of 'Abdu'l-Bahá, and visualize, while there is yet time, the dire consequences that must follow if this challenging and unhappy situation that faces the entire American nation is not definitely remedied. (Shoghi Effendi, *The Advent of Divine Justice*, ¶57)

Every believer, without any distinction, has his own part in the Divine Plan established by Bahá'u'lláh. Every one has his duties and responsibilities, and those are commensurate with his gifts and capacities. Let the friends therefore banish from their hearts every feeling of superiority complex. They are all but servants unto Him. (On behalf of Shoghi Effendi, letter dated 20 December 1936, to an individual believer)

Your interracial work, and the response it has awakened in some of the friends in your community, have particularly rejoiced his heart, and confirmed his hopes for the future role which the believers will be called upon to play in the establishment of racial unity and peace in America. The obstacles blocking their activities in this field are by no means easy to overcome, specially in these days when racialism is making such a headway in the West. But we Bahá'ís are sure of the eventual outcome of the forces which are now so seriously counteracting our efforts for the spread and establishment of Bahá'u'lláh's teachings on world unity and peace. (On behalf of Shoghi Effendi, letter dated 2 June 1934, to an individual believer)

All over the world the fires of prejudice are kindled, as if they would burn their brightest in defiance of the new order of oneness of mankind which Bahá'u'lláh has brought. The Bahá'ís face a tremendous task—but a task in which they know they will be victorious. They must demonstrate among themselves that they have done away with all sense of the false barriers which hitherto have kept men apart; then others will believe them and look to them for guidance. This requires true dedication and effort on the part of both the colored and white believers. They each have much to learn and much to overcome, as you both so clearly realize. (On behalf of Shoghi Effendi, letter dated 17 March 1943, to an individual believer)

He does not doubt—though it grieves him to have to admit it—that there are believers who have not overcome their racial prejudices. The Bahá'ís are not perfect, but they have made a great step forward by embracing the Faith of God. We must be patient with each other, and realize that each one of us has some faults to overcome, of one kind or another.

You he feels need to use greater wisdom and forbearance in dealing with your fellow-Bahá'ís and with difficult situations. To be courageous—as you evidently are—to rebel against the injustices of race prejudice and fight them, is not enough you must also show some patience for those who suffer from this terrible American ailment of Negro prejudice and act with wisdom in overcoming it instead of going at it so vehemently that you alienate the Bahá'ís instead of leading them to greater manifestations of the Bahá'í spirit of brotherhood and racial amity . . . (On behalf of Shoghi Effendi, letter dated 1949, to an individual believer, in *Lights of Guidance*, no. 1801)

White American Bahá'ís, he feels, although they have very much less preju-dice than the American people, are nevertheless tainted to some extent with this national evil, perhaps wholly unconsciously so. Therefore, it behooves every believer of white extraction to carefully study his own attitude, and to see whether he is condescending in his relations with his fellow-Bahá'ís of Negro extraction, whether he ever unconsciously insults them by using the term 'nigger' or being patronizingly kind, whether he invites them freely to his home, and makes friends of them to such a point that he no longer knows whether they are colored or white, but only thinks of them as Bill or Mary, so to speak. (On behalf of Shoghi Effendi, letter dated 27 May 1957, to the Bahá'í Inter-Racial Teaching Committee)

Nothing will so deeply affect the hearts of people who have been hurt and offended by the attitude of white supremacy as to consort with them as full equals—as indeed they are. . . . (On behalf of Shoghi Effendi, letter dated 2 February 1956, to an individual believer)

Redouble your efforts in connection with the promotion of interracial amity and understanding. *Urge* the believers to show more affection, confidence, fellowship and loving kindness to the colored believers. No trace of mistrust, no sense of superiority, no mark of discord and aloofness should characterize the relations of the white and colored believers. They should openly, bravely and sincerely follow the example of our Beloved and banish prejudice from their hearts. May He reinforce and bless your efforts in such an important field of work. (Shoghi Effendi, letter dated June 1927, addressed to Dr. Zia Bagdadi)

Another vital problem in America is the color question. Just as in Germany the racial problem is a real challenge to the German believers, so also in the States this problem for the colored and the white is a challenge to the American Bahá'ís. While the colored Bahá'ís must have more confidence in the white, the latter must, in their turn, and particularly on informal occa-sions, show more consideration and friendliness towards the former. The

Bahá'í attitude towards this problem must in all cases be made definite and clear, although its solution requires a great measure of tact and wisdom. (On behalf of Shoghi Effendi, letter dated 16 March 1934, to an individual believer)

The Guardian feels very strongly that the Negro Bahá'ís have great responsibilities, both towards their own race and towards their fellow-believers. They must not only arise to teach the Cause to the members of their own race, but must do all in their power to ensure that within their Bahá'í Community itself the Negro and white believers understand and love each other and are truly as one soul in different bodies. Our allegiance as believers is to Bahá'u'lláh; we must fix our attention and devotion on Him, and His Will, and, heedless of the shortcomings of our fellow-Bahá'ís, act as He would have us towards them. (On behalf of Shoghi Effendi, letter dated 23 November 1941, to an individual believer)

He was very happy to hear of how active and devoted you and your family are in the service of the Faith—particularly to learn that you are of the Negro race, as it always rejoices his heart to receive news that the colored friends are assuming their full Bahá'í responsibilities, and demonstrating, in a country so tainted with race prejudice, the unity of the friends, of all races, in the Cause of God. (On behalf of Shoghi Effendi, letter dated 6 September 1946, to an individual believer)

He was especially glad to hear that the activities of the friends in eliminating racial differences is daily increasing and that they are achieving much more than in past days. Such progress is naturally very slow for there are strong feelings on both sides that have to be overcome. It is a training that must spread over a period of many years. Shoghi Effendi hopes that the Bahá'ís will gradually be considered the leading religious movement working for this aim. This forms an important element in the teachings of Bahá'u'lláh and 'Abdu'l-Bahá and the world at large should know that it is so. (On behalf of Shoghi Effendi, letter dated 11 March 1931, to an individual believer)

Racial and ethnic prejudices have been subjected to equally summary treatment by historical processes that have little patience left for such pretensions. Here, rejection of the past has been especially decisive. Racism is now tainted by its association with the horrors of the twentieth century to the degree that it has taken on something of the character of a spiritual disease. While surviving as a social attitude in many parts of the world—and as a blight on the lives of a significant segment of humankind—racial prejudice has become so universally condemned in principle that no body of people can any longer safely allow themselves to be identified with it. (The Universal House of Justice, *To the World's Religious Leaders,* p. 1)

Wherever a Bahá'í community exists, whether large or small, let it be distinguished for its abiding sense of security and faith, its high standard of rectitude, its complete freedom from all forms of prejudice, the spirit of love among its members and for the closely knit fabric of its social life. (The Universal House of Justice, *Messages, 1963–1986,* no. 63.5)

Bahá'u'lláh tells us that prejudice in its various forms destroys the edifice of humanity. We are adjured by the Divine Messenger to eliminate all forms of prejudice from our lives. Our outer lives must show forth our beliefs. The world must see that, regardless of each passing whim or current fashion of the generality of mankind, the Bahá'í lives his life according to the tenets of his Faith. We must not allow the fear of rejection by our friends and neighbors to deter us from our goal: to live the Bahá'í life. Let us strive to blot out from our lives every last trace of prejudice—racial, religious, political, economic, national, tribal, class, cultural, and that which is based on differences of education or age. We shall be distinguished from our non-Bahá'í associates if our lives are adorned with this principle.

If we allow prejudice of any kind to manifest itself in us, we shall be guilty before God of causing a setback to the progress and real growth of the Faith of Bahá'u'lláh. It is incumbent upon every believer to endeavor with a fierce determination to eliminate this defect from his thoughts and acts. It is the duty of the institutions of the Faith to inculcate this principle in the hearts of the friends through every means at their disposal including summer schools, conferences, institutes and study classes.

The fundamental purpose of the Faith of Bahá'u'lláh is the realization of the organic unity of the entire human race. Bearing this glorious destiny in mind, and with entire reliance on the promises of the Blessed Beauty, we should follow His exhortation:

We love to see you at all times consorting in amity and concord within the paradise of My good-pleasure, and to inhale from your acts the fragrance of friendliness and unity, of loving-kindness and fellowship. (The Universal House of Justice, *Messages 1963–1986*, no. 117.2–5)

The Universal House of Justice received your letter . . . regarding class prejudice in the Bahá'í community, and it has asked us to comment as follows. . . .

The problems related to class prejudice which you have experienced and observed are noted, and the suggestions you offer for working toward their remedy are truly appreciated. As you know, the Bahá'ís are distinguished not by their perfection or their immunity from the negative influences of the wider society in which they live, but by their acceptance of Bahá'u'lláh's vision and willingness to work toward it. Each of us must strike a balance between realistically facing our community's shortcomings, and focusing on Bahá'u'lláh's Teachings rather than our fellow believers as our standard of faith. This comment is not intended to belittle your concerns, but rather to place them in perspective so that you may not become discouraged as you strive toward the ideal.

You are encouraged to share your thoughtful suggestions for raising awareness of this issue with your Local Spiritual Assembly, your National Spiritual Assembly and fellow individual believers. The first step in eradicating any prejudice is education at the local level about the existence of the problem rather than legislation of a particular policy from afar. As you suggest, the Nineteen Day Feast is a perfect forum for beginning consultation on such matters, and further opportunities for education through larger gatherings can always be suggested to the institutions. . . . (On behalf of the Universal House of Justice, letter dated 20 January 1994, to an individual believer)

The Universal House of Justice has received your letter . . . discussing the many difficulties faced by people of color in America, with particular reference to the Bahá'í community. . . .

Even if all you describe is so, you share in common with your fellow believers the unique bounty of having recognized the Supreme Manifestation of God, Bahá'u'lláh. This fact empowers you and them to engage in a necessary process of spiritual transformation, a process which is slow and sometimes can be painful. The most significant contribution one can make to the progress of such a transformation is first to deal with one's own spiritual deficiencies, then to attempt lovingly, patiently and confidently to encourage others in their strivings to adhere to the principles of the Cause. However, such encouragement is most effective not through words alone, but especially to the extent one's own ". . . inner life and private character mirror forth in their manifold aspects the splendor of those eternal principles proclaimed by Bahá'u'lláh."

Regarding relations between the races, in "The Advent of Divine Justice," Shoghi Effendi has clearly indicated the attitude and actions which will enable the friends, black or white, to deal with this entrenched and seemingly intractable problem. You also may wish to read about the life of the Hand of the Cause Louis Gregory to see how 'Abdu'l-Bahá's unbounded love so transformed him that he in turn became a potent instrument in effecting transformation in others, enabling him to triumph over racial prejudice at one of the saddest and worst periods of racial discrimination in the history of the United States. Look with the eye of fairness at how much things have changed for the better since that time, and be confident that the example Mr. Gregory set, if followed, can effect greater changes than have already occurred.

There is no way in which one can retreat to one's ethnic circle and find peace by building a fence around it. The goal is unity. In this new period of human history when the earth with all its diversity of peoples has become a single neighborhood, each Bahá'í must resolutely face the challenge of achieving unity and making peace. The House of Justice has noted that the National Spiritual Assembly of the United States has initiated a race unity campaign, which it hopes will go far in removing the blight of race prejudice from the American people. It hopes that you will lend your cooperation and energy to this work, which has ramifications not only for the people of America but, potentially, for the planet as a whole. (On behalf of the Universal House of Justice, letter dated 2 September 1992, to an individual believer)

With regard to the question of what public role might be played by the Bahá'í Faith in America to ameliorate in the immediately foreseeable future the plight of African-American males, the size and influence of the Bahá'í community are, alas, too limited for it to have a determining impact on conditions which have, after all, been hundreds of years in the making. As is well known, since at least the middle of the last century significant numbers of Americans, both black and white, have long labored, often with immense resourcefulness, to counteract the baleful legacy of racism in their country, in all its complex dimensions, structural and otherwise. Indeed, when one meditates on the sweep of United States history, one can see how unlikely it is that the bitter predicament of black males will be quickly or easily resolved. The obstacles are not of such character that, for example, legal reforms could dissolve them. This is not a counsel of despair. Nor is it an equivocation or a suggestion that the requirements of divine justice ought to be deferred. Nor is it to say that Bahá'ís have no critical role to play. On the contrary, the concern is with Bahá'í fundamentals, with looking deeply into underlying causes and identifying strategic lines of action which make the wisest use of our limited resources at this point in the development of the Bahá'í community.

If we are to avoid becoming entrammeled in the enervating coils of cynicism which are a characteristic of this age of transition, we must, as the "custodians of . . . the forces of love," ground our efforts in indomitable faith. In the future the Cause of God will spread throughout America; millions will be enlisted under its banner and race prejudice will finally be exorcised from the body politic. Of this have no doubt. It is inexorable, because it is the Will of Almighty God. However, as the House of Justice has been trying to get the friends to understand for some time, the necessary precondition to translation of our community's social vision into reality is a massive expansion in the number of committed, deepened believers who are well-grounded in the essentials of the Cause. Those who fail to comprehend the urgency assigned to the objective of achieving a large expansion have obviously failed to appreciate the moral imperative behind this aim.

Parallel to the process of large-scale enrollment, the institutions of the Faith, including those at the grassroots of the community, will gradually come to function with greater efficiency and increasing harmony, thereby enhancing their potential in stimulating the processes of social development.

Concerning the comparison you have drawn in your letter between the situation of the Bahá'í community in Iran and the African-American people generally, it is noteworthy that, while the plight of the Iranian friends is grievous, it is also in some essential respects far more tractable. Furthermore, since the community is organized around the divine Teachings and empowered by the Word of God, the effects of victimization on the Iranian believers is likely to prove, in the long view, less devastating than the effects of that which has been inflicted upon the African-Americans.

Moreover, it is wholly conceivable that a tiny handful of secular and clerical rulers who control the government there could, more or less at the stroke of a pen, effectively emancipate that community from the bulk of its practical difficulties. Nonetheless, we are the only ones in the world who would so persistently direct the focus of international attention toward achieving the aim of lifting the shackles from our co-religionists. There is no one else to take the lead.

The House of Justice sympathizes with your frustrations. It feels, however, that the best contribution which the friends can make is to carry on with work of the kind you are already doing, demonstrating the Bahá'í spirit to others, showing their love for mankind and patiently, determinedly working to bring about a change in the hearts and minds of those they are able to reach. It is a question of being in this struggle for the long term, of advancing the issue as much as feasible, given the conditions with which one has to work. In this respect, the powerful example of the Hand of the Cause Louis Gregory is an invaluable source of inspiration and encouragement. . . . (On behalf of the Universal House of Justice, letter dated 1 April 1996, to an individual believer)

The Universal House of Justice sympathizes with your view that the situation in America has not changed as hoped, but as the beloved Guardian has told us in the *Advent of Divine Justice*, no profound and lasting change will come about unless certain spiritual prerequisites are met. These prerequisites have yet to be achieved by the broad public, and Bahá'ís themselves have often been slow to put them into practice.

Your suggestion that some form of anthropology should be taught to all children is a good one, because when young people have access to accurate, biological information, when they learn how amorphous and uncertain such terms as "race" have been in terms of their precise scientific usage, this information will tend to inoculate them against some of the cruder, but nevertheless insidious, arguments used by racists to bolster their positions. Indeed, we should welcome any sound method for removing the encumbrances to a fruitful effort in resolving racial prejudices.

That the term "race," as used in its ordinary sense to describe one of the major, broad divisions of mankind, should be substituted by a new word, is interesting, but it will be hard to judge at this stage the effectiveness of such a change in view of the history of other changes within our own lifetimes. For instance, as pointed out in your letter, among the black people in the United States, the adjective of choice has changed from colored to Negro, to black, to Afro-American to African-American, and still no resolution has been reached in determining a universally acceptable and appropriate terminology for describing the race. This demonstrates really that the results sought are less inherent in terminologies than in the transformation of hearts which will be brought about only through the power of the Blessed Beauty and in the manner described by the beloved Guardian. (The Universal House of Justice, letter dated 23 May 1990, to an individual believer)

The Black Men's Gathering was inspired by a thought to stimulate African-Americans to respond to the urgent call to action of the Divine Plan and so overcome the crippling effects of a long history of oppression. The participants in the Gathering have wisely concentrated their energies on pursuing the requirements of that charter. Indeed, the fulfillment of their highest hopes for the advancement of the race depends on the extent to which they maintain their dedication to the Five Year Plan and succeeding enterprises that the House of Justice will devise in a continuing effort to accomplish the Master's scheme for world redemption. What the Gathering does so well is to instill in its participants the desire to strive to realize the potentialities they possess—both from their natural endowments as creatures of God and from the wisdom afforded them by the experience of their particular history—for contributing significantly to that effort. Such consecrated endeavor is the only way by which they can arrive at the furthermost goal of the common destiny of the entire human race: the Kingdom of God on earth. (On behalf of the Universal House of Justice, letter dated 3 June 2007)

The letter from the participants of 2011 Black Men's Gathering has been warmly received by the Universal House of Justice. It was pleased to note that a portion of the gathering was devoted to a study of the 28 December 2010 message concerning the new Five Year Plan, as well as the letters dated 1 April 1996, 3 June 2007, and 10 April 2011, which have particular relevance to African American believers.

A quarter century ago, the Black Men's Gathering was established with the aim of soothing hearts that had sustained slow-healing wounds and cultivating capacity for participation in a world-embracing mission. The approach involved drawing together a small number of participants from across the country with a capable facilitator. As you well know, in the Bahá'í Faith, the watchword of which is the oneness of humanity, it is no small exception to make arrangements for an assemblage that excludes others by race and gender. Yet, acknowledging the uncommon circumstances, the House of Justice lent its support to your endeavor with high hopes and expectations. For these many years, the Gathering has served its members as a bulwark against the forces of racial prejudice afflicting your nation, and, indeed, attacking the Bahá'í community itself, creating an environment in which injuries could be tended, bonds of unity strengthened, sparks of spirituality fanned into flames, and the capacity for assuming the responsibility for the work of the Cause gradually developed through experience in the field of action. The House of Justice hopes that, from the various communications you have studied, you have perceived that the time has now come for the friends who have benefited from the Gathering to raise their sights to new horizons.

The impact of the unfoldment of the Divine Plan is making itself felt in all continents of the world. The result is not only demonstrated in the growth in numbers and the invigoration of community life, but also in the stirrings of the society-building power of the Faith, as discussed in the 28 December message. During the last Plan, Africa particularly distinguished itself through its achievements. In the Democratic Republic of the Congo, more than 90 intensive programs of growth emerged. In the single cluster of Tiriki West in Kenya, more than 500 empowered individuals established a pattern of community life that embraced some 5,000 souls. Reports received from junior youth groups made it evident that thousands of young minds and spirits were galvanized and transformed as young people displayed a new attitude toward their communities, their families, and their education, determined to resist and cast aside the burdensome yoke of social ills such as tribalism. And in the establishment of hundreds of community schools across a dozen countries, the friends demonstrated their ability to apply Bahá'u'lláh's teachings to an embryonic educational network that made its mark on the spiritual, social, and material education of children, in many instances surpassing the performance of government schools.

The experience of the last five years and the recent guidance of the House of Justice should make it evident that in the instruments of the Plan you now have within your grasp everything that is necessary to raise up a new people and eliminate racial prejudice as a force within your society, though the path ahead remains long and arduous. The institute process is the primary vehicle by which you can transform and empower your people, indeed all the peoples of your nation. You have the capacity to serve as, and to prepare others to be, educators of children, animators of junior youth, teachers of the Faith, tutors of study circles, participants in elevated discourse, and initiators of social action. Let the well-prepared army you have assembled advance from its secure fortress to conquer the hearts of your fellow citizens. What is needed is concerted, persistent, sacrificial action, cycle after cycle, in cluster after cluster, by an ever-swelling number of consecrated individuals.

In the next year you will observe the centenary of the visit of 'Abdu'l-Bahá to your shores and will recall His tireless and heroic exertions to quicken the peoples of America—in particular His fearless assault on racial barriers. Follow in His noble path, so that by the end of this new Plan and the one to follow, you will have an abundant harvest of victories to offer in His name by the centenary of His passing in 2021.

Rest assured of the supplications of the House of Justice at the Sacred Threshold that the Almighty will confirm and reinforce your devoted efforts to bring the light of Bahá'u'lláh's Message to an ever-increasing number of receptive souls. (On behalf of the Universal House of Justice, letter dated 28 August 2011, addressed to the participants of the Black Men's Gathering)

AVERTING THE DANGERS OF DISUNITY, PREJUDICE, AND RACISM

O people of Justice! Be as brilliant as the light, and as splendid as the fire that blazed in the Burning Bush. The brightness of the fire of your love will no doubt fuse and unify the contending peoples and kindreds of the earth, whilst the fierceness of the flame of enmity and hatred cannot but result in strife and ruin. (Bahá'u'lláh, *Gleanings from the Writings of Bahá'u'lláh*, no. 43.7)

For a single purpose were the Prophets, each and all, sent down to earth; for this was Christ made manifest, for this did Bahá'u'lláh raise up the call of the Lord: that the world of man should become the world of God, this nether realm the Kingdom, this darkness light, this satanic wickedness all the virtues of heaven—and unity, fellowship and love be won for the whole human race, that the organic unity should reappear and the bases of discord be destroyed and life everlasting and grace everlasting become the harvest of mankind.

. . . Look about thee at the world: here unity, mutual attraction, gathering together, engender life, but disunity and inharmony spell death. When thou dost consider all phenomena, thou wilt see that every created thing hath come into being through the mingling of many elements, and once this collectivity of elements is dissolved, and this harmony of components is dissevered, the life form is wiped out. ('Abdu'l-Bahá, *Selections from the Writings of 'Abdu'l-Bahá*, no. 15.4–5)

Reflect ye as to other than human forms of life and be ye admonished thereby: those clouds that drift apart cannot produce the bounty of the rain, and are soon lost; a flock of sheep, once scattered, falleth prey to the wolf, and birds that fly alone will be caught fast in the claws of the hawk. What greater demonstration could there be that unity leadeth to flourishing life, while dissension and withdrawing from the others, will lead only to misery; for these are the sure ways to bitter disappointment and ruin. ('Abdu'l-Bahá, *Selections from the Writings of 'Abdu'l-Bahá*, no. 221.8)

The body politic may be likened to the human organism. As long as the various members and parts of that organism are coordinated and cooperating in harmony, we have as a result the expression of life in its fullest degree. When these members lack coordination and harmony, we have the reverse, which in the human organism is disease, dissolution, death. Similarly, in the body politic of humanity dissension, discord and warfare are always destructive and inevitably fatal. All created beings are dependent upon peace and coordination, for every contingent and phenomenal being is a composition of distinct elements. As long as there is affinity and cohesion among these constituent elements, strength and life are manifest; but when dissension and repulsion arise among them, disintegration follows. This is proof that peace and amity, which God has willed for His children, are the saving factors of human society, whereas war and strife, which violate His ordinances, are the cause of death and destruction. ('Abdu'l-Bahá, *The Promulgation of Universal Peace*, pp. 136–37)

Consider: Unity is necessary to existence. Love is the very cause of life; on the other hand, separation brings death. In the world of material creation, for instance, all things owe their actual life to unity. The elements which compose wood, mineral, or stone, are held together by the law of attraction. If this law should cease for one moment to operate these elements would not hold together, they would fall apart, and the object would in that particular form cease to exist. The law of attraction has brought together certain elements in the form of this beautiful flower, but when that attraction is withdrawn from this center the flower will decompose, and, as a flower, cease to exist.

So it is with the great body of humanity. The wonderful Law of Attraction, Harmony and Unity, holds together this marvelous Creation.

As with the whole, so with the parts; whether a flower or a human body, when the attracting principle is withdrawn from it, the flower or the man dies. It is therefore clear that attraction, harmony, unity and Love, are the cause of life, whereas repulsion, discord, hatred and separation bring death.

We have seen that whatever brings division into the world of existence causes death. Likewise in the world of the spirit does the same law operate. ('Abdu'l-Bahá, *Paris Talks*, no. 42.5–8)

A meeting such as this* seems like a beautiful cluster of precious jewels— pearls, rubies, diamonds, sapphires. It is a source of joy and delight. Whatever is conducive to the unity of the world of mankind is most acceptable and praiseworthy; whatever is the cause of discord and disunion is saddening and deplorable. Consider the significance of unity and harmony.

---

*An interracial meeting that 'Abdu'l-Bahá addressed on 24 April 1912 at the home of Mrs. Andrew J. Dyer in Washington, D.C.

This evening I will speak to you upon the subject of existence and nonexistence, life and death. Existence is the expression and outcome of composition and combination. Nonexistence is the expression and outcome of division and disintegration. If we study the forms of existence in the material universe, we find that all created things are the result of composition. Material elements have grouped together in infinite variety and endless forms. Each organism is a compound; each object is an expression of elemental affinity. We find the complex human organism simply an aggregation of cellular structure; the tree is a composite of plant cells; the animal, a combination and grouping of cellular atoms or units, and so on. Existence or the expression of being is, therefore, composition; and nonexistence is decomposition, division, disintegration. When elements have been brought together in a certain plan of combination, the result is the human organism; when these elements separate and disperse, the outcome is death and nonexistence. Life is, therefore, the product of composition; and death signifies decomposition.

Likewise, in the world of minds and souls, fellowship, which is an expression of composition, is conducive to life, whereas discord, which is an expression of decomposition, is the equivalent of death. Without cohesion among the individual elements which compose the body politic, disintegration and decay must inevitably follow and life be extinguished. Ferocious animals have no fellowship. The vultures and tigers are solitary, whereas domestic animals live together in complete harmony. The sheep, black and white, associate without discord. Birds of various species and colors wing their flight and feed together without a trace of enmity or disagreement. Therefore, in the world of humanity it is wise and seemly that all the individual members should manifest unity and affinity. In the clustered jewels of the races may the blacks be as sapphires and rubies and the whites as diamonds and pearls. The composite beauty of humanity will be witnessed in their unity and blending. How glorious the spectacle of real unity among mankind! How conducive to peace, confidence and happiness if races and nations were united in fellowship and accord! The Prophets of God were sent into the world upon this mission of unity and agreement: that these long-separated sheep might flock together. When the sheep separate, they are exposed to danger, but in a flock and under protection of the shepherd they are safe from the attack of all ferocious enemies. ('Abdu'l-Bahá, *The Promulgation of Universal Peace*, pp. 76–78)

. . . religious, racial, political, economic and patriotic prejudices destroy the edifice of humanity. As long as these prejudices prevail, the world of humanity will not have rest. For a period of 6,000 years history informs us about the world of humanity. During these 6,000 years the world of humanity has not been free from war, strife, murder and bloodthirstiness. In every period war has been waged in one country or another and that war was due to either religious prejudice, racial prejudice, political prejudice or patriotic prejudice. It has therefore been ascertained and proved that all prejudices are destructive of the human edifice. As long as these prejudices persist, the struggle for existence must remain dominant, and bloodthirstiness and rapacity continue. Therefore, even as was the case in the past, the world of humanity cannot be saved from the darkness of nature and cannot attain illumination except through the abandonment of prejudices and the acquisition of the morals of the Kingdom. ('Abdu'l-Bahá, *Selections from the Writings of 'Abdu'l-Bahá*, no. 71.1)

Again, as to religious, racial, national and political bias: all these prejudices strike at the very root of human life; one and all they beget bloodshed, and the ruination of the world. So long as these prejudices survive, there will be continuous and fearsome wars. ('Abdu'l-Bahá, *Selections from the Writings of 'Abdu'l-Bahá*, no. 202.10)

The most important teaching of His Highness Bahá'u'lláh is to leave behind racial, religious, national and patriotic prejudices. Until these prejudices are entirely removed from the people of the world, the realm of humanity will not find rest. Nay, rather, discord and bloodshed will increase day by day, and the foundation of the prosperity of the world of man will be destroyed. ('Abdu'l-Bahá, from a Tablet addressed to Mrs. Antoinette Crump Cone, translated 24 February 1912 by Mírzá Ahmad Sohrab, *Star of the West*, vol. 7, p. 122)

The glad tidings of the progress of the Cause of God in that country is the cause of happiness. I hope that the Congress of the White and the Black, which has been instituted, will have great influence on the inhabitants of America, so that everyone may confess and bear witness that the teachings of Bahá'u'lláh assemble the Black, the White, the Yellow, the Red and the Brown under the shade of the pavilion of the oneness of the world of humanity; and that if His teachings be not enforced, the antagonism between the Black and the White in America will give rise to great calamities. The salve for this wound and the remedy for this disease are none other than the breaths of holiness. If the hearts be attracted to the heavenly bounties, surely the White and Black will, in a short time, according to the teachings of Bahá'u'lláh, put away hatred and animosity and establish love and fellowship. ('Abdu'l-Bahá, from a recently translated Tablet)

'Abdu'l-Bahá said: ". . . If the races do not come to an agreement, there can be no question or doubt of bloodshed. When I was in America, I told the white and colored people that it was incumbent upon them to be united or else there would be the shedding of blood. I did not say more than this that they might not be saddened. But, indeed, there is a greater danger than only the shedding of blood. It is the destruction of America. Because aside from the racial prejudice there is another agitating factor. It is that of America's enemies. These enemies are agitating both sides, that is, they are stirring up the white race against the colored race and the colored race against the white race. But of this the Americans are submerged in the sea of ignorance. They will regret it. But of what use will their regret be after the destruction of America? Will it be of any use then?"

I told him of a letter which I had received from Chicago during the week, stating that two houses belonging to colored Bahá'ís had been bombed with dynamite. 'Abdu'l-Bahá said: "I foretell things before they happen and I write about them before they occur. The destruction of two or three houses is of no importance, but the importance lies in what is coming, which is the destruction of America. The Arabs have many proverbs. For instance, 'Heavy rains begin with drops before it pours,' and 'The dancer starts with shaking the shoulder, then the whole body.' Now is the time for the Americans to take up this matter and unite both the white and the colored races. Otherwise, hasten ye towards destruction! Hasten ye toward devastation!" (From a letter written by Zia M. Baghdádí, containing the reported words of 'Abdu'l-Bahá, in *Star of the West*, vol. 12, no. 6, pp. 120–21)

To bring the white and the black together is considered impossible and unfeasible, but the breaths of the Holy Spirit will bring about this union.

. . . the enmity and hatred which exist between the white and the black races is very dangerous and there is no doubt that it will end in bloodshed unless the influence of the Word of God, the breaths of the Holy Spirit and the teachings of Bahá'u'lláh are diffused amongst them and harmony is established between the two races.

They must destroy the foundation of enmity and rancor and lay the basis of love and affinity. The power of the Teachings of Bahá'u'lláh will remove this danger from America. ('Abdu'l-Bahá quoted in a letter dated 4 February 1985, on behalf of the Universal House of Justice to the National Spiritual Assembly of the United States)

"This question of the union of the white and the black is very important," He ['Abdu'l-Bahá] warns, "for if it is not realized, erelong great difficulties will arise, and harmful results will follow." "If this matter remaineth without change," is yet another warning, "enmity will be increased day by day, and the final result will be hardship and may end in bloodshed." (Shoghi Effendi, *The Advent of Divine Justice*, ¶56)

Races, alienated more than ever before, are filled with mistrust, humiliation and fear, and seem to prepare themselves for a fresh and fateful encounter. (Shoghi Effendi, *Bahá'í Administration*, pp. 67–68)

No less serious [than American moral laxity, crass materialism, and the arms race] is the stress and strain imposed on the fabric of American society through the fundamental and persistent neglect, by the governed and governors alike, of the supreme, the inescapable and urgent duty—so repeatedly and graphically represented and stressed by ʻAbduʼl-Bahá in His arraignment of the basic weaknesses in the social fabric of the nation—of remedying, while there is yet time, through a revolutionary change in the concept and attitude of the average white American toward his Negro fellow citizen, a situation which, if allowed to drift, will, in the words of ʻAbduʼl-Bahá, cause the streets of American cities to run with blood, aggravating thereby the havoc which the fearful weapons of destruction, raining from the air, and amassed by a ruthless, a vigilant, a powerful and inveterate enemy, will wreak upon those same cities.

The American nation, of which the community of the Most Great Name forms as yet a negligible and infinitesimal part, stands, indeed, from whichever angle one observes its immediate fortunes, in grave peril. The woes and tribulations which threaten it are partly avoidable, but mostly inevitable and God-sent, for by reason of them a government and people clinging tenaciously to the obsolescent doctrine of absolute sovereignty and upholding a political system, manifestly at variance with the needs of a world already contracted into a neighborhood and crying out for unity, will find itself purged of its anachronistic conceptions, and prepared to play a preponderating role, as foretold by ʻAbduʼl-Bahá, in the hoisting of the standard of the Lesser Peace, in the unification of mankind, and in the establishment of a world federal government on this planet. These same fiery tribulations will not only firmly weld the American nation to its sister nations in both hemispheres, but will through their cleansing effect, purge it thoroughly of the accumulated dross which ingrained racial prejudice, rampant materialism, widespread ungodliness and moral laxity have combined, in the course of successive generations, to produce, and which have prevented her thus far from assuming the role of world spiritual leadership forecast by ʻAbduʼl-Bahá's unerring pen—a role which she is bound to fulfill through travail and sorrow. (Shoghi Effendi, *Citadel of Faith*, p. 126)

He hopes that especially in the Amity work you will be guided to do the very best, for that is the outstanding social problem of that country. If that issue remains and drags and the existing distrust among the colored and white be left to wax stronger, as the Master said, the streets will actually run with blood. From our point of view, this problem can only be tackled from a spiritual angle, for only by a spiritual awakening can this misunderstanding and prejudice vanish. We are often apt to follow the modern attitude of mind and consider economic issues the common denominator of all our problems. With their spiritual approach, the Bahá'ís could achieve more than any other movement. (On behalf of Shoghi Effendi, letter dated 7 December 1930 to an individual believer, included in a letter dated 4 February 1985, on behalf of the Universal House of Justice to the National Spiritual Assembly of the United States)

The recent riots in Los Angeles and other cities are one more compelling reminder of the warnings uttered repeatedly by 'Abdu'l-Bahá during His visit to North America, and frequently echoed by Shoghi Effendi in his writings, about the dangerous consequences of racial prejudice. They also underscore the timeliness of the statement on racial unity which you issued at the Bahá'í National Convention in 1991.

In the wake of the disturbances which threaten to engulf other areas, we reiterate more strongly than before the encouragement we expressed for your campaign to combat racism in the United States. It is highly fitting that during this Holy Year, which marks the centenary of the ascension of the Manifestation of God Who made the oneness of humankind the pivotal principle and goal of His Faith, you should sally forth in a mighty effort to rally the forces which will in His Name and in obedience to His command assist in eradicating this evil from the fair name of your country. (The Universal House of Justice, letter dated 11 May 1992, to the National Spiritual Assembly of the United Sates)

Racism, one of the most baneful and persistent evils, is a major barrier to peace. Its practice perpetrates too outrageous a violation of the dignity of human beings to be countenanced under any pretext. Racism retards the unfoldment of the boundless potentialities of its victims, corrupts its perpetrators, and blights human progress. Recognition of the oneness of mankind, implemented by appropriate legal measures, must be universally upheld if this problem is to be overcome. (The Universal House of Justice, *The Promise of World Peace,* ¶29)

When Bahá'u'lláh proclaimed His Message to the world in the nineteenth century He made it abundantly clear that the first step essential for the peace and progress of mankind was its unification. As He says, "The well-being of mankind, its peace and security are unattainable unless and until its unity is firmly established." To this day, however, you will find most people take the opposite point of view: they look upon unity as an ultimate, almost unattainable goal and concentrate first on remedying all the other ills of mankind. If they did but know it, these other ills are but various symptoms and side effects of the basic disease—disunity. (The Universal House of Justice, letter dated 8 December 1967 to an individual believer, in *Wellspring of Guidance, Messages 1963–1968,* p. 131)

Avoiding Strife and Overcoming Estrangement

O friends! Be not careless of the virtues with which ye have been endowed, neither be neglectful of your high destiny. Suffer not your labors to be wasted through the vain imaginations which certain hearts have devised. Ye are the stars of the heaven of understanding, the breeze that stirreth at the break of day, the soft-flowing waters upon which must depend the very life of all men, the letters inscribed upon His sacred scroll. With the utmost unity, and in a spirit of perfect fellowship, exert yourselves, that ye may be enabled to achieve that which beseemeth this Day of God. Verily I say, strife and dissension, and whatsoever the mind of man abhorreth are entirely unworthy of his station. Center your energies in the propagation of the Faith of God. (Bahá'u'lláh, *Gleanings from the Writings of Bahá'u'lláh,* no. 96.3)

The distinguishing feature that marketh the preeminent character of this Supreme Revelation consisteth in that We have, on the one hand, blotted out from the pages of God's holy Book whatsoever hath been the cause of strife, of malice and mischief amongst the children of men, and have, on the other, laid down the essential prerequisites of concord, of understanding, of complete and enduring unity. Well is it with them that keep My statutes. (Bahá'u'lláh, *Gleanings from the Writings of Bahá'u'lláh*, no. 43.10)

Nothing whatever can, in this Day, inflict a greater harm upon this Cause than dissension and strife, contention, estrangement and apathy, among the loved ones of God. Flee them, through the power of God and His sovereign aid, and strive ye to knit together the hearts of men, in His Name, the Unifier, the All-Knowing, the All-Wise. (Bahá'u'lláh, *Gleanings from the Writings of Bahá'u'lláh*, no. 5.5)

O contending peoples and kindreds of the earth! Set your faces towards unity, and let the radiance of its light shine upon you. Gather ye together, and for the sake of God resolve to root out whatever is the source of contention amongst you. (Bahá'u'lláh, *Gleanings from the Writings of Bahá'u'lláh*, no. 111.1)

Shut your eyes to estrangement, then fix your gaze upon unity. Cleave tenaciously unto that which will lead to the well-being and tranquility of all mankind. This span of earth is but one homeland and one habitation. It behoveth you to abandon vainglory which causeth alienation and to set your hearts on whatever will ensure harmony. (Bahá'u'lláh, *Tablets of Bahá'u'lláh*, p. 67)

It is Our wish and desire that every one of you may become a source of all goodness unto men, and an example of uprightness to mankind. Beware lest ye prefer yourselves above your neighbors. Fix your gaze upon Him Who is the Temple of God amongst men. He, in truth, hath offered up His life as a ransom for the redemption of the world. He, verily, is the All-Bountiful, the Gracious, the Most High. If any differences arise amongst you, behold

Me standing before your face, and overlook the faults of one another for My name's sake and as a token of your love for My manifest and resplendent Cause. We love to see you at all times consorting in amity and concord within the paradise of My good-pleasure, and to inhale from your acts the fragrance of friendliness and unity, of loving-kindness and fellowship. Thus counselleth you the All-Knowing, the Faithful. We shall always be with you; if We inhale the perfume of your fellowship, Our heart will assuredly rejoice, for naught else can satisfy Us. (Bahá'u'lláh, *Gleanings from the Writings of Bahá'u'lláh*, no. 146.1)

Bend thou with tenderness over the servitors of the All-Merciful, that thou mayest hoist the sail of love upon the ark of peace that moveth across the seas of life. Let nothing grieve thee, and be thou angered at none. ('Abdu'l-Bahá, *Selections from the Writings of 'Abdu'l-Bahá*, no. 9.3)

Be in perfect unity. Never become angry with one another. Let your eyes be directed toward the kingdom of truth and not toward the world of creation. Love the creatures for the sake of God and not for themselves. You will never become angry or impatient if you love them for the sake of God. Humanity is not perfect. There are imperfections in every human being, and you will always become unhappy if you look toward the people themselves. But if you look toward God, you will love them and be kind to them, for the world of God is the world of perfection and complete mercy. Therefore, do not look at the shortcomings of anybody; see with the sight of forgiveness. The imperfect eye beholds imperfections. The eye that covers faults looks toward the Creator of souls. He created them, trains and provides for them, endows them with capacity and life, sight and hearing; therefore, they are the signs of His grandeur. ('Abdu'l-Bahá, *The Promulgation of Universal Peace*, p. 128)

How good it is if the friends be as close as sheaves of light, if they stand together side by side in a firm unbroken line. For now have the rays of reality from the Sun of the world of existence, united in adoration all the worshippers of this light; and these rays have, through infinite grace, gathered all peoples together within this wide-spreading shelter; therefore must all souls become as one soul, and all hearts as one heart. Let all be set free from the multiple identities that were born of passion and desire, and in the oneness of their love for God find a new way of life. ('Abdu'l-Bahá, *Selections from the Writings of 'Abdu'l-Bahá*, no. 36.3)

It behooveth all the beloved of God to become as one, to gather together under the protection of a single flag, to stand for a uniform body of opinion, to follow one and the same pathway, to hold fast to a single resolve. Let them forget their divergent theories and put aside their conflicting views since, God be praised, our purpose is one, our goal is one. We are the servants of one Threshold, we all draw our nourishment from the same one Source, we all are gathered in the shade of the same high Tabernacle, we all are sheltered under the one celestial Tree. ('Abdu'l-Bahá, *Selections from the Writings of 'Abdu'l-Bahá*, no. 193.7)

O ye lovers of this wronged one! Cleanse ye your eyes, so that ye behold no man as different from yourselves. See ye no strangers; rather see all men as friends, for love and unity come hard when ye fix your gaze on otherness. And in this new and wondrous age, the Holy Writings say that we must be at one with every people; that we must see neither harshness nor injustice, neither malevolence, nor hostility, nor hate, but rather turn our eyes toward the heaven of ancient glory. For each of the creatures is a sign of God, and it was by the grace of the Lord and His power that each did step into the world; therefore they are not strangers, but in the family; not aliens, but friends, and to be treated as such.

Wherefore must the loved ones of God associate in affectionate fellowship with stranger and friend alike, showing forth to all the utmost loving-kindness, disregarding the degree of their capacity, never asking whether they deserve to be loved. In every instance let the friends be considerate and infinitely kind. Let them never be defeated by the malice of the people, by their aggression and their hate, no matter how intense. If others hurl their darts against you, offer them milk and honey in return; if they poison your lives, sweeten their souls; if they injure you, teach them how to be comforted; if they inflict a wound upon you, be a balm to their sores; if they sting you, hold to their lips a refreshing cup. ('Abdu'l-Bahá, *Selections from the Writings of 'Abdu'l-Bahá*, no. 8.7–8)

Now ponder this: Animals, despite the fact that they lack reason and understanding, do not make colors the cause of conflict. Why should man, who has reason, create conflict? This is wholly unworthy of him. Especially white and black are the descendants of the same Adam; they belong to one household. In origin they were one; they were the same color. Adam was of one color. Eve had one color. All humanity is descended from them. Therefore, in origin they are one. These colors developed later due to climates and regions; they have no significance whatsoever. Therefore, today I am very happy that white and black have gathered together in this meeting. I hope this coming together and harmony reaches such a degree that no distinctions shall remain between them, and they shall be together in the utmost harmony and love. ('Abdu'l-Bahá, *The Promulgation of Universal Peace*, p. 61)

I swear this by the beauty of the Lord: whensoever I hear good of the friends, my heart filleth up with joy; but whensoever I find even a hint that they are on bad terms one with another, I am overwhelmed by grief. Such is the condition of 'Abdu'l-Bahá. Then judge from this where your duty lieth. ('Abdu'l-Bahá, *Selections from the Writings of 'Abdu'l-Bahá*, no. 198.10)

. . . peace must first be established among individuals, until it leadeth in the end to peace among nations. Wherefore, O ye Bahá'ís, strive ye with all your might to create, through the power of the Word of God, genuine love, spiritual communion and durable bonds among individuals. This is your task. ('Abdu'l-Bahá, *Selections from the Writings of 'Abdu'l-Bahá*, no. 201.2)

... it is the desire of the Lord God that the loved ones of God and the hand-maids of the Merciful in the West should come closer together in harmony and unity as day followeth day, and until this is accomplished, the work will never go forward. ('Abdu'l-Bahá, *Selections from the Writings of 'Abdu'l-Bahá*, no. 41.2)

Until such time, however, as the friends establish perfect unity among them-selves, how can they summon others to harmony and peace?

That soul which hath itself not come alive,

Can it then hope another to revive? ('Abdu'l-Bahá, *Selections from the Writings of 'Abdu'l-Bahá*, no. 221.5)

If this Cause cannot unite two individuals, how can we expect it to unite the world? (Shoghi Effendi, quoted in *Bahá'í News*, no. 13, p. 3)

If we Bahá'ís cannot attain to cordial unity among ourselves, then we fail to realize the main purpose for which the Báb, Bahá'u'lláh, and the Beloved Master lived and suffered.

In order to achieve this cordial unity one of the first essentials insisted on by Bahá'u'lláh and 'Abdu'l-Bahá is that we resist the natural tendency to let our attention dwell on the faults and failings of others rather than on our own. Each of us is responsible for one life only, and that is our own. Each of us is immeasurably far from being "perfect as our heavenly Father is perfect" and the task of perfecting our own life and character is one that requires all our atten-tion, our will-power and energy. If we allow our attention and energy to be taken up in efforts to keep others right and remedy their faults, we are wasting precious time. We are like ploughmen each of whom has his team to manage and his plough to direct, and in order to keep his furrow straight he must keep his eye on his goal and concentrate on his own task. If he looks to this side and that to see how Tom and Harry are getting on and to criticize their ploughing, then his own furrow will assuredly become crooked.

On no subject are the Bahá'í teachings more emphatic than on the neces-sary to abstain from fault-finding and backbiting while being ever eager to discover and root out our own faults and overcome our own failings.

If we profess loyalty to Bahá'u'lláh, to our Beloved Master and our dear Guardian, then we must show our love by obedience to these explicit teachings. Deeds not words are what they demand, and no amount of fervor in the use of expressions of loyalty and adulation will compensate for failure to live in the spirit of the teachings. (On behalf of Shoghi Effendi, letter dated 12 May 1925, to an individual believer, in *The Compilation of Compilations*, no. 1288)

We must never dwell too much on the attitudes and feelings of our fellow believers towards us. What is most important is to foster love and harmony and ignore any rebuffs we may receive; in this way the weakness of human nature and the peculiarity or attitude of any particular person is not magnified, but pales into insignificance in comparison with our joint service to the Faith we all love. (On behalf of Shoghi Effendi, letter dated 19 September 1948, to an individual believer, in *Lights of Guidance*, no. 397)

The friends must be patient with each other and must realize that the Cause is still in its infancy and its institutions are not yet functioning perfectly. The greater the patience, the loving understanding and the forbearance the believers show towards each other and their shortcomings, the greater will be the progress of the whole Bahá'í Community at large. (On behalf of Shoghi Effendi, letter dated 27 February 1943, to an individual, quoted in a letter compiled by the research department of the Universal House of Justice, 7 February 1993)

One of the greatest problems in the Cause is the relation of the believers to each other; for their immaturity (shared with the rest of humanity) and imperfections retard the work, create complications, and discourage each other. And yet we must put up with these things and try to combat them through love, patience, and forgiveness individually and proper administrative action collectively. (On behalf of Shoghi Effendi, letter dated 26 March 1948, to an individual believer)

You have complained of the unsatisfactory conditions prevailing in the . . . Bahá'í Community; the Guardian is well aware of the situation of the Cause there, but is confident that whatever the nature of the obstacles that confront the Faith they will be eventually overcome. You should, under no circumstances, feel discouraged, and allow such difficulties, even though they may have resulted from the misconduct, or the lack of capacity and vision of certain members of the Community, to make you waver in your faith and basic loyalty to the Cause. Surely, the believers, no matter how qualified they may be, whether as teachers or administrators, and however high their intellectual and spiritual merits, should never be looked upon as the standard whereby to evaluate and measure the divine authority and mission of the Faith. It is to the Teachings themselves, and to the lives of the Founders of the Cause that the believers should look for their guidance and inspiration, and only by keeping strictly to such a true attitude can they hope to establish their loyalty to Bahá'u'lláh upon an enduring and unassailable basis. You should take heart, therefore, and with unrelaxing vigilance and unremitting effort endeavour to play your full share in the gradual unfoldment of this Divine World Order. (On behalf of Shoghi Effendi, letter dated 23 August 1939, to an individual believer, in *The Compilation of Compilations*, vol. II, no. 1292)

Nothing is more contrary to the spirit of the Cause than discord and strife, which are the inevitable outcome of selfishness and greed. Pure detachment and selfless service, these should be the sole motives of every true believer. And unless each and every one of the friends succeeds in translating such qualities into living action, no hope of further progress can be entertained. It is now that unity of thought and action is most needed. It is now, when the Cause is entering a new phase of development, when its Administration is being gradually consolidated amid the welter and chaos of a tottering civilization, that the friends should present a united front to those forces of internal dissension, which, if not completely wiped out, will bring our work to inevitable destruction. (On behalf of Shoghi Effendi, letter dated 24 September 1933, to an individual believer, in *The Compilation of Compilations*, vol. II, no. 1279)

All should be ready and willing to set aside every personal sense of griev-ance—justified or unjustified—for the good of the Cause, because the people will never embrace it until they see in its Community life mirrored what is so conspicuously lacking in the world; love and unity. (On behalf of Shoghi Effendi, letter dated 13 May 1945, to the National Spiritual Assem-bly of Australia and New Zealand, quoted in a letter written on behalf of the Universal House of Justice, letter dated 19 August 1985, to the National Spiritual Assembly of Bolivia, in *Lights of Guidance*, no. 548)

Bahá'u'lláh . . . recognizes that human beings are fallible. He knows that, in our weakness, we shall repeatedly stumble when we try to walk in the path He has pointed out to us. If all human beings became perfect the moment they accepted the call of Bahá'u'lláh this world would be another world. It is in light of our frailty that 'Abdu'l-Bahá appealed to the friends everywhere to love each other and stressed the emphatic teaching of Bahá'u'lláh that each of us should concentrate upon improving his or her own life and ignore the faults of others. How many times the Master stressed the need for unity, for without it His Father's Cause could not go forward.

You have been blessed by recognizing Bahá'u'lláh as the Manifestation of God: your responsibility therefore is to God, irrespective of the actions of your fellow-believers. If every devoted believer withdrew from the Cause as soon as he found the sins of his fellow-Bahá'ís unbearable, who would be left to serve Bahá'u'lláh? All are struggling, with greater or less success to express in their lives the signs and standards that God has laid before them. (On behalf of the Universal House of Justice, letter dated 24 July 1973, to an individual believer)

The Universal House of Justice has received your letter . . . conveying your concern about the expression of racial and other prejudices prevailing among Bahá'ís, and indicating your impatience at the slowness of the believers to begin to manifest to a greater degree, both in their individual and community lives, the attributes described in our Teachings governing interpersonal relationships. The House of Justice points out that one of the goals of the Five Year Plan given to every National Spiritual Assembly is to develop "the distinctive character of Bahá'í life, particularly in the local communities." It is important, therefore, that in addition to the tasks of expansion and consolidation, the friends should consciously be working towards a more closely knit loving association. The attainment of this objective, calling as it does for the regeneration by the individual of his character, must be a continuing effort, and your own loving endeavours, along with those of your fellow believers, are essential. (On behalf of The Universal House of Justice, letter dated 5 March 1979, to an individual believer)

That a lack of consciousness and sensitivity to the race issue should manifest itself among certain segments of the Bahá'í community is troubling, but, given the scope and duration of the problem, is not altogether surprising. The community of the Most Great Name has the divine instructions and the crystal example of 'Abdu'l-Bahá to enable it to make its way from the wilderness of disunity, suspicion and estrangement into the bright sunlight of authentic fellowship, but the journey of transformation is steep and long.

The Central Figures of our Faith, in countless Tablets, illuminate the theme of unity, and by advice and admonition sketch the path toward its achievement. 'Abdu'l-Bahá made it the centerpiece of His public talks during His transcontinental American journey in 1912, even addressing an early meeting of the National Association for the Advancement of Colored People. Shoghi Effendi, writing to the American Bahá'í community in 1938 gave a trenchant analysis of racism and of the means through which it may be effectively resolved (see *The Advent of Divine Justice* 1984 edition, pages 33–41); it is an analysis which should be carefully studied, even memorized, by anyone seriously concerned with this subject. And, in its turn, the House of Justice has repeatedly drawn the attention of the friends to the importance of what the Guardian has termed the "most vital and challenging issue" in various communications, including its Riḍván Messages and in the Promise of World Peace. Finally, your National Assembly has recently directed a national race unity campaign to focus attention and resources on this issue, and it has been working to stimulate the community to renewed engagement with this deeply rooted problem.

However, there are practical limits to what can be accomplished through appeals and exhortations. Ultimately, any real progress depends upon the sustained, audacious and sincere efforts of the rank and file of believers, guided and motivated by the Sacred Writings and the letters of Shoghi Effendi, working in harmony with their Local Spiritual Assemblies, using Bahá'í consultation, to bring about a change in attitude and behavior. Clearly, all elements of the community must eventually be drawn into this activity. The problem did not appear overnight, however, and the process of healing centuries-old wounds will take time, tremendous perseverance and effort.

It is recommended that you read the biography of the Hand of the Cause Louis Gregory, *To Move the World,* for the insights and inspiration which his courageous example affords. The House of Justice is confident that if you will turn your heart to Bahá'u'lláh, study the Teachings, and undertake to sincerely apply the remedy outlined therein, that you can yourself make a worthy contribution to the amelioration of this scourge which has so long beset the American people.

Regarding Gospel music, the enthusiastic reception accorded the Gospel Choir which performed at the World Congress is evidence that the Bahá'í community is opening itself to music which can richly enhance the quality and spiritual atmosphere of its devotional activities.

As you arise in the path of service, to lend your share to the eradication of this long-standing evil, be assured of the ardent, loving prayers of the House of Justice in the Holy Shrines on your behalf. (On behalf of The Universal House of Justice, letter dated 3 July 1973, to an individual believer)

The Universal House of Justice has received your letter . . . regarding the atmosphere in the United States and your suggestion that it may be timely for the House of Justice to write a letter that would address the "pain of racism" and the consequent "hopelessness and despair" which its persistence occasions. We are to provide the following comments.

The intense focus which you personally have brought to bear on the challenge of dealing with the vital issue of racism in the United States is highly commendable. Action is what is needed. The House of Justice is confident that, as the friends arise, guided by the Writings and the instructions of the beloved Guardian, this enduring, seemingly intractable problem will be ameliorated. It is not certain, however, whether yet another letter will produce the effect you desire. The friends already have in hand copious quotations on the subject from the Central Figures of our Faith together with the interpretations and exhortations of Shoghi Effendi and the further elucidations and calls to action issued by the House of Justice. These have been compiled, as you are perhaps aware, in a volume of some length published by the National Assembly of the United States, in 1986, under the title *The Power of Unity*. And that Assembly has also itself provided a comprehensive statement on the matter, *The Vision of Race Unity*.

The solution to so deep-seated a problem will obviously depend, in large part, on a massive expansion in the number of believers to enable the Bahá'í community to exert the practical influence necessary to bring about profound social change. At the level of the individual, there is no substitute for personal example and for daily renewal of one's spirit through immersion in the Holy Writings and prayer. Studying the life of the Hand of the Cause Louis Gregory also provides a useful and inspiring perspective. (On behalf of the Universal House of Justice, letter dated 20 January 1994, to an individual believer)

At the very core of the aims of the Faith are the establishment of justice and unity in the world, the removal of prejudice and enmity from among all people, the awakening of compassion and understanding in the hearts of all men and women, and the raising of all souls to a new level of spirituality and behavior through the vitalizing influence of divine Revelation. The course set forth by Bahá'u'lláh for the attainment of these aims is the double task of simultaneously building an ideal society and perfecting the behavior of individuals. For this dual and reciprocal transformation He has not only revealed laws, principles and truths attuned to the needs of this age, but has established the very nucleus and pattern of those institutions which are to evolve into the structure of the divinely purposed world society.

Central to your perception of the statements made by the believers about whom you are concerned are their assertions that they are entirely obedient to the spirit of the Covenant and the institutions of the Faith; that they are merely voicing their disagreement with certain decisions and policies made by these institutions; are protesting against what they perceive to be unjust or improper actions by some people who occupy prominent administrative positions; and are suggesting modifications to Bahá'í procedures to prevent such perceived abuses of authority. These assertions, however, overlook certain important Bahá'í principles which provide the methods and channels for the voicing of such grievances or disagreements, and which are designed to lead to resolution of problems while preserving the unity of the community. . . .

The laws, commandments, injunctions and exhortations we have all agreed to obey and follow as Bahá'ís include a clearly defined approach to decision-making and to the implementation of decisions. You are, undoubtedly, well familiar with the various aspects of this approach, which is built on the conviction that the path of unity is the only path that can lead to the civilization envisioned by Bahá'u'lláh. So strong is the emphasis on unity that, for example, once a decision has been made by an Assembly, everyone is expected to support that decision wholeheartedly, relying confidently on 'Abdu'l-Bahá's assurance that, even if the decision is wrong, "as it is in unity the truth will be revealed and the wrong made right." This principle of unity is supplemented by other, related guidelines covering such issues as how criticism can be expressed, how the wrongdoing of members of the community is to be corrected, how the principle of justice is to be applied and appeals admitted, and how the integrity of individuals, the institutions and the Cause is to be upheld.

In adhering to such teachings Bahá'ís recognize that individuals do not become wholly virtuous on accepting the Faith. It takes time for them to grow spiritually out of their personal imperfections and out of the structural and behavioral assumptions of the societies in which they have been raised, which color their view of the world. The institutions of the Cause, which the believers have been raising in obedience to the law of Bahá'u'lláh, in accordance with the pattern set forth by 'Abdu'l-Bahá and the expositions of Shoghi Effendi, and under the guidance of the Universal House of Justice, are still in their embryonic stage and not infrequently fall short of the ideal for which they are striving. There is also the possibility of certain individuals' misusing the positions of authority to which they are elected or appointed within the structure of the Administrative Order. Again and again Shoghi Effendi, in his letters, called upon the Bahá'ís to be patient and forbearing, both with one another and with their Assemblies, but in serious cases of malfunctioning by either institutions or individuals, neither the Guardian nor the Universal House of Justice has hesitated to take remedial action. Bahá'í administration has provisions to cope with such human frailties and is designed to enable the believers to build Bahá'u'lláh's new World Order in the midst of their imperfections, but without conflicts which would destroy the entire edifice. (On behalf of the Universal House of Justice, letter dated 2 July 1996, to an individual believer)

APPRECIATING THE DIVERSITY OF THE HUMAN FAMILY

Bahá'u'lláh has proclaimed the oneness of the world of humanity. He has caused various nations and divergent creeds to unite. He has declared that difference of race and color is like the variegated beauty of flowers in a garden. If you enter a garden, you will see yellow, white, blue, red flowers in profusion and beauty—each radiant within itself and although different from the others, lending its own charm to them. Racial difference in the human kingdom is similar. If all the flowers in a garden were of the same color, the effect would be monotonous and wearying to the eye.

Therefore, Bahá'u'lláh hath said that the various races of humankind lend a composite harmony and beauty of color to the whole. Let all associate, therefore, in this great human garden even as flowers grow and blend together side by side without discord or disagreement between them. ('Abdu'l-Bahá, *The Promulgation of Universal Peace*, p. 94)

The Creator of all is One God.

From this same God all creation sprang into existence, and He is the one goal, towards which everything in nature yearns. This conception was embodied in the words of Christ, when He said, "I am the Alpha and the Omega, the beginning and the end." Man is the sum of Creation, and the Perfect Man is the expression of the complete thought of the Creator—the Word of God.

Consider the world of created beings, how varied and diverse they are in species, yet with one sole origin. All the differences that appear are those of outward form and color. This diversity of type is apparent throughout the whole of nature.

Behold a beautiful garden full of flowers, shrubs, and trees. Each flower has a different charm, a peculiar beauty, its own delicious perfume and beautiful color. The trees too, how varied are they in size, in growth, in foliage—and what different fruits they bear! Yet all these flowers, shrubs and trees spring from the self-same earth, the same sun shines upon them and the same clouds give them rain.

So it is with humanity. It is made up of many races, and its peoples are of different color, white, black, yellow, brown and red—but they all come from the same God, and all are servants to Him. This diversity among the children of men has unhappily not the same effect as it has among the vegetable creation, where the spirit shown is more harmonious. Among men exists the diversity of animosity, and it is this that causes war and hatred among the different nations of the world.

Differences which are only those of blood also cause them to destroy and kill one another. Alas! that this should still be so. Let us look rather at the beauty in diversity, the beauty of harmony, and learn a lesson from the vegetable creation. If you beheld a garden in which all the plants were the same as to form, color and perfume, it would not seem beautiful to you at all, but, rather, monotonous and dull. The garden which is pleasing to the eye and which makes the heart glad, is the garden in which are growing side by side flowers of every hue, form and perfume, and the joyous contrast of color is what makes for charm and beauty. So is it with trees. An orchard full of fruit trees is a delight; so is a plantation planted with many species of shrubs. It is just the diversity and variety that constitutes its charm; each flower, each tree, each fruit, beside being beautiful in itself, brings out by contrast the qualities of the others, and shows to advantage the special loveliness of each and all.

Thus should it be among the children of men! ('Abdu'l-Bahá, *Paris Talks*, no. 15.1–7)

A critic may object, saying that peoples, races, tribes and communities of the world are of different and varied customs, habits, tastes, character, inclinations and ideas, that opinions and thoughts are contrary to one another, and how, therefore, is it possible for real unity to be revealed and perfect accord among human souls to exist?

In answer we say that differences are of two kinds. One is the cause of annihilation and is like the antipathy existing among warring nations and conflicting tribes who seek each other's destruction, uprooting one another's families, depriving one another of rest and comfort and unleashing carnage. The other kind which is a token of diversity is the essence of perfection and the cause of the appearance of the bestowals of the Most Glorious Lord.

Consider the flowers of a garden: though differing in kind, color, form and shape, yet, inasmuch as they are refreshed by the waters of one spring, revived by the breath of one wind, invigorated by the rays of one sun, this diversity increaseth their charm, and addeth unto their beauty. Thus when that unifying force, the penetrating influence of the Word of God, taketh effect, the difference of customs, manners, habits, ideas, opinions and dispositions embellisheth the world of humanity. This diversity, this difference is like the naturally created dissimilarity and variety of the limbs and organs of the human body, for each one contributeth to the beauty, efficiency and perfection of the whole. When these different limbs and organs come under the influence of man's sovereign soul, and the soul's power pervadeth the limbs and members, veins and arteries of the body, then difference reinforceth harmony, diversity strengtheneth love, and multiplicity is the greatest factor for co-ordination.

How unpleasing to the eye if all the flowers and plants, the leaves and blossoms, the fruits, the branches and the trees of that garden were all of the same shape and color! Diversity of hues, form and shape, enricheth and adorneth the garden, and heighteneth the effect thereof. In like manner, when divers shades of thought, temperament and character, are brought together under the power and influence of one central agency, the beauty and glory of human perfection will be revealed and made manifest. ('Abdu'l-Bahá, *Selections from the Writings of 'Abdu'l-Bahá,* no. 225.22–25)

My hope is that the white and the black will be united in perfect love and fellowship, with complete unity and brotherhood. Associate with each other, think of each other, and be like a rose garden. Anyone who goes into a rose garden will see various roses, white, pink, yellow, red, all growing together and replete with adornment. Each one accentuates the beauty of the other. Were all of one color, the garden would be monotonous to the eye. If they were all white or yellow or red, the garden would lack variety and attractiveness; but when the colors are varied, white, pink, yellow, red, there will be the greatest beauty. Therefore, I hope that you will be like a rose garden. Although different in colors, yet—praise be to God!—you receive rays from the same sun. From one cloud the rain is poured upon you. You are under the training of one Gardener, and this Gardener is kind to all. Therefore, you must manifest the utmost kindness towards each other, and you may rest assured that whenever you are united, the confirmations of the Kingdom of Abhá will reach you, the heavenly favors will descend, the bounties of God will be bestowed, the Sun of Reality will shine, the cloud of mercy will pour its showers, and the breeze of divine generosity will waft its fragrances upon you.

I hope you will continue in unity and fellowship. How beautiful to see blacks and whites together! I hope, God willing, the day may come when I shall see the red men, the Indians, with you, also Japanese and others. Then there will be white roses, yellow roses, red roses, and a very wonderful rose garden will appear in the world. ('Abdu'l-Bahá, *The Promulgation of Universal Peace,* pp. 602–3)

95

Praise be to God, today the splendor of the Word of God hath illumined every horizon, and from all sects, races, tribes, nations, and communities souls have come together in the light of the Word, assembled, united and agreed in perfect harmony. Oh! What a great number of meetings are held adorned with souls from various races and diverse sects! Anyone attending these will be struck with amazement, and might suppose that these souls are all of one land, one nationality, one community, one thought, one belief and one opinion; whereas, in fact, one is an American, the other an African, one cometh from Asia and another from Europe, one is a native of India, another is from Turkestan, one is an Arab, another a Tajik, another a Persian and yet another a Greek. Notwithstanding such diversity they associate in perfect harmony and unity, love and freedom; they have one voice, one thought and one purpose. Verily, this is from the penetrative power of the Word of God! If all the forces of the universe were to combine they would not be able thus to gather a single assemblage so imbued with the sentiments of love, affection, attraction and enkindlement as to unite the members of different races and to raise up from the heart of the world a voice that shall dispel war and strife, uproot dissension and disputation, usher in the era of universal peace and establish unity and concord amongst men. ('Abdu'l-Bahá, *Selections from the Writings of 'Abdu'l-Bahá*, no. 225.26)

It is clear that human realities differ one from another, that opinions and perceptions vary, and that this divergence of thoughts, opinions, understandings, and sentiments among individuals is an essential requirement. For differences of degree in creation are among the essential requirements of existence, which is resolved into countless forms. We stand therefore in need of a universal power which can prevail over the thoughts, opinions, and sentiments of all, which can annul these divisions and bring all souls under the sway of the principle of the oneness of humanity. And it is clear and evident that the greatest power in the human world is the love of God. It gathers divers peoples under the shade of the tabernacle of oneness and fosters the greatest love and fellowship among hostile and contending peoples and nations. ('Abdu'l-Bahá, *Some Answered Questions*, no. 84.4)

Maintaining Unity in Diversity

The diversity in the human family should be the cause of love and harmony, as it is in music where many different notes blend together in the making of a perfect chord. If you meet those of different race and color from yourself, do not mistrust them and withdraw yourself into your shell of conventionality, but rather be glad and show them kindness. Think of them as different colored roses growing in the beautiful garden of humanity, and rejoice to be among them.

Likewise, when you meet those whose opinions differ from your own, do not turn away your face from them. All are seeking truth, and there are many roads leading thereto. Truth has many aspects, but it remains always and forever one.

Do not allow difference of opinion, or diversity of thought to separate you from your fellow-men, or to be the cause of dispute, hatred and strife in your hearts.

Rather, search diligently for the truth and make all men your friends.

Every edifice is made of many different stones, yet each depends on the other to such an extent that if one were displaced the whole building would suffer; if one is faulty the structure is imperfect.

Bahá'u'lláh has drawn the circle of unity, He has made a design for the uniting of all the peoples, and for the gathering of them all under the shelter of the tent of universal unity. This is the work of the Divine Bounty, and we must all strive with heart and soul until we have the reality of unity in our midst, and as we work, so will strength be given unto us. Leave all thought of self, and strive only to be obedient and submissive to the Will of God. In this way only shall we become citizens of the Kingdom of God, and attain unto life everlasting. ('Abdu'l-Bahá, *Paris Talks,* no. 15.7–12)

O peoples of the world! The Sun of Truth hath risen to illumine the whole earth, and to spiritualize the community of man. Laudable are the results and the fruits thereof, abundant the holy evidences deriving from this grace. This is mercy unalloyed and purest bounty; it is light for the world and all its peoples; it is harmony and fellowship, and love and solidarity; indeed it is compassion and unity, and the end of foreignness; it is the being at one, in complete dignity and freedom, with all on earth.

The Blessed Beauty saith: 'Ye are all the fruits of one tree, the leaves of one branch.' Thus hath He likened this world of being to a single tree, and all its peoples to the leaves thereof, and the blossoms and fruits. It is needful for the bough to blossom, and leaf and fruit to flourish, and upon the interconnection of all parts of the world-tree, dependeth the flourishing of leaf and blossom, and the sweetness of the fruit.

For this reason must all human beings powerfully sustain one another and seek for everlasting life; and for this reason must the lovers of God in this contingent world become the mercies and the blessings sent forth by that clement King of the seen and unseen realms. ('Abdu'l-Bahá, *Selections from the Writings of 'Abdu'l-Bahá*, no. 1.1–3)

Praise be to God, the hearts of the friends are united and linked together, whether they be from the east or the west, from north or from south, whether they be German, French, Japanese, American, and whether they pertain to the white, the black, the red, the yellow or the brown race. Variations of color, of land and of race are of no importance in the Bahá'í Faith; on the contrary, Bahá'í unity overcometh them all and doeth away with all these fancies and imaginations. ('Abdu'l-Bahá, *Selections from the Writings of 'Abdu'l-Bahá*, no. 75.1)

Let there be no misgivings as to the animating purpose of the world-wide Law of Bahá'u'lláh. Far from aiming at the subversion of the existing foundations of society, it seeks to broaden its basis, to remold its institutions in a manner consonant with the needs of an ever-changing world. It can conflict with no legitimate allegiances, nor can it undermine essential loyalties. Its purpose is neither to stifle the flame of a sane and intelligent patriotism in men's hearts, nor to abolish the system of national autonomy so essential if the evils of excessive centralization are to be avoided. It does not ignore, nor does it attempt to suppress, the diversity of ethnical origins, of climate, of history, of language and tradition, of thought and habit, that differentiate the peoples and nations of the world. It calls for a wider loyalty, for a larger aspiration than any that has animated the human race. It insists upon the subordination of national impulses and interests to the imperative claims of a unified world. It repudiates excessive centralization on one hand, and disclaims all attempts at uniformity on the other. Its watchword is unity in diversity. (Shoghi Effendi, *The World Order of Bahá'u'lláh*, p. 41)

When a person becomes a Bahá'í, he gives up the past only in the sense that he is a part of this new and living Faith of God, and must seek to pattern himself, in act and thought, along the lines laid down by Bahá'u'lláh. The fact that he is by origin a Jew or a Christian, a black man or a white man, is not important anymore, but, as you say, lends color and charm to the Bahá'í community in that it demonstrates unity in diversity. (On behalf of Shoghi Effendi, letter dated 12 March 1949, addressed to an individual believer)

We stand for unity through diversity and we hold in contempt every attempt at uniformity or at complete separateness. (On behalf of Shoghi Effendi, letter dated 3 June, 1933, to an individual believer)

. . . the Cause is for every nation, not just America, and each people can and must contribute some of the finest elements of its own genius and race to the Faith. (On behalf of Shoghi Effendi, letter dated 19 August 1952, to an individual believer)

The Guardian was very pleased to learn of the progress done by the Indian N.S.A. in its efforts to consolidate, widen and maintain the scope of its national activities. The difficulties in your way are tremendous. The differences of language and of social and intellectual background do, undoubtedly, render the work somewhat difficult to carry out and may temporarily check the efficient and smooth working of the national administrative machinery of the Faith. They, nevertheless, impart to the deliberations of the National Assembly a universality which they would be otherwise lacking, and give to its members a breadth of view which is their duty to cultivate and foster. It is not uniformity which we should seek in the formation of any national or local assembly. For the bedrock of the Bahá'í administrative order is the principle of unity in diversity, which has been so strongly and so repeatedly emphasized in the writings of the Cause. Differences which are not fundamental and contrary to the basic teachings of the Cause should be maintained, while the underlying unity of the administrative order should be at any cost preserved and insured. Unity, both of purpose and of means is, indeed, indispensable to the safe and speedy working of every Assembly, whether local or national. (On behalf of Shoghi Effendi, letter dated 2 January 1934, to the National Spiritual Assembly of India and Burma, in *Dawn of a New Day*, pp. 47–48)

Bahá'ís should obviously be encouraged to preserve their inherited cultural identities, as long as the activities involved do not contravene the principles of the Faith. The perpetuation of such cultural characteristics is an expression of unity in diversity. (On behalf of the Universal House of Justice, letter dated 26 May 1982, to the National Spiritual Assembly of Malaysia, in *Lights of Guidance*, no. 1880.2)

Yet, it is clear, too, from the Teachings that every people, through its inherent potentialities and particular range of experience, will make its own distinct contribution to the creation of a new civilization. To the extent that African-Americans who embrace the new Revelation arise to do their part by adhering to the Teachings will the gifts which are uniquely theirs be realized in the splendors of the Golden Age. The "pupil of the eye," Bahá'u'lláh's metaphoric reference to Black people, will no doubt acquire clear meaning as they conscientiously strive over time to fulfill the divine purpose for which the Blessed Beauty came. There can be no doubt that Americans of African descent can find in themselves the capacity, so well developed as a result of their long encounter with injustice, to recognize and respond to the vision of love and justice brought by the Promised One of all ages. Imbued with that vision, past and present sufferings are transformed into measures of patience, wisdom and compassion—qualities so essential to the effort to moderate the discordant ways of a confused world and aid the healing of its spiritual ills.

What better than the transformed character of a bruised people to smooth the course, to offer perspectives for new beginnings toward world order! (On behalf of the Universal House of Justice, letter dated 3 June 2007, to an individual believer)

The Bahá'í Faith seeks to maintain cultural diversity while promoting the unity of all peoples. Indeed, such diversity will enrich the tapestry of human life in a peaceful world society. The House of Justice supports the view that in every country it is quite appropriate for the cultural traditions of the people to be observed within the Bahá'í community as long as they are not contrary to the teachings. The general attitude of the Faith towards the traditional practices of various peoples is expressed in the following statement of Shoghi Effendi's, published in *The World Order of Bahá'u'lláh*, U.S. 1982 edition, pages 41–42. "Let there be no misgivings as to the animating purpose of the world-wide Law of Bahá'u'lláh. . . . It does not ignore, nor does it attempt to suppress, the diversity of ethnical origins, of climate, of history, of language and tradition, of thought and habit, that differentiate the peoples and nations of the world. . . . Its watchword is unity in diversity such as 'Abdu'l-Bahá Himself has explained:

'Consider the flowers of a garden. . . . Diversity of hues, form and shape enricheth and adorneth the garden, and heighteneth the effect thereof.'"

Of course, many cultural elements everywhere inevitably will disappear or be merged with related ones from their societies, yet the totality will achieve that promised diversity within world unity. We can expect much cultural diversity in the long period before the emergence of a world commonwealth of nations in the Golden Age of Peace of Bahá'u'lláh's new world order. Much wisdom and tolerance will be required, and much time must elapse until the advent of that great day.

At the present time, the challenge to every Bahá'í community is to avoid suppression of those culturally-diverse elements which are not contrary to the teachings, while establishing and maintaining such a high degree of unity that others are attracted to the Cause of God. (On behalf of the Universal House of Justice, letter dated 25 July 1988, to a National Spiritual Assembly)

. . . a primary challenge to Bahá'ís is to preserve and improve those whole-some aspects of tribal and family custom that are in accord with the Bahá'í Teachings and to dispense with those that are not. Such a challenge must be embraced with the understanding that the Book of God is the standard by which to weigh all forms of behaviour. While unwavering action is necessary, wisdom and tact and patience must, of course, be exercised. Let it be under-stood, too, that Africans are not alone in the struggle to change certain age-old practices. People everywhere have customs which must be abandoned so as to clear the path along which their societies must evolve towards that glorious, new civilization which is to be the fruit of Bahá'u'lláh's stupendous Revelation. Indeed, in no society on earth can there be found practices which adequately mirror the standards of His Cause. His own truth-bearing Words clarify the matter: "The summons and the message which We gave were never intended to reach or to benefit one land or one people only. Mankind in its entirety must firmly adhere to whatsoever hath been revealed and vouchsafed unto it. Then and only then will it attain unto true liberty. The whole earth is illuminated with the resplendent glory of God's Revelation." (The Universal House of Jus-tice, letter dated Riḍvan 1996, to the Bahá'ís of Africa)

We appreciate the careful thought you have given to the subject of indige-nous populations. The Bahá'í International Community should maintain its involvement with this issue, continuing the emphasis on the need for unity in diversity—a unity which implies mutual tolerance among the var-ious populations, a recognition by dominant populations of the freedom of indigenous peoples to exercise their rights in all legitimate varieties of ways, and the corollary recognition of indigenous peoples themselves that such freedom carries with it the responsibility of recognizing the rights of all others to the same expressions. The implications for indigenous peoples also include: realization of the virtues of cross-cultural influences; appreciation of the values of other cultures as accruing to the wealth of human experience and the freedom of all to share in such values without necessarily giving up their respective identities; avoidance of parochial attitudes which degener-ate into ethnic and cultural prejudices; and, above all, appreciation of the necessity to maintain a global perspective within which the particulars of indigenous expression can find an enduring context. (The Universal House of Justice, letter dated 19 July 1985, to the Bahá'í International Community UN office, in *Cultural Diversity in the Age of Maturity,* no. 41)

. . . the Bahá'í Faith aims to demonstrate its power to create unified organic units in which cultural diversity is fostered, which are free from parochial attitudes and from ethnic or cultural prejudices, and in which all believers regard each other as true brothers and sisters. As the Faith progresses, the contrast is growing in many parts of the world, between the fragmented and mutually-antagonistic elements of society on the one hand, and the unified and harmonious Bahá'í community on the other hand. (The Universal House of Justice, letter dated 25 July 1988, to the Bahá'ís of the United States)

CREATING MARRIAGES OF DIVERSITY

O ye two believers in God! The Lord, peerless is He, hath made woman and man to abide with each other in the closest companionship, and to be even as a single soul. They are two helpmates, two intimate friends, who should be concerned about the welfare of each other.

If they live thus, they will pass through this world with perfect contentment, bliss, and peace of heart, and become the object of divine grace and favor in the Kingdom of heaven. But if they do other than this, they will live out their lives in great bitterness, longing at every moment for death, and will be shamefaced in the heavenly realm.

Strive, then, to abide, heart and soul, with each other as two doves in the nest, for this is to be blessed in both worlds. ('Abdu'l-Bahá, *Selections from the Writings of 'Abdu'l-Bahá,* no. 92.1–3)

O ye two who have believed in Him!

. . . I pray God that ye may at all times be in the utmost love and harmony, and be a cause for the spirituality of the human world. This union will unquestionably promote love and affection between the black and the white, and will affect and encourage others. These two races will unite and merge together, and there will appear and take root a new generation sound in health and beauteous in countenance. ('Abdu'l-Bahá, authorized translation of Tablet, quoted in letter dated 15 April 1985, on behalf of the Universal House of Justice to the Bahá'í Publishing Trust of the United States)

God's wisdom hath decreed that partners to a marriage should be of distant origins. That is, the further removed the relationship between husband and wife is, the stronger, the more beautiful and the healthier will their offspring be. ('Abdu'l-Bahá, from a previously unpublished Tablet, translated 24 November 1980)

In marriage the more distant the blood-relationship the better, for such distance in family ties between husband and wife provides the basis for the well-being of humanity and is conducive to fellowship among mankind. ('Abdu'l-Bahá, quoted in a letter dated 15 April 1985, on behalf of the Universal House of Justice to the Bahá'í Publishing Trust of the United States)

Thou must endeavor that they intermarry. There is no greater means to bring about affection between the white and the black than the influence of the Word of God. Likewise marriage between these two races will wholly destroy and eradicate the root of enmity. ('Abdu'l-Bahá, quoted in a letter dated 30 September 1985, on behalf of the Universal House of Justice to the Bahá'í Publishing Trust of the United States)

. . . your statement to the effect that the principle of the oneness of mankind prevents any true Bahá'í from regarding race itself as a bar to union is in complete accord with the Teachings of the Faith on this point. For both Bahá'u'lláh and 'Abdu'l-Bahá never disapproved of the idea of interracial marriage, nor discouraged it. The Bahá'í Teachings, indeed, by their very nature transcend all limitations imposed by race, and as such can and should never be identified with any particular school of racial philosophy. (Shoghi

Effendi, letter dated 27 January 1935, to the National Spiritual Assembly of the United States and Canada, in *Lights of Guidance*, no. 1288)

The Bahá'ís should welcome the Negroes to their homes, make every effort to teach them, associate with them, even marry them if they want to. We must remember that 'Abdu'l-Bahá Himself united in Bahá'í marriage a colored and a white believer. He could not do more. (On behalf of Shoghi Effendi, letter dated 27 May 1957, to the Bahá'í Inter-racial Teaching Committee)

Also with regard to the problem of inter-marriage between the Zoroastrian and Hindu Bahá'ís, this is a highly delicate and vital question, as important as the problem of the black and white in America. The friends should all realize that racial considerations do not, in the light of the Bahá'í Teachings, constitute any hindrance to any kind of intercourse between the believers. . . . While the goal is quite clear yet, wisdom and caution are needed in order to carry this ideal into full practice. (On behalf of Shoghi Effendi, in *Dawn of a New Day*, p. 198)

. . . as you no doubt know, Bahá'u'lláh has stated that the purpose of marriage is to promote unity, so you should bear this in mind when dealing with your non-Bahá'í relatives; they cannot be expected to feel the way we do on questions of racial amity, and we must not force our views on them, but rather lovingly and wisely seek to educate them. (On behalf of Shoghi Effendi, letter dated 30 August 1957, to an individual believer)

THE NECESSITY FOR COURAGE AND WISDOM

Do not despair! Work steadily. Sincerity and love will conquer hate. How many seemingly impossible events are coming to pass in these days! Set your faces steadily towards the Light of the World. Show love to all; "Love is the breath of the Holy Spirit in the heart of Man." Take courage! God never forsakes His children who strive and work and pray! Let your hearts be filled with the strenuous desire that tranquility and harmony may encircle all this warring world. So will success crown your efforts, and with the universal brotherhood will come the Kingdom of God in peace and goodwill. ('Abdu'l-Bahá, *Paris Talks*, no. 6.12)

The oneness of mankind is the fundamental basis upon which the World Order of Bahá'u'lláh is built. Therefore the Bahá'ís must carry into their lives and into their activities the ideals which Bahá'u'lláh has taught of the unity of the human race.

At such a time as this the believers must take a very firm and strong stand on the racial issue so that there may be no misunderstanding on anyone's part as to just how the Bahá'ís view this all-important subject.

This does not mean that the Bahá'ís should enter into specific controversies which may rage; but it does mean that we should take our stand in behalf of the unity of the human family and the oneness of mankind; and there is no reason why we should not let the people know. This of course requires great consideration and consultation amongst the believers and particularly the local Assemblies in the areas involved.

The Guardian is praying that this serious problem may find solution in the hearts of the people because its ultimate solution rests with the individual who has become imbued with the ideal of unity and in that field there is no place for segregation. (On behalf of Shoghi Effendi, letter dated 27 October 1957, to an individual believer, in *Bahá'í News*, vol. 4, no. 324)

The believers must realize that the forces of prejudice are, along with so many other evil practices, growing at present stronger in the darkness surrounding humanity. The Bahá'ís must exercise not only tact and judgment, but courage and confidence in the aid of Bahá'u'lláh, which He will vouchsafe to those who attempt to live up to His teachings, in their whole approach to this racial question. Too much hesitance, too great timidity in the face of public opinion, can be just as bad as too much disregard of the actual situation and the problems it involves. (On Behalf of Shoghi Effendi, letter dated 23 December 1941, to an individual believer, in *Lights of Guidance*, no. 1813)

In connection with the developments reported in the "Washington Post"—copies of which you were kind enough to send the Guardian—concerning the concert which was given by the famous colored singer Miss Anderson; these events, which clearly show how deep-rooted and intense is racial prejudice in America, should awaken the friends to a deeper realization of the unique responsibility that is theirs, as the founders of the New World Order of Bahá'u'lláh, to combat courageously and relentlessly the false racial doctrines, and inveterate racial hatreds that so sadly poison the hearts and minds of their fellow-countrymen, and of such increasingly growing number of the peoples and nations of the world. More than ever today it is their vital duty to proclaim, boldly and unequivocally, the essential and underlying unity of all human races, and to demonstrate how the unifying Spirit released in this age through Bahá'u'lláh has succeeded in making this ideal a living and working reality. (On behalf of Shoghi Effendi, letter dated 14 May 1939, to the National Spiritual Assembly of the United States and Canada)

Regarding the solution of the racial problem; the believers should of course realize that the principle of the oneness of mankind which is the cornerstone of the message of Bahá'u'lláh is wholly incompatible with all forms of racial prejudice. Loyalty to this foundation principle of the Faith is the paramount duty of every believer and should be therefore wholehearted and unqualified. For a Bahá'í, racial prejudice, in all its forms, is simply a negation of faith, an attitude wholly incompatible with the very spirit and actual teachings of the Cause.

But while the friends should faithfully and courageously uphold this Bahá'í principle of the essential unity of all human races, yet in the methods they adopt for its application and further realization on the social plane they should act with tact, wisdom and moderation. These two attitudes are by no means exclusive. Bahá'ís do not believe that the spread of the Cause and its principles and teachings can be effected by means of radical and violent methods. While they are loyal to all those teachings, yet they believe in the necessity of resorting to peaceful and friendly means for the realization of their aims. (On behalf of Shoghi Effendi, letter dated 22 November 1936, to an individual believer, in *Lights of Guidance*, no. 1812.1–2)

It is difficult for the friends to always remember that in matter[s] where race enters, a hundred times more consideration and wisdom in handling situations is necessary than when an issue is not complicated by this factor. (On behalf of Shoghi Effendi, letter dated 25 March, 1949, to an individual believer)

It is . . . evident that the principle of the oneness of Mankind—which is the main pivot round which all the teachings of Bahá'u'lláh revolve—precludes the possibility of considering race as a bar to any intercourse, be it social or otherwise. The Faith, indeed, by its very nature and purpose, transcends all racial limitations and differences, and proclaims the basic and essential unity of the entire human race. Racial prejudice, of whatever nature and character, is therefore severely condemned, and as such should be wiped out by the friends in all their relations, whether private or social. Its abolition, however, should be done gradually and with extreme caution and wisdom. To act too precipitately and abruptly in such matters can lead to serious misunderstandings regarding the aims and purposes of the Cause, and the methods adopted by the friends for their promotion and establishment.

The believers, therefore, while firmly adhering to the teachings of the Faith regarding the underlying unity of all human races, should at the same time be careful not to proceed too quickly and unwisely in carrying them out, and even in expounding them to the non-Bahá'ís. (On behalf of Shoghi Effendi, letter dated 16 February 1935, to an individual believer)

Regarding the whole manner of teaching the Faith in the South: the Guardian feels that, although the greatest consideration should be shown the feelings of white people in the South whom we are teaching, under no circumstances should we discriminate in their favor, consider them more valuable to the Cause than their Negro fellow-southerners, or single them out to be taught the Message first. To pursue such a policy, however necessary and even desirable it may superficially seem, would be to compromise the true spirit of our Faith, which permits us to make no such distinctions in offering its tenets to the world. The Negro and white races should be offered, simultaneously, on a basis of equality, the Message of Bahá'u'lláh. Rich or poor, known or unknown, should be permitted to hear of this Holy Faith in this, humanity's greatest hour of need.

This does not mean that we should go against the laws of the state, pursue a radical course which will stir up trouble, and cause misunderstanding. On the contrary, the Guardian feels that, where no other course is open, the two races should be taught separately until they are fully conscious of the implications of being a Bahá'í, and then be confirmed and admitted to voting membership. Once, however, this has happened, they cannot shun each other's company, and feel the Cause to be like other Faiths in the South, with separate white and black compartments. . . .

'Abdu'l-Bahá Himself set the perfect example to the American believers in this matter—as in every other. He was tactful, but the essence of courage, and showed no favoritism to the white people as opposed to their dark-skinned compatriots. No matter how sincere and devoted the white believers in the South may be, there is no reason why they should be the ones to decide when and how the Negro Southerner shall hear of the Cause of God; both must be taught by whoever rises to spread the Message in those parts. (On behalf of Shoghi Effendi, letter dated 5 July 1942, addressed to an individual believer)

As regards the interracial meetings held in your home; the Guardian wishes you by all means to maintain them, and to invite those white believers who are willing to assist you in this great work to participate in these gatherings. But, as always, you should take great care not to openly wound the feelings of the noncolored population. The racial problem, whether in America or elsewhere should, indeed, be tackled with the utmost tact and moderation, but also with conscious, firm and absolute loyalty to the spirit as well as to the actual word of the Bahá'í teaching of the Oneness of Mankind. (On behalf of Shoghi Effendi, letter dated 26 January, to an individual believer, attached to letter dated 4 February 1985, on behalf of the Universal House of Justice to the National Spiritual Assembly of the United States)

Concerning the racial problem; the Guardian's considered view is still the same as the one already presented to the believers by him in his letters to the friends, namely that the solution to this problem has to be applied with the utmost caution, tact and wisdom and not through precipitate and violent action. The authorities, in particular, should not be offended and given the impression that the Bahá'í Cause stands for radical and revolutionary action in such matters. The friends should always follow the principle of moderation, and proceed through peaceful means and reject every form of violent action. (On behalf of Shoghi Effendi, letter dated 18 May, to an individual believer, attached to letter dated 4 February 1985, on behalf of the Universal House of Justice to the National Spiritual Assembly of the United States)

The race problem which is beyond doubt one of the most burning issues of the day cannot be solved at once and by means of violent and precipitate action. The friends must act gradually, and with patience without being, however, in the least disloyal to the basic Bahá'í principle of the oneness of the human race and of humanity as a whole. Great care should be taken not to displease, much less to challenge, the authorities. Too precipitate an action might offend them, and make them suspicious of the motives of the friends. (On behalf of Shoghi Effendi, letter dated 16 May 1936, to an individual believer, attached to letter dated 4 February 1985, on behalf of the Universal House of Justice to the National Spiritual Assembly of the United States)

Now, as to the methods which the friends should adopt for the application of this principle [of the oneness of mankind]; the Guardian has invariably urged the believers to act with the utmost wisdom, tact and moderation. It is not only fruitless, but actually harmful to the best interests of the Cause to publicly and violently attack the racial corruptions and traditions prevalent among such a large section of the American people. The friends should first start by applying the principle of the oneness of races within their own community, and thus set before the world outside a noble and inspiring example. Every trace of racial prejudice should be banished by the friends in their community life, and also in their private life, so much so that they should come to gradually forget the very existence of the racial problem as such. Such an attitude is bound to strongly impress every outsider and draw his attention to the Cause, and convince him of the sublimity and practicability of its Teachings. (On behalf of Shoghi Effendi, letter dated 11 November 1936, to an individual believer)

Service for Social Transformation

Promoting Harmony and Unity

Become as true brethren in the one and indivisible religion of God, free from distinction, for verily God desireth that your hearts should become mirrors unto your brethren in the Faith, so that ye find yourselves reflected in them, and they in you. This is the true Path of God, the Almighty, and He is indeed watchful over your actions. (The Báb, *Selections from the Writings of the Báb*, no. 2:24:2)

He Who is the Eternal Truth hath, from the Dayspring of Glory, directed His eyes towards the people of Bahá, and is addressing them in these words: "Address yourselves to the promotion of the well-being and tranquillity of the children of men. Bend your minds and wills to the education of the peoples and kindreds of the earth, that haply the dissensions that divide it may, through the power of the Most Great Name, be blotted out from its face, and all mankind become the upholders of one Order, and the inhabitants of one City. Illumine and hallow your hearts; let them not be profaned by the thorns of hate or the thistles of malice. Ye dwell in one world, and have been created through the operation of one Will. Blessed is he who mingleth with all men in a spirit of utmost kindliness and love." (Bahá'u'lláh, *Gleanings from the Writings of Bahá'u'lláh*, no. 156.1)

Raise ye a clamor like unto a roaring sea; like a prodigal cloud, rain down the grace of heaven. Lift up your voices and sing out the songs of the Abhá Realm. Quench ye the fires of war, lift high the banners of peace, work for the oneness of humankind and remember that religion is the channel of love unto all peoples. ('Abdu'l-Bahá, *Selections from the Writings of 'Abdu'l-Bahá*, no. 17.4)

Praise thou God that at last, through the divine teachings, thou hast obtained both sight and insight to the highest degree, and hast become firmly rooted in certitude and faith. It is my hope that others as well will achieve illumined eyes and hearing ears, and attain to everlasting life: that these many rivers, each flowing along in diverse and separated beds, will find their way back to the circumambient sea, and merge together and rise up in a single wave of surging oneness; that the unity of truth, through the power of God, will make these illusory differences to vanish away. This is the one essential: for if unity be gained, all other problems will disappear of themselves. ('Abdu'l-Bahá, *Selections from the Writings of 'Abdu'l-Bahá*, no. 15.2)

Wherefore must the loved ones of God associate in affectionate fellowship with stranger and friend alike, showing forth to all the utmost loving-kindness, disregarding the degree of their capacity, never asking whether they deserve to be loved. In every instance let the friends be considerate and infinitely kind. Let them never be defeated by the malice of the people, by their aggression and their hate, no matter how intense. If others hurl their darts against you, offer them milk and honey in return; if they poison your lives, sweeten their souls; if they injure you, teach them how to be comforted; if they inflict a wound upon you, be a balm to their sores; if they sting you, hold to their lips a refreshing cup. ('Abdu'l-Baha, *Selections from the Writings of 'Abdu'l-Bahá*, no. 8.8)

O army of God! Beware lest ye harm any soul, or make any heart to sorrow; lest ye wound any man with your words, be he known to you or a stranger, be he friend or foe. Pray ye for all; ask ye that all be blessed, all be forgiven. Beware, beware, lest any of you seek vengeance, even against one who is thirsting for your blood. Beware, beware, lest ye offend the feelings of another, even though he be an evil-doer, and he wish you ill. Look ye not upon the creatures, turn ye to their Creator. See ye not the never-yielding people, see but the Lord of Hosts. Gaze ye not down upon the dust, gaze upward at the shining sun, which hath caused every patch of darksome earth to glow with light. ('Abdu'l-Bahá, *Selections from the Writings of 'Abdu'l-Bahá*, no. 35.11)

Wherefore must the friends of God, with utter sanctity, with one accord, rise up in the spirit, in unity with one another, to such a degree that they will become even as one being and one soul. On such a plane as this, physical bodies play no part, rather doth the spirit take over and rule; and when its power encompasseth all then is spiritual union achieved. Strive ye by day and night to cultivate your unity to the fullest degree. Let your thoughts dwell on your own spiritual development, and close your eyes to the deficiencies of other souls. Act ye in such wise, showing forth pure and goodly deeds, and modesty and humility, that ye will cause others to be awakened. ('Abdu'l-Bahá, *Selections from the Writings of 'Abdu'l-Bahá*, no. 174.5)

Consort together in brotherly love, be ready to lay down your lives one for the other, and not only for those who are dear to you, but for all humanity. Look upon the whole human race as members of one family, all children of God; and, in so doing, you will see no difference between them. ('Abdu'l-Bahá, *Paris Talks*, no. 53.11)

Wherefore, O ye beloved of the Lord, bestir yourselves, do all in your power to be as one, to live in peace, each with the others: for ye are all the drops from but one ocean, the foliage of one tree, the pearls from a single shell, the flowers and sweet herbs from the same one garden. And achieving that, strive ye to unite the hearts of those who follow other faiths.

For one another must ye give up even life itself. To every human being must ye be infinitely kind. Call none a stranger; think none to be your foe. Be ye as if all men were your close kin and honored friends. Walk ye in such wise that this fleeting world will change into a splendor and this dismal heap of dust become a palace of delights. Such is the counsel of 'Abdu'l-Bahá, this hapless servant. ('Abdu'l-Bahá, *Selections from the Writings of 'Abdu'l-Bahá*, no. 221.11–12)

When you love a member of your family or a compatriot, let it be with a ray of the Infinite Love! Let it be in God, and for God! Wherever you find the attributes of God love that person, whether he be of your family or of another. Shed the light of a boundless love on every human being whom you meet, whether of your country, your race, your political party, or of any other nation, color or shade of political opinion. Heaven will support you while you work in this in-gathering of the scattered peoples of the world beneath the shadow of the almighty tent of unity.

You will be servants of God, who are dwelling near to Him, His divine helpers in the service, ministering to all Humanity. All Humanity! Every human being! Never forget this! ('Abdu'l-Bahá, *Paris Talks,* no. 9.21–22)

Become as waves of one sea, trees of one forest, growing in the utmost love, agreement and unity.

If you attain to such a capacity of love and unity, the Blessed Perfection will shower infinite graces of the spiritual Kingdom upon you, guide, protect and preserve you under the shadow of His Word, increase your happiness in this world and uphold you through all difficulties. ('Abdu'l-Bahá, *The Promulgation of Universal Peace,* p. 33)

May you become the quintessence of love. May you prove to be the effulgence of God, replete with the efficacy of the Holy Spirit and the cause of unity and fellowship in the world of humanity, for today mankind has the greatest need of love and agreement. If the world should remain as it is today, great danger will face it. But if reconciliation and unity are witnessed, if security and confidence be established, if with heart and soul we strive in order that the teachings of Bahá'u'lláh may find effective penetration in the realities of humankind, inducing fellowship and accord, binding together the hearts of the various religions and uniting divergent peoples, the world of mankind shall attain peace and composure, the will of God will become the will of man and the earth a veritable habitation of angels. ('Abdu'l-Bahá, *The Promulgation of Universal Peace*, p. 455)

I hope that thou mayest become a herald of the Kingdom and a means whereby the white and colored people shall close their eyes to racial differences and behold the reality of humanity, which is the universal unity. In other words, it is the oneness and wholeness of the human race, and the manifestation of the bounty of the Almighty. Look not upon thy frailty and thy limited capacity; look thou upon the Bounties and Providence of the Lord of the Kingdom, for His Confirmation is great, and His Power unparalleled and incomparable. Rely as much as thou canst upon the True One, and be thou resigned to the Will of God, so that like unto a candle thou mayest be enkindled in the world of humanity and like unto a star thou mayest shine and gleam from the Horizon of Reality and become the cause of the guidance of both races. ('Abdu'l-Bahá, in a Tablet addressed to Louis G. Gregory, received November 1909, attached to letter dated 30 September 1985, on behalf of the Universal House of Justice to the National Spiritual Assembly of the United States)

Thou hast written that there were several joyful and happy meetings—some for the white and some for the black. However, both races, praise be to God, are under the protection of the All-Knowing God; therefore, the lamps of unity must be lighted in these meetings in such a manner that no distinction may be perceived between the white and the black. Colors are nonessential characteristics, but the realities of men are essential. When there is unity of the essence, what power hath the ephemeral? When the light of reality is shining, what power hath the darkness of the unreal? If it be possible, gather together these two races—black and white—into one Assembly, and create such a love in the hearts that they shall not only unite, but blend into one reality. Know thou of a certainty that as a result differences and disputes between black and white will be totally abolished.

115

By the Will of God, may it be so! This is a most great service to humanity. ('Abdu'l-Bahá, authorized translation from a letter dated 15 April 1985, on behalf of the Universal House of Justice to the Bahá'í Publishing Trust of the United States)

Endeavor that the black and the white may gather in one meeting place, and with the utmost love, fraternally associate with each other, so that quarrels and strife may vanish from among the white and the black. . . . ('Abdu'l-Bahá, authorized translation from a letter dated 2 April 1985, on behalf of the Universal House of Justice to the National Spiritual Assembly of the United States)

Verily the faces of these [the members of the black race] are as the pupil of the eye; although the pupil is created black, yet it is the source of light. I hope God will make these black ones the glory of the white ones and as the wellspring of the light of love of God. And I ask God to assist them under all circumstances, that they may be encompassed with the favors of their Loving Lord throughout centuries and ages. ('Abdu'l-Bahá, authorized translation from a letter dated 30 September 1985, on behalf of the Universal House of Justice to the Bahá'í Publishing Trust of the United States)

THE REQUIREMENTS FOR TEACHING

Arise for the triumph of My Cause, and, through the power of thine utterance, subdue the hearts of men. Thou must show forth that which will ensure the peace and the well-being of the miserable and the downtrodden. Gird up the loins of thine endeavor, that perchance thou mayest release the captive from his chains, and enable him to attain unto true liberty. (Bahá'u'lláh, *Tablets of Bahá'u'lláh*, p. 84)

Now is the time for the lovers of God to raise high the banners of unity, to intone, in the assemblages of the world, the verses of friendship and love and to demonstrate to all that the grace of God is one. Thus will the tabernacles of holiness be upraised on the summits of the earth, gathering all peoples into the protective shadow of the Word of Oneness. This great bounty will dawn over the world at the time when the lovers of God shall arise to carry out His Teachings, and to scatter far and wide the fresh, sweet scents of universal love. ('Abdu'l-Bahá, *Selections from the Writings of 'Abdu'l-Bahá*, no. 7.3)

Be thou a summoner to love, and be thou kind to all the human race. Love thou the children of men and share in their sorrows. Be thou of those who foster peace. Offer thy friendship, be worthy of trust. Be thou a balm to every sore, be thou a medicine for every ill. Bind thou the souls together. Recite thou the verses of guidance. Be engaged in the worship of thy Lord, and rise up to lead the people aright. Loose thy tongue and teach, and let thy face be bright with the fire of God's love. Rest thou not for a moment, seek thou to draw no easeful breath. Thus mayest thou become a sign and symbol of God's love, and a banner of His grace. ('Abdu'l-Bahá, *Selections from the Writings of 'Abdu'l-Bahá*, no. 10.2)

O ye beloved of the Lord! In this sacred Dispensation, conflict and contention are in no wise permitted. Every aggressor deprives himself of God's grace. It is incumbent upon everyone to show the utmost love, rectitude of conduct, straightforwardness and sincere kindliness unto all the peoples and kindreds of the world, be they friends or strangers. So intense must be the spirit of love and loving kindness, that the stranger may find himself a friend, the enemy a true brother, no difference whatsoever existing between them. For universality is of God and all limitations earthly. Thus man must strive that his reality may manifest virtues and perfections, the light whereof may shine upon everyone. . . .

Wherefore, O my loving friends! Consort with all the peoples, kindreds and religions of the world with the utmost truthfulness, uprightness, faithfulness, kindliness, good-will and friendliness, that all the world of being may be filled with the holy ecstasy of the grace of Bahá, that ignorance, enmity, hate and rancor may vanish from the world and the darkness of estrangement amidst the peoples and kindreds of the world may give way to the Light of Unity. ('Abdu'l-Bahá, *Will and Testament of 'Abdu'l-Bahá,* p. 27)

Therefore, the believers of God throughout all the republics of America, through the divine power, must become the cause of the promotion of heavenly teachings and the establishment of the oneness of humanity. Every one of the important souls must arise, blowing over all parts of America the breath of life, conferring upon the people a new spirit, baptizing them with the fire of the love of God, the water of life, and the breaths of the Holy Spirit so that the second birth may become realized. ('Abdu'l-Bahá, *Tablets of the Divine Plan,* no. 14.6)

. . . it is the desire of the Lord God that the loved ones of God and the handmaids of the Merciful in the West should come closer together in harmony and unity as day followeth day, and until this is accomplished, the work will never go forward. The Spiritual Assemblies are collectively the most effective of all instruments for establishing unity and harmony. This matter is of the utmost importance; this is the magnet that draweth down the confirmations of God. If once the beauty of the unity of the friends—this Divine Beloved—be decked in the adornments of the Abhá Kingdom, it is certain that within a very short time those countries will become the Paradise of the All-Glorious, and that out of the west the splendors of unity will cast their bright rays over all the earth. ('Abdu'l-Bahá, *Selections from the Writings of 'Abdu'l-Bahá,* no. 41.2)

. . . unity, according to the Master is the essential prerequisite to all forms of service to the Cause. God's blessings will be cut off from us and our efforts will be fruitless, should there be lack of unity among the friends. (On behalf of Shoghi Effendi, letter dated 27 December 1931, to Juliet Thompson)

You may be sure he will pray for the unity of the . . . believers, as this is of paramount importance, and upon it depends the development of the

Cause there, and the success of every teaching effort. The thing the friends need—everywhere—is a greater love for each other, and this can be acquired by greater love for Bahá'u'lláh; for if we love Him deeply enough, we will never allow personal feelings and opinions to hold His Cause back; we will be willing to sacrifice ourselves to each other for the sake of the Faith, and be, as the Master said, one soul in many bodies. (On behalf of Shoghi Effendi, letter dated 5 September 1946, in *The Compilation of Compilations,* vol. II, no. 1310)

Without the spirit of real love for Bahá'u'lláh, for His Faith and its Institutions, and the believers for each other, the Cause can never really bring in large numbers of people. For it is not preaching and rules the world wants, but love and action. (On behalf of Shoghi Effendi, letter dated 25 October 1948, in *The Compilation of Compilations,* vol. II, no. 1324)

Unless and until the believers really come to realize they are one spiritual family, knit together by a bond more lasting than mere physical ties can ever be, they will not be able to create that warm community atmosphere which alone can attract the hearts of humanity, frozen for lack of real love and feeling. (On behalf of Shoghi Effendi, letter dated 5 May 1943, in *The Compilation of Compilations,* vol. II, no. 1956)

Through example, loving fellowship, prayer, and kindness the friends can attract the hearts of such people and enable them to realize that this is the Cause of God in deed, not merely words! (On behalf of Shoghi Effendi, letter dated 24 February 1943, in *The Compilation of Compilations,* vol. II, no. 1955)

I have emphatically appealed through a recent letter to the American believers to banish from their hearts and minds every trace of racial prejudice—as an essential prerequisite of an effectual campaign conducted by them on behalf of racial amity. There is much to be accomplished by them as fellow-believers before they face the outside world and claim the attention of their fellowmen, as the exponents of these sublime Teachings of Bahá'u'lláh.

I trust they will realize their responsibilities and resolve to wage eternal battle with their natural instincts if they desire to ensure the efficacy of their concerted efforts in this field. (Shoghi Effendi, postscript to letter dated 5 September 1927, written on his behalf to the National Spiritual Assembly of the United States and Canada, attached to a letter dated 4 February 1985, on behalf of the Universal House of Justice to the National Spiritual Assembly of the United States)

He was also very pleased to hear about the new Negro element in the Cause, and he hopes that the Bahá'í Assemblies and Committees will utilize this new talent to the full. Perhaps great suffering for America could be averted if the Cause were not only more widely and quickly spread but the solidarity of races within its ranks more conspicuously demonstrated. He deeply appreciates your services in this important field of Bahá'í activity—racial unity. (On behalf of Shoghi Effendi, letter dated 13 March 1944, to an individual believer, attached to a letter dated 4 February 1985, on behalf of the Universal House of Justice to the National Spiritual Assembly of the United States)

The teaching campaign, now in full swing in the United States and Canada, should, under no circumstances affect the progress, or detract from the importance & urgency of the racial amity work that challenges & confronts the believers in that continent. (On behalf of Shoghi Effendi, letter dated 11 November 1936, addressed to Louis G. Gregory)

Concerning the racial amity conferences; the Guardian firmly believes that they constitute a vital and inseparable part of the teaching campaign now being carried on by the American believers. It is the duty of every loyal Bahá'í to do all that he possibly can to promote this phase of Bahá'í activity, without which no campaign of teaching can bear lasting results. (On behalf of Shoghi Effendi, letter dated 11 November 1936, to an individual believer)

You mentioned the Unity Conferences that were held there some time ago. This is a new and very promising plan for teaching the Cause to broad-minded and progressive people. The friends should do their level best to make this a success and try to bring definitely in the Cause persons attracted to the teachings through those meetings. Shoghi Effendi has great hopes in this new system of teaching and earnestly prays for its success. One thing to bear in mind is that the preparation for these Conferences and the work after them are very important and need great care before any result can be obtained. (On behalf of Shoghi Effendi, letter dated 15 December 1926, to an individual believer)

Dark days seem still ahead of the world, and outside of this Divine Refuge the people will not, we firmly believe, find inner conviction, peace and security. So they have a right to at least hear of the Cause. . . . (On behalf of Shoghi Effendi, letter dated 24 April 1949, to an individual believer, in *Bahá'í News*, vol. 1, no. 226)

It is our duty to redeem as many of our fellowmen as we possibly can, whose hearts are enlightened, before some great catastrophe overtakes them, in which they will either be hopelessly swallowed up or come out purified and strengthened, and ready to serve. The more believers there are to stand forth as beacons in the darkness whenever that time does come, the better; hence the supreme importance of the teaching work at this time. . . . (On behalf of Shoghi Effendi, in a letter dated 9 July 1957, to the National Spiritual Assemblies of South and West Africa, in *Lights of Guidance*, no. 453)

Teaching Diverse Populations

Let us scatter to the uttermost corners of the earth; sacrifice our personal interests, comforts, tastes and pleasures; mingle with the divers kindreds and peoples of the world; familiarize ourselves with their manners, traditions, thoughts and customs; arouse, stimulate and maintain universal interest in the Movement, and at the same time endeavor by all the means in our power, by concentrated and persistent attention, to enlist the unreserved allegiance and the active support of the more hopeful and receptive among our hearers. Let us too bear in mind the example which our beloved Master has clearly set before us. Wise and tactful in His approach, wakeful and attentive in His early intercourse, broad and liberal in all His public utterances, cautious and gradual in the unfolding of the essential verities of the Cause, passionate in His appeal yet sober in argument, confident in tone, unswerving in conviction, dignified in His manners—such were the distinguishing features of our Beloved's noble presentation of the Cause of Bahá'u'lláh. (Shoghi Effendi, *Bahá'í Administration*, p. 69)

Every laborer in those fields, whether as traveling teacher or settler, should, I feel, make it his chief and constant concern to mix, in a friendly manner, with all sections of the population, irrespective of class, creed, nationality, or color, to familiarize himself with their ideas, tastes, and habits, to study the approach best suited to them, to concentrate, patiently and tactfully, on a few who have shown marked capacity and receptivity, and to endeavor, with extreme kindness, to implant such love, zeal, and devotion in their hearts as to enable them to become in turn self-sufficient and independent promoters of the Faith in their respective localities. (Shoghi Effendi, *The Advent of Divine Justice*, ¶95)

. . . the fundamental prerequisite for any successful teaching enterprise . . . is to adapt the presentation of the fundamental principles of their Faith to the cultural and religious backgrounds, the ideologies, and the temperament of the divers races and nations whom they are called upon to enlighten and attract. The susceptibilities of these races and nations, from both the northern and southern climes, springing from either the Germanic or Latin stock, belonging to either the Catholic or Protestant communion, some democratic, others totalitarian in outlook, some socialistic, others capitalistic in their tendencies, differing widely in their customs and standards of living, should at all times be carefully considered, and under no circumstances neglected. (Shoghi Effendi, *Citadel of Faith*, p. 25)

By all means persevere and associate in a friendly spirit with other groups of young people, particularly of a different race or minority nationality, for such association will demonstrate your complete conviction of the oneness of mankind and attract others to the Faith, both young and old alike.

A spirit of prejudice-free, loving comradeship with others is what will open the eyes of people more than any amount of words. Combined with such deeds you can teach the Faith easily. (On behalf of Shoghi Effendi, in a letter dated 18 June 1945, to the Bahá'ís of Dayton, Ohio, in *The Compilation of Compilations*, vol. II, no. 1958)

In America, where racial prejudice is still so widely prevalent, it is the responsibility of the believers to combat and uproot it with all their force, first by endeavouring to introduce into the Cause as many . . . minority groups as they can approach and teach, and second by stimulating close fellowship and intercourse between them and the rest of the Community. (On behalf of Shoghi Effendi, letter dated 30 January 1941, to an individual believer)

It should be the paramount concern of your Committee to foster this aim through every means available. Not only the coloured people, who because of the increasing receptivity they are evincing to the Message and truly deserve special attention, but all other minorities, whether racial or religious, Jews, Red Indians, all alike should be contacted and confirmed. The greater the receptivity of a particular class or group, the stronger should wax the desire and determination of the believers to attract and teach its members. At a time when the whole world is steeped in prejudices of race, class, and nation, the Bahá'ís, by upholding firmly and loyally this cardinal principle of their Faith, can best hope to vindicate its truth, and establish its right to bring order and peace out of the chaos and strife of this war-torn world. (On behalf of Shoghi Effendi, letter dated 30 January 1941, to an individual believer, in *Lights of Guidance*, no. 1808.2)

Your Committee . . . should also, as part of its work, urge the Bahá'ís, wherever they may be, to devote more attention to the minorities. This is particularly true in places where there are universities where foreign students belonging to the black, yellow and brown races are studying. In this way, the friends cannot only obey one of the most beautiful principles of our Faith, to show hospitality to the stranger in our midst, but also demonstrate the universality of our Teachings, and the true brotherhood that animates us, and in addition, confirm Bahá'ís who may go back to the distant places of the earth—the Pacific, Africa, Asia, etc., and be of inestimable help to the newly-born Bahá'í Communities.

Likewise the friends should carry their friendship and their teachings to other minority groups in America, such as the Italians, the Jews, the Czechs, the Poles, the Russians, etc.

He hopes your Committee will constantly bear in mind these points, and that you will try to meet with as many people personally as possible. Teaching trips, lectures, example, have more effect than the circular of printed matter, which half the time is not properly read and assimilated. (On behalf of Shoghi Effendi, letter dated 27 May 1957, to the Bahá'í Inter-Racial Teaching Committee)

He feels that, as the main object of the Bahá'í Inter-racial work is to abolish prejudice against any and every race and minority group, it is, obviously proper for them to include in particular any group that is receiving especially bad treatment—such as the Japanese Americans are being subjected to. There is also no reason why work should not be done among, and in cooperation with, the Mexicans, the Chinese, and so on.

He has always been very anxious to have the Indians taught and enlisted under the banner of the Faith, in view of the Master's remarkable statements about the possibilities for their future and that they represent the aboriginal American population.

The Negroes, likewise, are one might say a key problem and epitomise the feelings of colour prejudice so rife in the United States. That is why he has constantly emphasized the importance of the Bahá'ís actively and continuously demonstrating that in the Faith this cruel and horrible taint of discrimination against, and contempt for, them does not exist but is, on the contrary, supplanted by a feeling of esteem for their great gifts and a complete lack of prejudice against associating with them in every field of life.

The work of the Race Unity Committee should include, as far as is feasible, contacts with all minority groups, and where ever there is a particularly stout prejudice against a special group—such as feeling against the Japanese in the Western states and the negroes in the Southern, etc.,—efforts should be made to counteract it by showing publicly the Bahá'í example of loving tolerance and brotherly association. (On behalf of Shoghi Effendi, letter dated 30 December 1945, to an individual believer, in *Lights of Guidance*, no. 1796)

No more laudable and meritorious service can be rendered the Cause of God, at the present hour, than a successful effort to enhance the diversity of the members of the American Bahá'í community by swelling the ranks of the Faith through the enrollment of the members of these races [the Negro, the Indian, the Eskimo, and Jewish]. A blending of these highly differentiated elements of the human race, harmoniously interwoven into the fabric of an all-embracing Bahá'í fraternity, and assimilated through the dynamic processes of a divinely appointed Administrative Order, and contributing each its share to the enrichment and glory of Bahá'í community life, is surely an achievement the contemplation of which must warm and thrill every Bahá'í heart. (Shoghi Effendi, *The Advent of Divine Justice*, ¶81)

He was particularly happy to see that some of the Indian believers were present at the Convention. He attaches the greatest importance to teaching the original inhabitants of the Americas the Faith. 'Abdu'l-Bahá Himself has stated how great are their potentialities, and it is their right, and the duty of the non-Indian Bahá'ís, to see that they receive the Message of God for this Day. One of the most worthy objectives of your Assembly must be the establishment of all-Indian Spiritual Assemblies. Other minorities should likewise be especially sought out and taught. (On behalf of Shoghi Effendi, in *A Special Measure of Love*, pp. 19–20)

Special attention must be focused on the work of converting the Indians to the Faith. The goal should be all-Indian assemblies, so that these much exploited and suppressed original inhabitants of the land may realize that they are equals and partners in the affairs of the Cause of God, and that Bahá'u'lláh is the Manifestation of God for them. (On behalf of Shoghi Effendi, in *A Special Measure of Love*, p. 19)

The original population of the United States was very dear to 'Abdu'l-Bahá's heart, and He foretold for the Indians a great future if they accepted and became enlightened by the Teachings of Bahá'u'lláh.

To believe in the Mouthpiece of God in His Day confers very great blessings, not only on individuals, but on races, and He hopes that you who are now numbered amongst the followers of Bahá'u'lláh will give His Message to many more of your tribe, and in this way hasten for your people a bright and happy future. (On behalf of Shoghi Effendi, letter dated 21 December 1947, to an individual believer, in *Lights of Guidance*, no. 1802)

As you know, the Master attached the utmost importance to the teaching of the Indians in America. The Guardian therefore hopes that your Assembly will devote considerable energy to this most important matter so that contacts are made with Indians in all of the countries under your jurisdiction and some of these Indians become confirmed in the Faith.

If the light of Divine Guidance enters properly into the lives of the Indians, it will be found that they will arise with a great power and will become an example of spirituality and culture to all of the people in these countries. (On behalf of Shoghi Effendi, letter dated 22 August 1957, to the National Spiritual Assembly of Central America and Mexico, in *Lights of Guidance*, no. 2029)

In the Tablets of the Divine Plan, the Master pays the utmost attention to this most important matter. He states that if the Power of the Holy Spirit today properly enters into the minds and hearts of the natives of the great American continents that they will become great standard bearers of the Faith, similar to the Nomads (Arabians) who become the most cultured and enlightened people under the Muhammadan civilization. (On behalf of Shoghi Effendi, letter dated 22 August 1957, to the National Spiritual Assembly of Brazil, Peru, Colombia, Ecuador, and Venezuela, in *Lights of Guidance,* no. 1776.4)

As to the racial aspects of your work Shoghi Effendi believes that no chances should be lost, for the Master stressed constantly the importance of reconciling the Negro and white people of North America. This field of service not only attracts the attention of innumerable persons to the Cause, but also furthers one of the ideals of the Faith, namely the abolition of racial prejudice. (On behalf of Shoghi Effendi, letter dated 18 December 1930, as an attachment from a letter dated 4 February 1985, on behalf of the Universal House of Justice to the National Spiritual Assembly of the United States)

The real means of eliminating race prejudice, is to spread and establish the Faith; for in it, there is no prejudice whatsoever, as the Faith itself holds as its cardinal principle, the Oneness of Humanity.

The Guardian will pray that you will be confirmed in your efforts to teach more Negroes. They have been subject so long to the prejudices of the majority peoples, that he hopes they will find their goal in the Cause of God. . . . The friends should concentrate on pure hearted people, and continue association and fellowship with them, until they themselves become active workers in the Cause of God. (On behalf of Shoghi Effendi, letter dated 20 December 1955 to an individual believer, attached to a letter dated 4 February 1985, on behalf of the Universal House of Justice to the National Spiritual Assembly of the United States)

He urges the friends to concentrate on teaching the negroes. They should be courageous in their racial stand, particularly as so many non-Bahá'ís and non-Bahá'í organizations are showing marked courage at this time . . . The friends must remember that the cardinal principle of their Faith is the Oneness of Mankind. This places an obligation on them far surpassing the obligation which Christian charity and brotherly love places upon the

Christians. They should demonstrate this spirit of oneness constantly and courageously. . . . (On behalf of Shoghi Effendi, letter dated 21 September 1957, to the American Bahá'ís)

Indeed if the friends could seek, and exert themselves, to become 100 per cent Bahá'ís they would see how greatly their influence over others would be increased, and how rapidly the Cause would spread. The world is seeking not a compromise but the embodiment of a high and shining ideal. The more the friends live up to our teachings in every aspect of their lives, in their homes, in business, in their social relationships, the greater will be the attraction they exercise over the hearts of others.

He is pleased to see you have naturally, with conviction and good will towards all, been mingling with and teaching the coloured people. When the Bahá'ís live up to their teachings as they should, although it may arouse the opposition of some it will arouse still more the admiration of fair-minded people. (On behalf of Shoghi Effendi, letter dated 23 January 1945, *The Compilation of Compilations*, vol. II, no. 1303)

The Message of this Day is directed to the whole of mankind, not to any particular section of it. The colored as well as the noncolored are both welcomed into the Bahá'í Community, and once they enter its ranks they are recognized as one and the same. Rather they should cease to look at the racial differences separating them, and should associate with each other in perfect peace, unity and fellowship.

The Bahá'ís should by all means endeavor to attract to the Faith as many members of the colored race as they possibly can, and thus demonstrate in deeds the universality of the Message of Bahá'u'lláh. It is only through this intermingling of races within the framework of His World Order that a lasting and just solution can be found to the perplexing racial issues confronting mankind. (On behalf of Shoghi Effendi, letter dated 19 November 1937, to an individual believer, quoted in a letter dated 4 February 1985, on behalf of the Universal House of Justice to the National Spiritual Assembly of the United States)

It is only natural that people should be able to pour out more freely their enthusiasm in the field of services that lies nearest to their heart, and if your departure would in no way affect the assembly status . . . he sees no reason why you should not go and teach among the Negroes, as this is a very important field of Bahá'í activity, especially so in these days when the racial question seems to be coming to a head in the United States. The more Negroes who become Bahá'ís, the greater the leaven will be within their own race, working for harmony and friendship between these two bodies of American citizens: the white and the colored. (On behalf of Shoghi Effendi, letter dated 18 December 1943, to an individual believer, quoted in a letter dated 4 February 1985, on behalf of the Universal House of Justice to the National Spiritual Assembly of the United States)

The qualities of heart so richly possessed by the Negro are much needed in the world today—their great capacity for faith, their loyalty and devotion to their religion when once they believe, their purity of heart. God has richly endowed them, and their great contribution to the Cause is much needed, especially as there is a lack of Negro Bahá'í teachers who can go out to their own people, along with their white brothers and sisters, and convince them of the active universality of our Faith. He will especially pray that you may confirm souls of capacity in this field. (On behalf of Shoghi Effendi, letter dated 27 September 1941, to two believers, in *Lights of Guidance,* no. 1809)

He is well aware that the conditions within the ranks of the believers in respect to race prejudice is [sic] far from being as it should be. However he feels very strongly that it presents a challenge to both white and colored believers.

As we neither feel nor acknowledge any distinction between the duties and privileges of a Bahá'í, whoever he may be, it is incumbent upon the Negro believers to rise above this great test which the attitude of some of their white brethren may present. They must prove their innate equality not by words but by deeds. They must accept the Cause of Bahá'u'lláh for the sake of the *Cause,* love it, and cling to it, and teach it, and fight for it as *their* own Cause, forgetful of the shortcomings of others. Any other attitude is unworthy of their faith.

Proud and happy in the praises which even Bahá'u'lláh Himself has bestowed upon them, they must feel He revealed Himself for them and every other downtrodden race, loves them, and will help them to attain their destiny.

The whole race question in America is a national one and of great importance. But the Negro friends must not waste their precious opportunity to serve the Faith, in these momentous days, by dwelling on the admitted shortcomings of the white friends. They must arise and serve and teach, confident of the future they are building, a future in which we know these barriers will have once and for all been overcome! (On behalf of Shoghi Effendi, letter dated 9 February 1942, addressed to Sadie Oglesby)

The Negro believers must be just as active as their white brothers and sisters in spreading the Faith, both among their own race and members of other races. It has been a great step forward in the Cause's development in America to have Negro pioneers go forth, and their work has been of the greatest help and very productive of results. (On behalf of Shoghi Effendi, letter dated 19 March 1944, to two individual believers, in *Lights of Guidance,* no. 1784)

He hopes that your Assembly will endeavour to reach the Eskimos with the Message; he fully realizes how difficult a task this is, but it is also one of great importance. If but one of these souls should become truly enkindled, he or she could then teach others in their own language and a manner suited to their minds. (On behalf of Shoghi Effendi, letter dated 19 November 1945, to the Spiritual Assembly of Anchorage, in *High Endeavours: Messages to Alaska,* p. 13)

'Abdu'l-Bahá was most anxious that the Eskimo people should be taught the Message of this New Day, and it is a source of happiness to all Bahá'ís that you, a member of that race, have arisen to spread these teachings.* God has surely guided your steps and blessed your search for divine Truth.

---

* Melba Call (King) was the first Eskimo to become a Bahá'í. While she was born and raised in Alaska, she was residing in New Mexico when she heard of the Faith and became a Bahá'í.

If people only realized it, the inner life of the spirit is that which counts, but they are so blinded by desires and so misled that they have brought upon themselves all the suffering we see at present in the world. The Bahá'ís seek to lead people back to a knowledge of their true selves and the purpose for which they were created, and thus to their greatest happiness and highest good. (On behalf of Shoghi Effendi, letter dated 24 July 1943, addressed to an individual believer, *High Endeavours: Messages to Alaska,* p. 7)

Your Assembly should bear in mind the necessity, in the future at any rate, of having firmly grounded local Assemblies in all of the States of Australia and New Zealand; and also the importance of increasing the representation of the minority races, such as the Aborigines and the Maoris, within the Bahá'í Community. Special effort should be made to contact these people and to teach them; and the Bahá'ís in Australia and New Zealand should consider that every one of them that can be won to the Faith is a precious acquisition. (On behalf of Shoghi Effendi, letter dated July 24 1945, to the National Spiritual Assembly of Australia and New Zealand, *Letters from the Guardian to Australia and New Zealand,* p. 124)

In connection with the teaching work throughout the Pacific area, he fully believes that in many cases the white society is difficult to interest in anything but its own superficial activities. The Bahá'ís must identify themselves on the one hand, as much as they reasonably can, with the life of the white people, so as not to become ostracized, criticized and eventually ousted from their hard-won pioneer posts. On the other hand, they must bear in mind that the primary object of their living there is to teach the native population the Faith. This they must do with tact and discretion, in order not to forfeit their foot-hold in these islands which are often so difficult of access.

Sound judgment, a great deal of patience and forbearance, faith and nobility of conduct, must distinguish the pioneers, and be their helpers in accomplishing the object of their journey to these far places.

He attaches great importance to teaching the aboriginal Australians, and also in converting more Maoris to the Faith, and hopes that the Bahá'ís will devote some attention to contacting both of these minority groups. (On behalf of Shoghi Effendi, letter dated 16 June 1954, to the National Spiritual Assembly of Australia and New Zealand, in *Letters from the Guardian to Australia and New Zealand,* p. 118)

The Guardian thinks perhaps a different approach to the aborigines might attract them; one of being interested in their lives and their folklore, and of trying to become their friend, rather than trying to change them or improve them. (On behalf of Shoghi Effendi, letter dated 9 April 1955, in *The Compilation of Compilations,* vol. II, no. 1990)

These people [the indigenous people], finding the Bahá'ís *sincerely* lacking in either prejudice—or that even worse attitude—condescension—might not only take interest in our Teachings, but also help us to reach their people in the proper way.

It is a great mistake to believe that because people are illiterate or live primitive lives, they are lacking in either intelligence or sensibility. On the contrary, they may well look on us, with the evils of our civilization, with its moral corruption, its ruinous wars, its hypocrisy and conceit, as people who merit watching with both suspicion and contempt. We should meet them as equals, well-wishers, people who admire and respect their ancient descent and who feel that they will be interested, as we are, in a /living religion/—and not in the dead forms of present-day churches. (On behalf of Shoghi Effendi, letter dated 21 September 1951, to The Comite Nacional de Ensenanza Bahá'í para los Indigenas de Sur America, in *Lights Of Guidance,* no. 1777)

The racial question all over Africa is very acute, but, while being wise and tactful, believers must realise that their standard is far from that of the white colonials. They have not gone there to uphold the white man's supremacy, but to give the Cause of God to, primarily, the black man whose home is Africa. (On behalf of Shoghi Effendi, letter dated 30 August 1951, to an individual believer, in *The Unfolding Destiny of the British Bahá'í Community*, p. 460)

He has spoken very strongly to some of the pilgrims here about the teaching work in that country, and impressed upon them that the whole object of the pioneers in going forth to Africa, is to teach the coloured people, and not the white people. This does not mean that they must refuse to teach the white people, which would be a foolish attitude. It does, however, mean that they should constantly bear in mind that it is to the native African that they are now carrying the Message of Bahá'u'lláh, in his own country, and not to people from abroad who have migrated there permanently or temporarily and are a minority, and many of them, judging by their acts, a very unsavoury minority. (On behalf of Shoghi Effendi, letter dated 4 June 1954, to the British Africa Committee, in *The Unfolding Destiny of the British Bahá'í Community*, p. 330)

The unsophisticated people of the world—and they form the large majority of its population—have the same right to know of the Cause of God as others. When the friends are teaching the Word of God they should be careful to give the Message in the same simplicity as it is enunciated in our Teachings. In their contacts they must show genuine and divine love. The heart of an unlettered soul is extremely sensitive; any trace of prejudice on the part of the pioneer or teacher is immediately sensed. (The Universal House of Justice, letter dated 13 July 1964, to all National Spiritual Assemblies, *Messages 1963–1986*, no. 18.3)

The paramount goal of the teaching work at the present time is to carry the Message of Bahá'u'lláh to every stratum of human society and every walk of life. An eager response to the teachings will often be found in the most unexpected quarters, and any such response should be quickly followed up, for success in a fertile area awakens a response in those who were at first uninterested.

The same presentation of the teachings will not appeal to everybody; the method of expression and the approach must be varied in accordance with the outlook and interest of the hearer. An approach which is designed to appeal to everybody will usually result in attracting the middle section, leaving both extremes untouched. No effort must be spared to ensure that the healing Word of God reaches the rich and the poor, the learned and the illiterate, the old and the young, the devout and the atheist, the dweller in the remote hills and islands, the inhabitant of the teeming cities, the suburban businessman, the laborer in the slums, the nomadic tribesman, the farmer, the university student; all must be brought consciously within the teaching plans of the Bahá'í community. (The Universal House of Justice, letter dated 31 October 1937, *Wellspring of Guidance, Messages 1963–1968*, p. 124)

We note that the new teaching methods you have developed, in reaching the waiting masses, have substantially influenced the winning of your goals, and we urge the American Bahá'ís, one and all, newly enrolled and believers of long standing, to arise, put their reliance in Bahá'u'lláh and armed with that supreme power, continue unabated their efforts to reach the waiting souls, while simultaneously consolidating the hard-won victories. New methods inevitably bring with them criticism and challenges no matter how successful they may ultimately prove to be. The influx of so many new believers is, in itself, a call to the veteran believers to join the ranks of those in this field of service and to give wholeheartedly of their knowledge and experience. Far from standing aloof, the American believers are called upon now, as never before, to grasp this golden opportunity which has been presented to them, to consult together prayerfully and widen the scope of their endeavors.

Efforts to reach the minorities should be increased and broadened to include all minority groups such as the Indians, Spanish-speaking people, Japanese and Chinese. Indeed, every stratum of American society must be reached and can be reached with the healing Message, if the believers will but arise and go forth with the spirit which is conquering the citadels of the southern states. Such a program, coupled as it must be with continuous consolidation, can be effectively carried out by universal participation on the part of every lover of Bahá'u'lláh. (The Universal House of Justice, letter dated 14 February 1972, to the National Spiritual Assembly of the United States, in *Messages, 1968–1973,* p. 85)

The Americas have been a melting pot and a meeting place for the races of men, and the need is acute for the fulfillment of God's promises of the realization of the oneness of mankind. Particularly do the Master and the Guardian point to the Afro-Americans and the Amerindians, two great ethnic groups whose spiritual powers will be released through their response to the Creative Word. But our Teachings must touch all, must include all peoples. And, in this hour of your tireless activity, what special rewards shall come to those who will arise, summoned by 'Abdu'l-Bahá's Words: "Now is the time to divest yourselves of the garment of attachment to this phenomenal realm, be wholly severed from the physical world, become angels of heaven, and travel and teach through all these regions." (The Universal House of Justice, letter dated May 1971, to the Caribbean Conference, in *Lights of Guidance,* no. 1778)

UPHOLDING JUSTICE: A PREREQUISITE TO UNITY

I beseech Thee, O my God, by all the transcendent glory of Thy Name, to clothe Thy loved ones in the robe of justice and to illumine their beings with the light of trustworthiness. Thou art the One that hath power to do as He pleaseth and Who holdeth within His grasp the reins of all things, visible and invisible. (Bahá'u'lláh, in *Bahá'í Prayers,* p. 173)

Assuredly we are today living in the Days of God. These are the glorious days on the like of which the sun hath never risen in the past. These are the days which the people in bygone times eagerly expected. What hath then befallen you that ye are fast asleep? These are the days wherein God hath caused the Day-Star of Truth to shine resplendent. What hath then caused you to keep your silence? These are the appointed days which ye have been yearningly awaiting in the past—the days of the advent of divine justice. Render ye thanks unto God, O ye concourse of believers. (The Báb, *Selections from the Writings of the Báb,* no. 6:11:5)

I testify, O my God, that Thou hast, from eternity, sent down upon Thy servants naught else except that which can cause them to soar up and be drawn near unto Thee, and to ascend into the heaven of Thy transcendent oneness. Thou hast established Thy bounds among them, and ordained them to stand among Thy creatures as evidences of Thy justice and as signs of Thy mercy, and to be the stronghold of Thy protection amongst Thy people, that no man may in Thy realm transgress against his neighbor. (Bahá'u'lláh, *Prayers and Meditations by Bahá'u'lláh*, no. 178.7)

The structure of world stability and order hath been reared upon, and will continue to be sustained by, the twin pillars of reward and punishment. . . . There can be no doubt whatever that if the daystar of justice, which the clouds of tyranny have obscured, were to shed its light upon men, the face of the earth would be completely transformed. (Bahá'u'lláh, *Gleanings from the Writings of Bahá'u'lláh*, no. 112.1)

By the righteousness of God! Justice is a powerful force. It is, above all else, the conqueror of the citadels of the hearts and souls of men, and the revealer of the secrets of the world of being, and the standard-bearer of love and bounty. (Bahá'u'lláh, *Epistle to the Son of the Wolf*, p. 32)

The light of men is Justice. Quench it not with the contrary winds of oppression and tyranny. The purpose of justice is the appearance of unity among men. The ocean of divine wisdom surgeth within this exalted word, while the books of the world cannot contain its inner significance. Were mankind to be adorned with this raiment, they would behold the daystar of the utterance, "On that day God will satisfy everyone out of His abundance,"* shining resplendent above the horizon of the world. (Bahá'u'lláh, *Tablets of Bahá'u'lláh*, p. 66)

---

* Qur'án 4:129

O Son of Spirit! The best beloved of all things in My sight is Justice; turn not away therefrom if thou desirest Me, and neglect it not that I may confide in thee. By its aid thou shalt see with thine own eyes and not through the eyes of others, and shalt know of thine own knowledge and not through the knowledge of thy neighbor. Ponder this in thy heart; how it behoveth thee to be. Verily justice is My gift to thee and the sign of My loving-kindness. Set it then before thine eyes.

They that are just and fair-minded in their judgement occupy a sublime station and hold an exalted rank. The light of piety and uprightness shineth resplendent from these souls. We earnestly hope that the peoples and countries of the world may not be deprived of the splendors of these two luminaries. (Bahá'u'lláh, *Tablets of Bahá'u'lláh*, p. 36)

O son of man! If thine eyes be turned towards mercy, forsake the things that profit thee, and cleave unto that which will profit mankind. And if thine eyes be turned towards justice, choose thou for thy neighbor that which thou choosest for thyself. Humility exalteth man to the heaven of glory and power, whilst pride abaseth him to the depths of wretchedness and degradation. (Bahá'u'lláh, *Epistle to the Son of the Wolf*, p. 29)

Be vigilant, that ye may not do injustice to anyone, be it to the extent of a grain of mustard seed. Tread ye the path of justice, for this, verily, is the straight path. (Bahá'u'lláh, *Gleanings from the Writings of Bahá'u'lláh*, no. 118.1)

Lay not on any soul a load which ye would not wish to be laid upon you, and desire not for any one the things ye would not desire for yourselves. This is My best counsel unto you, did ye but observe it. (Bahá'u'lláh, *Gleanings from the Writings of Bahá'u'lláh*, no. 66.8)

Be fair to yourselves and to others, that the evidences of justice may be revealed, through your deeds, among Our faithful servants. Beware lest ye encroach upon the substance of your neighbor. Prove yourselves worthy of his trust and confidence in you, and withhold not from the poor the gifts which the grace of God hath bestowed upon you. He, verily, shall recompense the charitable, and doubly repay them for what they have bestowed. No God is there but Him. All creation and its empire are His. He bestoweth His gifts on whom He will, and from whom He will He withholdeth them. He is the Great Giver, the Most Generous, the Benevolent. (Bahá'u'lláh, *Gleanings from the Writings of Bahá'u'lláh,* no. 128.9)

Justice, which consisteth in rendering each his due, dependeth upon and is conditioned by two words: reward and punishment. From the standpoint of justice, every soul should receive the reward of his actions, inasmuch as the peace and prosperity of the world depend thereon, even as He saith, exalted be His glory: "The structure of world stability and order hath been reared upon, and will continue to be sustained by, the twin pillars of reward and punishment." In brief, every circumstance requireth a different utterance and every occasion calleth for a different course of action. (Bahá'u'lláh, *The Tabernacle of Unity,* pp. 40–41)

Say: No man can attain his true station except through his justice. No power can exist except through unity. No welfare and no well-being can be attained except through consultation. (Bahá'u'lláh, translated from a Tablet in Arabic, in *The Compilation of Compilations,* vol. I, no. 167)

The second attribute of perfection is justice and impartiality. This means to have no regard for one's own personal benefits and selfish advantages, and to carry out the laws of God without the slightest concern for anything else. It means to see one's self as only one of the servants of God, the All-Possessing, and except for aspiring to spiritual distinction, never attempting to be singled out from the others. It means to consider the welfare of the community as one's own. It means, in brief, to regard humanity as a single individual, and one's own self as a member of that corporeal form, and to know of a certainty that if pain or injury afflicts any member of that body, it must inevitably result in suffering for all the rest. ('Abdu'l-Bahá, *The Secret of Divine Civilization,* ¶71)

Oh, friends of God, be living examples of justice! So that by the Mercy of God, the world may see in your actions that you manifest the attributes of justice and mercy.

Justice is not limited, it is a universal quality. Its operation must be carried out in all classes, from the highest to the lowest. Justice must be sacred, and the rights of all the people must be considered. Desire for others only that which you desire for yourselves. Then shall we rejoice in the Sun of Justice, which shines from the Horizon of God.

Each man has been placed in a post of honor, which he must not desert. A humble workman who commits an injustice is as much to blame as a renowned tyrant. Thus we all have our choice between justice and injustice.

I hope that each one of you will become just, and direct your thoughts towards the unity of mankind; that you will never harm your neighbors nor speak ill of any one; that you will respect the rights of all men, and be more concerned for the interests of others than for your own. Thus will you become torches of Divine justice, acting in accordance with the Teaching of Bahá'u'lláh, who, during His life, bore innumerable trials and persecutions in order to show forth to the world of mankind the virtues of the World of Divinity, making it possible for you to realize the supremacy of the spirit, and to rejoice in the Justice of God. ('Abdu'l-Bahá, *Paris Talks,* no. 49.14–17)

If man were to care for himself only he would be nothing but an animal, for only the animals are thus egoistic. If you bring a thousand sheep to a well to kill nine hundred and ninety-nine, the one remaining sheep would go on grazing, not thinking of the others and worrying not at all about the lost, never bothering that its own kind had passed away, or had perished or been killed. To look after one's self only is, therefore, an animal propensity. It is the animal propensity to live solitary and alone. It is the animal proclivity to look after one's own comfort. But man was created to be a man—to be fair, to be just, to be merciful, to be kind to all his species, never to be willing that he himself be well off while others are in misery and distress. This is an attribute of the animal and not of man. Nay, rather, man should be willing to accept hardships for himself in order that others may enjoy wealth; he should enjoy trouble for himself that others may enjoy happiness and well-being. This is the attribute of man. This is becoming of man. Otherwise man is not man—he is less than the animal.

The man who thinks only of himself and is thoughtless of others is undoubtedly inferior to the animal because the animal is not possessed of the reasoning faculty. The animal is excused; but in man there is reason, the faculty of justice, the faculty of mercifulness. Possessing all these faculties, he must not leave them unused. He who is so hard-hearted as to think only of his own comfort, such an one will not be called man.

Man is he who forgets his own interests for the sake of others. His own comfort he forfeits for the well-being of all. Nay, rather, his own life must he be willing to forfeit for the life of mankind. Such a man is the honor of the world of humanity. Such a man is the glory of the world of mankind. Such a man is the one who wins eternal bliss. Such a man is near to the threshold of God. Such a man is the very manifestation of eternal happiness. Otherwise, men are like animals, exhibiting the same proclivities and propensities as the world of animals. What distinction is there? What prerogatives, what perfection? None whatever! Animals are better even thinking only of themselves and negligent of the needs of others.

Consider how the greatest men in the world—whether among prophets or philosophers—all have forfeited their own comfort, have sacrificed their own pleasure for the well-being of humanity. They have sacrificed their own lives for the body politic. They have sacrificed their own wealth for that of the general welfare. They have forfeited their own honor for the honor of mankind. Therefore, it becomes evident that this is the highest attainment for the world of humanity.

We ask God to endow human souls with justice so that they may be fair, and may strive to provide for the comfort of all, that each member of humanity may pass his life in the utmost comfort and welfare. Then this material world will become the very paradise of the Kingdom, this elemental earth will be in a heavenly state and all the servants of God will live in the utmost joy, happiness and gladness. We must all strive and concentrate all our thoughts in order that such happiness may accrue to the world of humanity. ('Abdu'l-Bahá, *The Promulgation of Universal Peace*, pp. 441–42)

At a time when warfare and strife prevailed among nations, when enmity and hatred separated sects and denominations and human differences were very great, Bahá'u'lláh appeared upon the horizon of the East, proclaiming the oneness of God and the unity of the world of humanity. He promulgated the teaching that all mankind are the servants of one God; that all have come into being through the bestowal of the one Creator; that God is kind to all, nurtures, rears and protects all, provides for all and extends His love and mercy to all races and people. Inasmuch as God is loving, why should we be unjust and unkind? As God manifests loyalty and mercy, why should we show forth enmity and hatred? Surely the divine policy is more perfect than human plan and theory; for no matter how wise and sagacious man may become, he can never attain a policy that is superior to the policy of God. Therefore, we must emulate the attitude of God, love all people, be just and kind to every human creature. ('Abdu'l-Bahá, *The Promulgation of Universal Peace*, pp. 241–42)

The Almighty hath not created in man the claws and teeth of ferocious animals, nay rather hath the human form been fashioned and set with the most comely attributes and adorned with the most perfect virtues. The honor of this creation and the worthiness of this garment therefore require man to have love and affinity for his own kind, nay rather, to act towards all living creatures with justice and equity. ('Abdu'l-Bahá, *Selections from the Writings of 'Abdu'l-Bahá*, no. 225.12)

Bahá'u'lláh taught that an equal standard of human rights must be recognized and adopted. In the estimation of God all men are equal; there is no distinction or preferment for any soul in the dominion of His justice and equity. ('Abdu'l-Bahá, *The Promulgation of Universal Peace*, p. 252)

"No radiance," He [Bahá'u'lláh] declares, "can compare with that of justice. The organization of the world and the tranquility of mankind depend

141

upon it." "O people of God!" He exclaims, "That which traineth the world is Justice, for it is upheld by two pillars, reward and punishment. These two pillars are the sources of life to the world." "Justice and equity," is yet another assertion, "are two guardians for the protection of man. They have appeared arrayed in their mighty and sacred names to maintain the world in uprightness and protect the nations." "Bestir yourselves, O people," is His emphatic warning, "in anticipation of the days of Divine justice, for the promised hour is now come. Beware lest ye fail to apprehend its import, and be accounted among the erring." "The day is approaching," He similarly has written, "when the faithful will behold the daystar of justice shining in its full splendor from the dayspring of glory." (Shoghi Effendi, *The Advent of Divine Justice*, ¶42)

"God be praised!" 'Abdu'l-Bahá, in His turn, exclaims, "The sun of justice hath risen above the horizon of Bahá'u'lláh. For in His Tablets the foundations of such a justice have been laid as no mind hath, from the beginning of creation, conceived." "The canopy of existence," He further explains, "resteth upon the pole of justice, and not of forgiveness, and the life of mankind dependeth on justice and not on forgiveness."

Small wonder, therefore, that the Author of the Bahá'í Revelation should have chosen to associate the name and title of that House, which is to be the crowning glory of His administrative institutions, not with forgiveness but with justice, to have made justice the only basis and the permanent foundation of His Most Great Peace, and to have proclaimed it in His Hidden Words as "the best beloved of all things" in His sight. It is to the American believers, particularly, that I feel urged to direct this fervent plea to ponder in their hearts the implications of this moral rectitude, and to uphold, with heart and soul and uncompromisingly, both individually and collectively, this sublime standard—a standard of which justice is so essential and potent an element. (Shoghi Effendi, *The Advent of Divine Justice*, ¶43–44)

Wherever they reside, Bahá'ís endeavour to uphold the standard of justice, addressing inequities directed towards themselves or towards others, but only through lawful means available to them, eschewing all forms of violent protest. Moreover, in no way does the love they hold in their hearts for humanity run counter to the sense of duty they feel to expend their energies in service to their respective countries. (The Universal House of Justice, letter dated 2 March 2013, addressed to the Bahá'ís of Iran)

Together with the crumbling of barriers separating peoples, our age is witnessing the dissolution of the once insuperable wall that the past assumed would forever separate the life of Heaven from the life of Earth. The scriptures of all religions have always taught the believer to see in service to others not only a moral duty, but an avenue for the soul's own approach to God. Today, the progressive restructuring of society gives this familiar teaching new dimensions of meaning. As the age-old promise of a world animated by principles of justice slowly takes on the character of a realistic goal, meeting the needs of the soul and those of society will increasingly be seen as reciprocal aspects of a mature spiritual life. (The Universal House of Justice, letter dated April 2002, addressed to the World's Religious Leaders)

SAFEGUARDING THE RIGHTS AND PRIVILEGES OF MINORITY GROUPS

To discriminate against any race, on the ground of its being socially backward, politically immature, and numerically in a minority, is a flagrant violation of the spirit that animates the Faith of Bahá'u'lláh. The consciousness of any division or cleavage in its ranks is alien to its very purpose, principles, and ideals. Once its members have fully recognized the claim of its Author, and, by identifying themselves with its Administrative Order, accepted unreservedly the principles and laws embodied in its teachings, every differentiation of class, creed, or color must automatically be obliterated, and never be allowed, under any pretext, and however great the pressure of events or of public opinion, to reassert itself. If any discrimination is at all to be tolerated, it should be a discrimination not against, but rather in favor of the minority, be it racial or otherwise. Unlike the nations and peoples of the earth, be they of the East or of the West, democratic or authoritarian, communist or capitalist, whether belonging to the Old World or the New, who either ignore, trample upon, or extirpate, the racial, religious, or political minorities within the sphere of their jurisdiction, every organized community enlisted under the banner of Bahá'u'lláh should feel it to be its first and inescapable obligation to nurture, encourage, and safeguard every minority belonging to any faith, race, class, or nation within it. So great and vital is this principle that in such circumstances, as when an equal number of ballots have been cast in an election, or where the qualifications for any office are balanced as between the various races, faiths or nationalities within the community, priority should unhesitatingly be accorded the party representing the minority, and this for no other reason except to stimulate and encourage it, and afford it an opportunity to further the interests of the community. In the light of this principle, and bearing in mind the extreme desirability of having the minority elements participate and share responsibility in the conduct of Bahá'í activity, it should be the duty of every Bahá'í community so to arrange its affairs that in cases where individuals belonging to the divers minority elements within it are already qualified and fulfill the necessary requirements, Bahá'í representative institutions, be they Assemblies, conventions, conferences, or committees, may have represented on them as many of these divers elements, racial or otherwise, as possible. The adoption of such a course, and faithful adherence to it, would not only be a source of inspiration and encouragement to those elements that are numerically small and inadequately represented, but would demonstrate to the world at large the universality and representative character of the Faith of Bahá'u'lláh, and the freedom of His followers from the taint of those prejudices which have already wrought such havoc in the domestic affairs, as well as the foreign relationships, of the nations. (Shoghi Effendi, *The Advent of Divine Justice,* ¶53)

The friends should bear in mind that in our Faith, unlike every other society, the minority, to compensate for what might be treated as an inferior status, receives special attention, love and consideration. (On behalf of Shoghi Effendi, July 1957, in *A Special Measure of Love,* pp. 19–20)

He urges you all to devote particular attention to the contact with racial minorities. In a country which has such a large element of prejudice against its colored citizens as the United States, it is of the greatest importance that the Bahá'ís—and more especially the youth—should demonstrate actively our complete lack of prejudice and, indeed, our prejudice in favour of minorities. (On behalf of Shoghi Effendi, letter dated 11 November 1951, to the Senior Youth Session at Louhelen Bahá'í School, in *Lights of Guidance,* no. 2156)

The two races should ultimately be brought together, and be urged to associate with the utmost unity and fellowship, and be given full and equal opportunity to participate in the conduct of the teachings as well as administrative activities of the Faith. Nothing short of such an ultimate fusion of the two races can ensure the faithful application of that cornerstone principle of the Cause regarding the oneness of mankind. (On behalf of Shoghi Effendi, letter dated 22 March 1937, to the National Spiritual Assembly of the United States and Canada)

On principle no discrimination whatsoever should be made between the white and the colored believers in any administrative function or duty. The Cause stands above any racial consideration, for the core of its message is the principle of the oneness of mankind. The colored believers are entitled to the very same privileges and opportunities of service which their fellow-believers of the white race enjoy.

This principle is quite clear, and should be always emphasized without any compromise of any kind. Its application, however, to individual cases is the responsibility of the assemblies. (On behalf of Shoghi Effendi, letter dated 14 October 1937, to an individual believer, quoted in a letter dated 4 February 1985, on behalf of the Universal House of Justice to the National Spiritual Assembly of the United States)

To discriminate against any tribes because they are in a minority is a violation of the spirit that animates the Faith of Bahá'u'lláh. As followers of God's

Holy Faith it is our obligation to protect the just interests of any minority element within the Bahá'í community. In fact in the administration of our Bahá'í affairs, representatives of minority groups are not only enabled to enjoy equal rights and privileges, but they are even favoured and accorded priority. Bahá'ís should be careful never to deviate from this noble standard, even if the course of events or public opinion should bring pressure to bear upon them.

The principles in the Writings are clear, but usually it is when these principles are applied that questions arise. In all cases where the correct course of action is not clear believers should consult their National Spiritual Assembly who will exercise their judgement in advising the friends on the best course to follow. (The Universal House of Justice, letter dated 8 February 1970, to the National Spiritual Assemblies in Africa, *The Universal House of Justice, Messages 1963–1986*, p. 166, no. 77.11–12)

What is not clearly defined is "majority" and "minority." The Guardian refers to "various races, faiths or nationalities." Where this is obvious, e.g., in the United States a white American and a Negro, there is no problem. In all cases of doubt a re-vote should be held. (The Universal House of Justice, dated 30 June 1966, to a National Spiritual Assembly, in *Developing Distinctive Bahá'í Communities*)

Deeds: Translating the Teachings into Action

The days when idle worship was deemed sufficient are ended. The time is come when naught but the purest motive, supported by deeds of stainless purity, can ascend to the throne of the Most High and be acceptable unto Him. (The Báb, quoted in *The Dawn-Breakers*, from His address to the Letters of the Living, p. 93)

One righteous work performed in this Day, equalleth all the virtuous acts which for myriads of centuries men have practiced—nay, We ask forgiveness of God for such a comparison! (Bahá'u'lláh, The Kitáb-i-Íqán, ¶153)

146

The companions of God are, in this day, the lump that must leaven the peoples of the world. They must show forth such trustworthiness, such truthfulness and perseverance, such deeds and character that all mankind may profit by their example. (Bahá'u'lláh, quoted in *The Advent of Divine Justice*, ¶39)

O people of God! Do not busy yourselves in your own concerns; let your thoughts be fixed upon that which will rehabilitate the fortunes of mankind and sanctify the hearts and souls of men. This can best be achieved through pure and holy deeds, through a virtuous life and a goodly behavior. Valiant acts will ensure the triumph of this Cause, and a saintly character will reinforce its power. (Bahá'u'lláh, *Gleanings from the Writings of Bahá'u'lláh*, no. 43.4)

It behooveth the people of Bahá to render the Lord victorious through the power of their utterance and to admonish the people by their goodly deeds and character, inasmuch as deeds exert greater influence than words. (Bahá'u'lláh, *Tablets of Bahá'u'lláh*, p. 57)

Words must be followed by deeds. Whoso accepteth the words of the Friend is in truth a man of deeds; otherwise a dead carcass is verily of greater worth. (Bahá'u'lláh, *The Tabernacle of Unity*, p. 69)

It is incumbent upon every man of insight and understanding to strive to translate that which hath been written into reality and action.... (Bahá'u'lláh, *Gleanings from the Writings of Bahá'u'lláh*, no. 117.1)

O people! Words must be supported by deeds, for deeds are the true test of words. Without the former, the latter can never quench the thirst of the yearning soul, nor unlock the portals of vision before the eyes of the blind. The Lord of celestial wisdom saith: A harsh word is even as a sword thrust; a gentle word as milk. The latter leadeth the children of men unto knowledge and conferreth upon them true distinction. (Bahá'u'lláh, *The Tabernacle of Unity*, p. 8)

O SON OF MY HANDMAID! Guidance hath ever been given by words, and now it is given by deeds. Every one must show forth deeds that are pure and holy, for words are the property of all alike, whereas such deeds as these belong only to Our loved ones. Strive then with heart and soul to distinguish yourselves by your deeds. In this wise We counsel you in this holy and resplendent tablet. (Bahá'u'lláh, The Hidden Words, Persian, no. 76)

O CHILDREN OF ADAM! Holy words and pure and goodly deeds ascend unto the heaven of celestial glory. Strive that your deeds may be cleansed from the dust of self and hypocrisy and find favor at the court of glory; for ere long the assayers of mankind shall, in the holy presence of the Adored One, accept naught but absolute virtue and deeds of stainless purity. This is the daystar of wisdom and of divine mystery that hath shone above the horizon of the divine will. Blessed are they that turn thereunto. (Bahá'u'lláh, The Hidden Words, Persian, no. 69)

O SON OF DUST! Verily I say unto thee: Of all men the most negligent is he that disputeth idly and seeketh to advance himself over his brother. Say, O brethren! Let deeds, not words, be your adorning. (Bahá'u'lláh, The Hidden Words, Persian, no. 5)

To be purged from defilement is to be cleansed of that which is injurious to man and detracteth from his high station—among which is to take undue pleasure in one's own words and deeds, notwithstanding their unworthiness. True peace and tranquillity will only be realized when every soul will have become the well-wisher of all mankind. (Bahá'u'lláh, *The Tabernacle of Unity*, p. 7)

Love ye all religions and all races with a love that is true and sincere and show that love through deeds and not through the tongue; for the latter hath no importance, as the majority of men are, in speech, well-wishers, while action is the best. ('Abdu'l-Bahá, *Selections from the Writings of 'Abdu'l-Bahá*, no. 34.5)

All over the world one hears beautiful sayings extolled and noble precepts admired. All men say they love what is good, and hate everything that is evil! Sincerity is to be admired, whilst lying is despicable. Faith is a virtue, and treachery is a disgrace to humanity. It is a blessed thing to gladden the hearts of men, and wrong to be the cause of pain. To be kind and merciful is right, while to hate is sinful. Justice is a noble quality and injustice an iniquity. That it is one's duty to be pitiful and harm no one, and to avoid jealousy and malice at all costs. Wisdom is the glory of man, not ignorance; light, not darkness! It is a good thing to turn one's face toward God, and foolishness to ignore Him. That it is our duty to guide man upward, and not to mislead him and be the cause of his downfall. There are many more examples like unto these.

But all these sayings are but words and we see very few of them carried into the world of action. On the contrary, we perceive that men are carried away by passion and selfishness, each man thinking only of what will benefit himself even if it means the ruin of his brother. They are all anxious to make their fortune and care little or nothing for the welfare of others. They are concerned about their own peace and comfort, while the condition of their fellows troubles them not at all.

Unhappily this is the road most men tread.

But Bahá'ís must not be thus; they must rise above this condition. Actions must be more to them than words. By their actions they must be merciful and not merely by their words. They must on all occasions confirm by their actions what they proclaim in words. Their deeds must prove their fidelity, and their actions must show forth Divine light.

Let your actions cry aloud to the world that you are indeed Bahá'ís, for it is actions that speak to the world and are the cause of the progress of humanity.

If we are true Bahá'ís speech is not needed. Our actions will help on the world, will spread civilization, will help the progress of science, and cause the arts to develop. Without action nothing in the material world can be accomplished, neither can words unaided advance a man in the spiritual Kingdom. It is not through lip-service only that the elect of God have attained to holiness, but by patient lives of active service they have brought light into the world.

Therefore strive that your actions day by day may be beautiful prayers. Turn towards God, and seek always to do that which is right and noble. Enrich the poor, raise the fallen, comfort the sorrowful, bring healing to the sick, reassure the fearful, rescue the oppressed, bring hope to the hopeless, shelter the destitute!

This is the work of a true Bahá'í, and this is what is expected of him. If we strive to do all this, then are we true Bahá'ís, but if we neglect it, we are not followers of the Light, and we have no right to the name.

God, who sees all hearts, knows how far our lives are the fulfilment of our words. ('Abdu'l-Bahá, *Paris Talks,* no. 26.1–9)

A man may be a Bahá'í in name only. If he is a Bahá'í in reality, his deeds and actions will be decisive proofs of it. What are the requirements? Love for mankind, sincerity toward all, reflecting the oneness of the world of humanity, philanthropy, becoming enkindled with the fire of the love of God, attainment to the knowledge of God and that which is conducive to human welfare. ('Abdu'l-Bahá, *The Promulgation of Universal Peace,* p. 476)

What profit is there in agreeing that universal friendship is good, and talking of the solidarity of the human race as a grand ideal? Unless these thoughts are translated into the world of action, they are useless.

The wrong in the world continues to exist just because people talk only of their ideals, and do not strive to put them into practice. If actions took the place of words, the world's misery would very soon be changed into comfort.

A man who does great good, and talks not of it, is on the way to perfection.

The man who has accomplished a small good and magnifies it in his speech is worth very little.

If I love you, I need not continually speak of my love—you will know without any words. On the other hand if I love you not, that also will you know—and you would not believe me, were I to tell you in a thousand words, that I loved you.

People make much profession of goodness, multiplying fine words because they wish to be thought greater and better than their fellows, seeking fame in the eyes of the world. Those who do most good use fewest words concerning their actions. ('Abdu'l-Bahá, *Paris Talks*, no. 1.9–14)

What result is forthcoming from material rest, tranquillity, luxury and attachment to this corporeal world? It is evident that the man who pursues these things will in the end become afflicted with regret and loss.

Consequently, one must close his eyes wholly to these thoughts, long for eternal life, the sublimity of the world of humanity, the celestial developments, the Holy Spirit, the promotion of the Word of God, the guidance of the inhabitants of the globe, the promulgation of universal peace and the proclamation of the oneness of the world of humanity! This is the work! Otherwise like unto other animals and birds one must occupy himself with the requirements of this physical life, the satisfaction of which is the highest aspiration of the animal kingdom, and one must stalk across the earth like unto the quadrupeds. ('Abdu'l-Bahá, *Tablets of the Divine Plan*, no. 7.17–18)

God has conferred upon man the gift of guidance, and in thankfulness for this great gift certain deeds must emanate from him. To express his gratitude for the favors of God man must show forth praiseworthy actions. In response to these bestowals he must render good deeds, be self-sacrificing, loving the servants of God, forfeiting even life for them, showing kindness to all the creatures. ('Abdu'l-Bahá, *The Promulgation of Universal Peace*, p. 330)

The truth is that God has endowed man with virtues, powers and ideal faculties of which nature is entirely bereft and by which man is elevated, distinguished and superior. We must thank God for these bestowals, for these powers He has given us, for this crown He has placed upon our heads.

How shall we utilize these gifts and expend these bounties? By directing our efforts toward the unification of the human race. We must use these powers in establishing the oneness of the world of humanity; appreciate these virtues by accomplishing the unity of the white and colored races; devote this divine intelligence to the perfecting of amity and accord among all branches of the human family, so that under the protection and providence of God, the East and West may hold each other's hands and become as lovers. Then will mankind be as one nation, one race and kind—as waves of one ocean. ('Abdu'l-Bahá, *The Promulgation of Universal Peace*, pp. 69–70)

It is our duty and privilege to translate the love and devotion we have for our beloved Cause into deeds and actions that will be conducive to the highest good of mankind. (On behalf of Shoghi Effendi, letter dated 20 November 1924, to an individual believer, in *The Compilation of Compilations*, vol. II, no. 1269)

The Bahá'ís are the leaven of God, which must leaven the lump of their nation. In direct ratio to their success will be the protection vouchsafed, not only to them but to their country. These are the immutable laws of God, from which there is no escape: 'For unto whomsoever much is given, of him shall be much required.' (On behalf of Shoghi Effendi, letter dated 21 September 1957, to the National Spiritual Assembly of the United States, in *Lights of Guidance*, no. 454)

Upon our efforts depends in very large measure the fate of humanity. (The Universal House of Justice, *Wellspring of Guidance*, p. 120)

The power released by Bahá'u'lláh works at a quickening pace, speeding the processes of change which must usher in the new order He proclaimed. The declining state of society demonstrates it, the global yearning for new solutions to human problems confirms it. Much is at stake: the fortunes of humankind hang precariously in the balance. The Bahá'í community bears grave responsibilities toward the near and far future as movement toward the Lesser Peace accelerates. Now is the time for the friends to seize new opportunities to extend this range and influence of the Faith, to reach a new level of action in expanding the community and fortifying its foundations. It is indeed time for audacious action undeterred by a fear of mistakes, fired by the urgency of ministering to the pressing needs of humanity. Will the American Bahá'í community not see its chance to meet the challenge? Will its members not once again blaze a trail that can set in motion a myriad victories? (The Universal House of Justice, letter dated 19 May 1994, to the National Spiritual Assembly of the United States)

THE CONSEQUENCES OF INACTION AND MISDEEDS

Beware, O people of Bahá, lest ye walk in the ways of them whose words differ from their deeds. Strive that ye may be enabled to manifest to the peoples of the earth the signs of God, and to mirror forth His commandments. Let your acts be a guide unto all mankind, for the professions of most men, be they high or low, differ from their conduct. It is through your deeds that ye can distinguish yourselves from others. Through them the brightness of your light can be shed upon the whole earth. Happy is the man that heedeth My counsel, and keepeth the precepts prescribed by Him Who is the All-Knowing, the All-Wise. (Bahá'u'lláh, *Gleanings from the Writings of Bahá'u'lláh,* no. 139.8)

Some men and women glory in their exalted thoughts, but if these thoughts never reach the plane of action they remain useless: the power of thought is dependent on its manifestation in deeds. ('Abdu'l-Bahá, *Paris Talks,* no. 2.6)

The theories and policies, so unsound, so pernicious, which deify the state and exalt the nation above mankind, which seek to subordinate the sister races of the world to one single race, which discriminate between the black and the white, and which tolerate the dominance of one privileged class over all others—these are the dark, the false, and crooked doctrines for which any man or people who believes in them, or acts upon them, must, sooner or later, incur the wrath and chastisement of God. (Shoghi Effendi, *The Promised Day is Come,* ¶277)

This judgment of God, as viewed by those who have recognized Bahá'u'lláh as His Mouthpiece and His greatest Messenger on earth, is both a retributory calamity and an act of holy and supreme discipline. It is at once a visitation from God and a cleansing process for all mankind. Its fires punish the perversity of the human race, and weld its component parts into one organic, indivisible, world-embracing community. Mankind, in these fateful years, which at once signalize the passing of the first century of the Bahá'í Era and proclaim the opening of a new one, is, as ordained by Him Who is both the Judge and the Redeemer of the human race, being simultaneously called upon to give account of its past actions, and is being purged and prepared for its future mission. It can neither escape the responsibilities of the past, nor shirk those of the future. God, the Vigilant, the Just, the Loving, the All-Wise Ordainer, can, in this supreme Dispensation, neither allow the sins of an unregenerate humanity, whether of omission or of commission, to go unpunished, nor will He be willing to abandon His children to their fate, and refuse them that culminating and blissful stage in their long, their slow and painful evolution throughout the ages, which is at once their inalienable right and their true destiny. (Shoghi Effendi, *The Promised Day is Come*, ¶6)

It is because of this dual guilt, the things it has done and the things it has left undone, its misdeeds as well as its dismal and signal failure to accomplish its clear and unmistakable duty towards God, His Messenger, and His Faith, that this grievous ordeal, whatever its immediate political and economic causes, has laid its adamantine grip upon it.

God, however, as has been pointed out in the very beginning of these pages, does not only punish the wrongdoings of His children. He chastises because He is just, and He chastens because He loves. Having chastened them, He cannot, in His great mercy, leave them to their fate. Indeed, by the very act of chastening them He prepares them for the mission for which He has created them. "My calamity is My providence," He, by the mouth of Bahá'u'lláh, has assured them, "outwardly it is fire and vengeance, but inwardly it is light and mercy." (Shoghi Effendi, *The Promised Day is Come*, ¶283–84)

Humanity, through suffering and turmoil, is swiftly moving on towards its destiny; if we be loiterers, if we fail to play our part surely others will be called upon to take up our task as ministers to the crying needs of this afflicted world. (Shoghi Effendi, letter dated 24 September 1924, to the National Spiritual Assembly of America and Great Britain, in *Bahá'í Administration,* p. 66)

The Bahá'ís all over the world are subject sometimes to suffering, along with their fellow-men. Whatever vicissitudes befall their country, they will be protected though, and watched over by Bahá'u'lláh, and should not fear the future but rather fear any failure on their part to carry out the work of His Cause. (Shoghi Effendi, *Dawn of a New Day,* p. 202)

You mention the need of the Cause for capable and enlightened souls who would arise and help the promotion of our beloved Faith and the carrying through of its divine plans. This has been for long the earnest prayer of Shoghi Effendi but for some reason or other it does not seem to be realized. It may be because we have failed to do our best, in living the life, and promoting the spread of the Message to the best of our ability. We have first to create the material with which we have to work and then hope to succeed. In the Bayan the Báb says that every religion of the past was fit to become universal. The only reason why they fail to attain that mark was the incompetence of their followers. He then proceeds to give a definite promise that this would not be the fate of the revelation of "Him whom God would make manifest," that it will become universal and include all the people of the world. This shows that we will ultimately succeed. But could we not through our shortcoming, failures to sacrifice and reluctance to concentrate our efforts in spreading the Cause, retard the realization of that ideal. And what would that mean? It shall mean that we will be held responsible before God, that the race will remain longer in its state of waywardness, that wars would not be so soon averted, that human suffering will last longer. (On behalf of Shoghi Effendi, letter dated 20 February 1932, addressed to an individual believer)

PARTICIPATING IN HUMANITARIAN ORGANIZATIONS AND ACTIVITIES

Fully aware of the repeated statements of 'Abdu'l-Bahá that universality is of God, Bahá'ís in every land are ready, nay anxious, to associate themselves by word and deed with any association of men which, after careful scrutiny, they feel satisfied is free from every tinge of partisanship and politics and is wholly devoted to the interests of all mankind. In their collaboration with such associations they would extend any moral and material assistance they can afford, after having fulfilled their share of support to those institutions that affect directly the interests of the Cause. They should always bear in mind, however, the dominating purpose of such a collaboration which is to secure in time the recognition by those with whom they are associated of the paramount necessity and the true significance of the Bahá'í Revelation in this day. (Shoghi Effendi, letter dated 20 February 1927, to the National Spiritual Assembly of the United States and Canada, *Bahá'í Administration*, p. 125)

Let him survey the possibilities which the particular circumstances in which he lives offer him, evaluate their advantages, and proceed intelligently and systematically to utilize them for the achievement of the object he has in mind. Let him also attempt to devise such methods as association with clubs, exhibitions, and societies, lectures on subjects akin to the teachings and ideals of his Cause such as temperance, morality, social welfare, religious and racial tolerance, economic cooperation, Islam, and Comparative Religion, or participation in social, cultural, humanitarian, charitable, and educational organizations and enterprises which, while safeguarding the integrity of his Faith, will open up to him a multitude of ways and means whereby he can enlist successively the sympathy, the support, and ultimately the allegiance of those with whom he comes in contact. Let him, while such contacts are being made, bear in mind the claims which his Faith is constantly making upon him to preserve its dignity, and station, to safeguard the integrity of its laws and principles, to demonstrate its comprehensiveness and universality, and to defend fearlessly its manifold and vital interests. (Shoghi Effendi, *The Advent of Divine Justice*, ¶78)

Whilst chiefly engaged in the pursuit of their major task, consisting chiefly in the formation and the consolidation of Bahá'í administrative institutions, they should endeavour to participate, within recognized limits, in the work of institutions which, though unaware of the claim of the Bahá'í Cause, are prompted by a sincere desire to promote the spirit that animates the Faith. In the pursuit of their major task their function is to preserve the identity of the Cause and the purity of the mission of Bahá'u'lláh. In their minor undertaking their purpose should be to imbue with the spirit of power and strength such movements as in their restricted scope are endeavouring to achieve what is near and dear to the heart of every true Bahá'í. It would even appear at times to be advisable and helpful as a supplement to their work for the Bahá'ís to initiate any undertaking not specifically designated as Bahá'í, provided that they have ascertained that such an undertaking would constitute the best way of approach to those whose minds and hearts are as yet unprepared for a full acceptance of the claim of Bahá'u'lláh. These twofold obligations devolving upon organized Bahá'í communities, far from neutralizing the effects of one another or of appearing antagonistic in their aims, should be regarded as complementary and fulfilling, each in its way, a vital and necessary function. (Shoghi Effendi, letter dated 20 February 1927, to the National Spiritual Assembly of the United States and Canada, *The Compilation of Compilations,* vol. II, no. 1476.3)

Membership in non-political organizations . . . is, indeed, the best method of teaching indirectly the Message by making useful and frequent contacts with well-known and influential persons who, if not completely won to the Faith, can at least become of some effective use to it. (On behalf of Shoghi Effendi, *The Unfolding Destiny of the British Bahá'í Community,* p. 91)

It is surely very necessary that the friends should keep in touch with the modern social movements, but their main objective should be to draw more people to the spirit and teachings of the Cause. They should learn from the experience of others and not permit themselves to go (off) at a tangent, and finally be so absorbed in other movements as to forget the Cause of God. (On behalf of Shoghi Effendi, letter addressed to an individual believer, received 25 December 1931)

Our principal duty is undoubtedly to teach the Cause and help in the administration of its affairs. But that is not the only one. The Cause will not attain its aim and order in the great reign of peace unless its principles are put into practice. We have to assist the different movements which have progressive ideas and are striving for an aim similar to ours. (Shoghi Effendi, letter addressed to the Regional Committee for Canada, *Bahá'í News*, February 1926, no. 10)

He [the Guardian] does not see any objection to Bahá'í students taking part as Bahá'ís in a protest such as that mentioned in the clipping. On the contrary, he does not see how they could remain indifferent when fellow students were noticing our own Bahá'í attitude in such a vital issue and one we feel so strongly about.

He thinks that the quotation you cite, from *The Advent of Divine Justice* would certainly indicate that such a protest was justifiable as there was nothing political about it there was no reason for the Bahá'í students not to participate. (On behalf of Shoghi Effendi, letter dated 1 April 1948, in *White and Negro Alike: Stories of Bahá'í Pioneers Ellsworth and Ruth Blackwell*)

Movements for social progress and racial justice, as long as they are disassociated from both political and religious partisanship, should be supported by those Bahá'ís who feel urged to undertake such work. Consequently there is no reason why you should not work for the betterment of your race [African American] through channels that in no way conflict with our Bahá'í attitude.

However meritorious such work may be, we should, however, never lose sight of the fact that ultimately the only solution for the problems facing not only the Negro, but the entire human race, is that which Bahá'u'lláh has embodied in His teachings. The more various racial movements of reform make progress, the easier it will be for society to accept our enlightened teachings. But such movements can never alone solve the grave problems facing men today. (On behalf of Shoghi Effendi, letter dated 23 November 1941, to an individual believer)

In its letter of 23 January 1985 concerning the International Year of Peace, the Universal House of Justice urged Bahá'í communities to reach out to the non-Bahá'í public by finding ways of discussing the important issues of peace with others. One way to make such discussions relevant and effective is for the friends to know and acknowledge and pay just tribute to persons whose lives were dedicated to peaceful means of bettering social conditions.

One such person was the black American Martin Luther King, Jr. whose promotion of non-violent means of achieving racial equality in the United States cost him his life. The positive effects of his heroic efforts brought encouragement to downtrodden peoples throughout the world and earned him the Nobel Peace Prize in 1964. Four years later he was assassinated. His aspirations for a society in which the races can live in harmony are perhaps best expressed in the famous speech he delivered at a gathering of some 250,000 people in the capital of the United States in 1963. A copy is enclosed.

The House of Justice has asked us to call your attention to Dr. King for these reasons. His widow, Mrs. Coretta Scott King, a non-Bahá'í, has written to the House of Justice that a national public holiday has been officially designated in the United States in honor of Dr. King. She intends to make an appeal that on 20 January 1986, the first observance of this holiday, "nations and liberation movements all over the world cease all violent actions, seek amnesty and reconciliation both within and outside of their national boundaries, and encourage all of their citizens to recommit themselves to work for international peace, universal justice and the elimination of hunger and poverty in the world." The House of Justice feels that Mrs. King has a noble intention to which the friends can lend their moral and spiritual support. Since that date on which action is desired falls within the International Year of Peace, Spiritual Assemblies may consider holding peace conferences on 20 January, or close to that date, and naturally include in the presentations at these conferences references to the life and work of Dr. King. An alternative might be to devote the Bahá'í programs on World Religion Day, 19 January, to peace and on these occasions pay tribute to Dr. King.

The thought of the House of Justice in suggesting such action is not to promote the holiday for Dr. King, and it does not expect Bahá'í communities everywhere to commemorate his life annually; rather, it wishes to indicate to the friends a legitimate occasion, as illustrated by Mrs. King's plan, when the Bahá'í peace activities can be associated with the worthy activities of others. (On behalf of The Universal House of Justice, letter dated 5 August 1985, to all National Spiritual Assemblies)

We understand that the Bahá'ís support the Martin Luther King Day in the United States primarily as an indication of its encouragement of the uplift-ment of the black people in the United States and not necessarily as an effort to promote "the Martin Luther King movement." Similarly, 'Abdu'l-Bahá, during His visit to America, spoke before the fourth annual meeting of the National Association for the Advancement of Colored People (N.A.A.C.P.), which does not mean that He was supporting the explicit program of that particular organization, but rather, that He was affirming the principles which the N.A.A.C.P. seeks to uphold. (On behalf of The Universal House of Justice, letter dated 26 August 1991, to an individual believer)

So it is that Bahá'ís do their utmost at all times to heed the counsel of Bahá'u'lláh, "Shut your eyes to estrangement, then fix your gaze upon unity." "That one indeed is a man," He exhorts His followers, "who, today, dedi-cateth himself to the service of the entire human race." "Be anxiously con-cerned with the needs of the age ye live in," is His admonition, "and centre your deliberations on its exigencies and requirements." "The supreme need of humanity is cooperation and reciprocity," 'Abdu'l-Bahá has indicated. "The stronger the ties of fellowship and solidarity amongst men, the greater will be the power of constructiveness and accomplishment in all the planes of human activity." "So powerful is the light of unity," Bahá'u'lláh declares, "that it can illuminate the whole earth."

It is with such thoughts in mind that Bahá'ís enter into collaboration, as their resources permit, with an increasing number of movements, organizations, groups and individuals, establishing partnerships that strive to transform society and further the cause of unity, promote human welfare, and contribute to world solidarity. Indeed, the standard set by passages such as the above inspires the Bahá'í community to become actively engaged in as many aspects of contemporary life as feasible. In choosing areas of collaboration, Bahá'ís are to bear in mind the principle, enshrined in their teachings, that means should be consistent with ends; noble goals cannot be achieved through unworthy means. Specifically, it is not possible to build enduring unity through endeavours that require contention or assume that an inherent conflict of interests underlies all human interactions, however subtly. It should be noted here that, despite the limitations imposed by adherence to this principle, the community has not experienced a shortage of opportunities for collaboration; so many people in the world today are working intensely towards one or another aim which Bahá'ís share. In this respect, they also take care not to overstep certain bounds with their colleagues and associates. They are not to regard any joint undertaking as an occasion to impose religious convictions. Self-righteousness and other unfortunate manifestations of religious zeal are to be utterly avoided. Bahá'ís do, however, readily offer to their collaborators the lessons they have learned through their own experience, just as they are happy to incorporate into their community-building efforts insights gained through such association. (The Universal House of Justice, letter dated 2 March 2013, to the Bahá'ís of Iran)

Also relevant to such participation is greater appreciation and application of Bahá'u'lláh's insights on moderation. "In all matters moderation is desirable," He states. "If a thing is carried to excess, it will prove a source of evil." This call for moderation includes in particular the manner of speech if a just conclusion is to be achieved. "Human utterance is an essence which aspireth to exert its influence and needeth moderation," Bahá'u'lláh writes. "One word is like unto springtime causing the tender saplings of the rose-garden of knowledge to become verdant and flourishing, while another word is even as a deadly poison," He explains. "It behoveth a prudent man of wisdom to speak with utmost leniency and forbearance so that the sweetness of his words may induce everyone to attain that which befitteth man's station." By moderation, Bahá'u'lláh is in no way referring to mere compromise, the dilution of truth, or a hypocritical or utopian consensus. The moderation He calls for demands an end to destructive excesses that have plagued humanity and fomented ceaseless contention and turmoil. Moderation in deliberation and action stands in contrast to the arbitrary imposition of views through power or insistence upon ideological aims, both of which obstruct the search for truth and sow the seeds of continuing injustice. A moderate perspective is a practical and principled standpoint from which one can recognize and adopt valid and insightful ideas whatever their source, without prejudice. "Whoso cleaveth to justice, can, under no circumstances, transgress the limits of moderation," Bahá'u'lláh states. "He discerneth the truth in all things, through the guidance of Him Who is the All-Seeing."

The House of Justice trusts that, in pursuing the many facets of their work of community building, social action, and involvement in the discourses of society, individuals, communities, and institutions will continually grow in their capacity to make a distinctive and effective contribution to addressing the multitudinous problems afflicting society and the planet, including those associated with climate change. (On behalf of the Universal House of Justice, letter dated 29 November 2017, to three individual believers)

COMBATTING THE NEGATIVE FORCES IN OUR SOCIETY

The tests of every dispensation are in direct proportion to the greatness of the Cause, and as heretofore such a manifest Covenant, written by the Supreme Pen, hath not been entered upon, the tests are proportionately more severe. ('Abdu'l-Bahá, *Selections from the Writings of 'Abdu'l-Bahá*, no. 185.1)

The American Bahá'í Community, the leaven destined to leaven the whole, cannot hope, at this critical juncture in the fortunes of a struggling, perilously situated, spiritually moribund nation, to either escape the trials with which this nation is confronted, nor claim to be wholly immune from the evils that stain its character. (Shoghi Effendi, *Citadel of Faith*, p. 127)

A rectitude of conduct which, in all its manifestations, offers a striking contrast to the deceitfulness and corruption that characterize the political life of the nation and of the parties and factions that compose it; a holiness and chastity that are diametrically opposed to the moral laxity and licentiousness which defile the character of a not inconsiderable proportion of its citizens; an interracial fellowship completely purged from the curse of racial prejudice which stigmatizes the vast majority of its people—these are the weapons which the American believers can and must wield in their double crusade, first to regenerate the inward life of their own community, and next to assail the long-standing evils that have entrenched themselves in the life of their nation. The perfection of such weapons, the wise and effective utilization of every one of them, more than the furtherance of any particular plan, or the devising of any special scheme, or the accumulation of any amount of material resources, can prepare them for the time when the Hand of Destiny will have directed them to assist in creating and in bringing into operation that World Order which is now incubating within the worldwide administrative institutions of their Faith.

In the conduct of this twofold crusade the valiant warriors struggling in the name and for the Cause of Bahá'u'lláh must, of necessity, encounter stiff resistance, and suffer many a setback. Their own instincts, no less than the fury of conservative forces, the opposition of vested interests, and the objections of a corrupt and pleasure-seeking generation, must be reckoned with, resolutely resisted, and completely overcome. As their defensive measures for the impending struggle are organized and extended, storms of abuse and ridicule, and campaigns of condemnation and misrepresentation, may be unloosed against them. Their Faith, they may soon find, has been assaulted, their motives misconstrued, their aims defamed, their aspirations derided, their institutions scorned, their influence belittled, their authority undermined, and their Cause, at times, deserted by a few who will either be incapable of appreciating the nature of their ideals, or unwilling to bear the brunt of the mounting criticisms which such a contest is sure to involve. "Because of 'Abdu'l-Bahá," the beloved Master has prophesied, "many a test will be visited upon you. Troubles will befall you, and suffering afflict you."

Let not, however, the invincible army of Bahá'u'lláh, who in the West, and at one of its potential storm centers is to fight, in His name and for His sake, one of its fiercest and most glorious battles, be afraid of any criticism that might be directed against it. Let it not be deterred by any condemnation with which the tongue of the slanderer may seek to debase its motives. Let it not recoil before the threatening advance of the forces of fanaticism, of orthodoxy, of corruption, and of prejudice that may be leagued against it. The voice of criticism is a voice that indirectly reinforces the proclamation of its Cause. Unpopularity but serves to throw into greater relief the contrast between it and its adversaries, while ostracism is itself the magnetic power that must eventually win over to its camp the most vociferous and inveterate amongst its foes. Already in the land where the greatest battles of the Faith have been fought, and its most rapacious enemies have lived, the march of events, the slow yet steady infiltration of its ideals, and the fulfillment of its prophecies, have resulted not only in disarming and in transforming the character of some of its most redoubtable enemies, but also in securing their firm and unreserved allegiance to its Founders. So complete a transformation, so startling a reversal of attitude, can only be effected if that chosen vehicle which is designed to carry the Message of Bahá'u'lláh to the hungry, the restless, and unshepherded multitudes is itself thoroughly cleansed from the defilements which it seeks to remove. (Shoghi Effendi, *The Advent of Divine Justice*, ¶59–61)

How great, therefore, how staggering the responsibility that must weigh upon the present generation of the American believers, at this early stage in their spiritual and administrative evolution, to weed out, by every means in their power, those faults, habits, and tendencies which they have inherited from their own nation, and to cultivate, patiently and prayerfully, those distinctive qualities and characteristics that are so indispensable to their effective participation in the great redemptive work of their Faith. Incapable as yet, in view of the restricted size of their community and the limited influence it now wields, of producing any marked effect on the great mass of their countrymen, let them focus their attention, for the present, on their own selves, their own individual needs, their own personal deficiencies and weaknesses, ever mindful that every intensification of effort on their part will better equip them for the time when they will be called upon to eradicate in their turn such evil tendencies from the lives and the hearts of the entire body of their fellow-citizens. Nor must they overlook the fact that the World Order, whose basis they, as the advance-guard of the future Bahá'í generations of their countrymen, are now laboring to establish, can never be reared unless and until the generality of the people to which they belong has been already purged from the divers ills, whether social or political, that now so severely afflict it. (Shoghi Effendi, *The Advent of Divine Justice*, ¶34)

The gross materialism that engulfs the entire nation at the present hour; the attachment to worldly things that enshrouds the souls of men; the fears and anxieties that distract their minds; the pleasure and dissipations that fill their time, the prejudices and animosities that darken their outlook, the apathy and lethargy that paralyze their spiritual faculties—these are among the formidable obstacles that stand in the path of every would-be warrior in the service of Bahá'u'lláh, obstacles which he must battle against and surmount in his crusade for the redemption of his own countrymen.

To the degree that the home front crusader is himself cleansed of these impurities, liberated from these petty preoccupations and gnawing anxieties, delivered from these prejudices and antagonisms, emptied of self, and filled by the healing and the sustaining power of God, will he be able to combat the forces arrayed against him, magnetize the souls of those whom he seeks to convert, and win their unreserved, their enthusiastic and enduring allegiance to the Faith of Bahá'u'lláh.

Delicate and strenuous though the task may be, however arduous and prolonged the effort required, whatsoever the nature of the perils and pitfalls that beset the path of whoever arises to revive the fortunes of a Faith struggling against the rising forces of materialism, nationalism, secularism, racialism, ecclesiasticism, the all-conquering potency of the grace of God, vouchsafed through the Revelation of Bahá'u'lláh, will, undoubtedly, mysteriously and surprisingly, enable whosoever arises to champion His Cause to win complete and total victory. (Shoghi Effendi, *Citadel of Faith*, p. 148)

It is precisely by reason of the patent evils which, notwithstanding its [the United States] other admittedly great characteristics and achievements, an excessive and binding materialism has unfortunately engendered within it that the Author of their Faith and the Center of His Covenant have singled it out to become the standard-bearer of the New World Order envisaged in their writings. It is by such means as this that Bahá'u'lláh can best demonstrate to a heedless generation His almighty power to raise up from the very midst of a people, immersed in a sea of materialism, a prey to one of the most virulent and long-standing forms of racial prejudice, and notorious for its political corruption, lawlessness and laxity in moral standards, men and women who, as time goes by, will increasingly exemplify those essential virtues of self-renunciation, of moral rectitude, of chastity, of indiscriminating fellowship, of holy discipline, and of spiritual insight that will fit them for the preponderating share they will have in calling into being that World Order and that World Civilization of which their country, no less than the entire human race, stands in desperate need. (Shoghi Effendi, *The Advent of Divine Justice*, ¶32)

The friends must, at all times, bear in mind that they are, in a way, like soldiers under attack. The world is at present in an exceedingly dark condition spiritually; hatred and prejudice, of every sort, are literally tearing it to pieces. We, on the other hand, are the custodians of the opposite forces, the forces of love, of unity, of peace and integration, and we must constantly be on our guard, whether as negative forces enter into our midst. In other words we must beware lest the darkness of society become reflected in our acts and attitudes, perhaps all unconsciously. Love for each other, the deep sense that we are a new organism, the dawn-breakers for a New World Order, must constantly animate our Bahá'í lives, and we must pray to be protected from the contamination of society which is so diseased with prejudice. (On behalf of Shoghi Effendi, letter dated 5 February 1947, to the Spiritual Assembly of Atlanta, in *Lights of Guidance*, no. 1347)

We cannot segregate the human heart from the environment outside us and say that once one of these is reformed everything will be improved. Man is organic with the world. His inner life moulds the environment and is itself also deeply affected by it. The one acts upon the other and every abiding change in the life of man is the result of these mutual reactions.

No movement in the world directs its attention upon both these aspects of human life and has full measures for their improvement save the teachings of Bahá'u'lláh. And this is its distinctive feature. If we desire therefore the good of the world we should strive to spread those teachings and also practice them in our own life. Through them will the human heart be changed and also our social environment provides the atmosphere in which we can grow spiritually and reflect in full the light of God shining through the revelation of Bahá'u'lláh. (On behalf of Shoghi Effendi, letter dated 17 February 1933, to an individual believer, in *The Compilation of Compilations*, vol. I, p. 84, no. 3.3)

. . . in a world of inter-dependent peoples and nations the advantage of the part is best to be reached by the advantage of the whole, and that no abiding benefit can be conferred upon the component parts if the general interests of the entity itself are ignored or neglected. (Shoghi Effendi, *The World Order of Bahá'u'lláh*, p. 198)

The believers, to better understand their own internal condition, should realize that the forces of darkness in the world are so prevalent and strong that their morbid and turbulent influence is felt by all. They should therefore consciously strive to be more loving, more united, more dedicated and prayerful than ever before, in order to fight against the atmosphere of present day society which is unloving, disunited, careless of right and wrong, and heedless of God. (On behalf of Shoghi Effendi, letter dated 20 March 1946, to the National Spiritual Assembly of the United States and Canada, in *Lights of Guidance*, no. 1346)

These, indeed, are the days when heroism is needed on the part of the believers. Self-sacrifice, courage, indomitable hope and confidence are the characteristics they should show forth, because these very attributes cannot but fix the attention of the public and lead them to enquire what, in a world so hopelessly chaotic and bewildered, leads these people to be so assured, so confident, so full of devotion? Increasingly, as time goes by, the characteristics of the Bahá'ís will be that which captures the attention of their fellow-citizens. They must show their aloofness from the hatreds and recriminations which are tearing at the heart of humanity, and demonstrate by deed and word their profound belief in the future peaceful unification of the entire human race. (On behalf of Shoghi Effendi, letter dated 26 October 1941, in *Lights of Guidance*, no. 1348)

The decline of religious and moral restraints has unleashed a fury of chaos and confusion that already bears the signs of universal anarchy. Engulfed in this maelstrom, the Bahá'í world community, pursuing with indefeasible unity and spiritual force its redemptive mission, inevitably suffers the disruption of economic, social and civil life which afflicts its fellowmen throughout the planet. It must also bear particular tribulations. (The Universal House of Justice, letter dated Naw-Rúz 1979, to the Bahá'ís if the World, *Messages, 1963–1986*, no. 221.1)

We all know how often the Master and the beloved Guardian called upon the friends to consciously strive to be more loving, more united, more dedicated and prayerful than ever before in order to overcome the atmosphere of present-day society which is unloving, disunited, careless of right and wrong and heedless of God. ". . . when we see the increasing darkness in the world today," the Guardian's secretary wrote on his behalf, "we can fully realize that unless the Message of Bahá'u'lláh reaches into the hearts of men and transforms them, there can be no peace and no spiritual progress in the future." (The Universal House of Justice, letter dated 16 November 1969, to the Bahá'ís of the World, *Messages, 1963–1986*, no. 73.4)

In many letters and on many occasions the beloved Guardian warned that the disintegrating process will penetrate deeper and deeper into the very core of human society and that much suffering is in store ere mankind is fused by the fires of universal affliction into one organic commonwealth. Even when universal suffrage and all other rights presently sought by civil rights movements are fully attained, they still remains for the Bahá'ís the unaccomplished task of cleansing humanity, by precept and example, of every trace of racial prejudice. Nothing but the Faith of God can accomplish this. (The Universal House of Justice, letter dated 30 March 1965, to the National Spiritual Assembly of the United States, in *Lights of Guidance*, no. 456)

TRANSFORMING SOCIETY

The All-Knowing Physician hath His finger on the pulse of mankind. He perceiveth the disease, and prescribeth, in His unerring wisdom, the remedy. Every age hath its own problem, and every soul its particular aspiration. The remedy the world needeth in its present-day afflictions can never be the same as that which a subsequent age may require. Be anxiously concerned with the needs of the age ye live in, and center your deliberations on its exigencies and requirements. (Bahá'u'lláh, *Gleanings from the Writings of Bahá'u'lláh*, no. 106.1)

Note ye how easily, where unity existeth in a given family, the affairs of that family are conducted; what progress the members of that family make, how they prosper in the world. Their concerns are in order, they enjoy comfort and tranquility, they are secure, their position is assured, they come to be envied by all. Such a family but addeth to its stature and its lasting honor, as day succeedeth day. And if we widen out the sphere of unity a little to include the inhabitants of a village who seek to be loving and united, who associate with and are kind to one another, what great advances they will be seen to make, how secure and protected they will be. Then let us widen out the sphere a little more, let us take the inhabitants of a city, all of them together: if they establish the strongest bonds of unity among themselves, how far they will progress, even in a brief period and what power they will exert. And if the sphere of unity be still further widened out, that is, if the inhabitants of a whole country develop peaceable hearts, and if with all their hearts and souls they yearn to cooperate with one another and to live in unity, and if they become kind and loving to one another, that country will achieve undying joy and lasting glory. Peace will it have, and plenty, and vast wealth.

Note then: if every clan, tribe, community, every nation, country, territory on earth should come together under the single-hued pavilion of the oneness of mankind, and by the dazzling rays of the Sun of Truth should proclaim the universality of man; if they should cause all nations and all creeds to open wide their arms to one another, establish a World Council, and proceed to bind the members of society one to another by strong mutual ties, what would happen then? There is no doubt whatsoever that the divine Beloved, in all His endearing beauty, and with Him a massive host of heavenly confirmations and human blessings and bestowals, would appear in His full glory before the assemblage of the world. ('Abdu'l-Bahá, *Selections from the Writings of 'Abdu'l-Bahá*, no. 221.9–10)

The great and fundamental teachings of Bahá'u'lláh are the oneness of God and unity of mankind. This is the bond of union among Bahá'ís all over the world. They become united among themselves, then unite others. It is impossible to unite unless united. Christ said, "Ye are the salt of the earth; but if the salt has lost his savor, wherewith shall it be salted?" This proves there were dissensions and lack of unity among His followers. Hence His admonition to unity of action.

Now must we, likewise, bind ourselves together in the utmost unity, be kind and loving to each other, sacrificing all our possessions, our honor, yea, even our lives for each other. Then will it be proved that we have acted according to the teachings of God, that we have been real believers in the oneness of God and unity of mankind. ('Abdu'l-Bahá, *The Promulgation of Universal Peace*, pp. 215–16)

Not by merely imitating the excesses and laxity of the extravagant age they live in; not by the idle neglect of the sacred responsibilities it is their privilege to shoulder; not by the silent compromise of the principles dearly cherished by 'Abdu'l-Bahá; not by their fear or unpopularity or their dread of censure can they hope to rouse society from its spiritual lethargy, and serve as a model to a civilization the foundations of which the corrosion of prejudice has well-nigh undermined. By the sublimity of their principles, the warmth of their love, the spotless purity of their character, and the depth of their devoutness and piety, let them demonstrate to their fellow-countrymen the ennobling reality of a power that shall weld a disrupted world.

We can prove ourselves worthy of our Cause only if in our individual conduct and corporate life we sedulously imitate the example of our beloved Master, Whom the terrors of tyranny, the storms of incessant abuse, the oppressiveness of humiliation, never caused to deviate a hair's breadth from the revealed Law of Bahá'u'lláh.

Such is the path of servitude, such is the way of holiness He chose to tread to the very end of His life. Nothing short of the strictest adherence to His glorious example can safely steer our course amid the pitfalls of this perilous age, and lead us on to fulfill our high destiny. (Shoghi Effendi, letter dated 12 April 1927, to the National Spiritual Assembly of the United States and Canada, *Bahá'í Administration*, p. 132)

Do not for a moment hesitate or slacken in your efforts for such a glorious cause—and encourage the friends to exemplify the harmony and good will that should characterize the relations of races to one another, before attempting to summon the multitude to its urgent call. Let them search their own hearts, purge their own minds before attempting the regeneration of mankind. I will pray that your words may influence and inspire the souls and that the Almighty may guide every step you take. (Shoghi Effendi, Postscript to letter dated 11 September 1927, written on behalf of Shoghi Effendi to an individual believer, quoted in a letter dated 4 February 1985, on behalf of the Universal House of Justice to the National Spiritual Assembly of the United States)

... the object of life to a Bahá'í is to promote the oneness of mankind. The whole object of our lives is bound up with the lives of all human beings; not a personal salvation we are seeking, but a universal one. . . . Our aim is to produce a world civilization which will in turn react on the character of the individual. (Shoghi Effendi, quoted by Rúḥíyyih Khánum, in *Bahá'í World*, vol. 15, p. 776)

... [Shoghi Effendi] feels that the friends should constantly be encouraged to bear in mind certain salient facts: Bahá'u'lláh has brought a new system and new laws and standards of personal as well as racial conduct into the world. Although outside agencies have been to a certain extent illumined by the radiance of His message and doctrines, and are exerting efforts to bring the world into that orbit of universal peace and harmony He has set for it, these outside forces cannot achieve what only the followers of His Faith can. The believers must not take their eyes off their own immediate tasks of patiently consolidating their administrative institutions, building up new Assemblies . . . and labouring to perfect the Bahá'í pattern of life, for these are things that no other group of people in the world can do or will do, and they alone are able to provide the spiritual foundation and example on which the larger world schemes must ultimately rest.

At the same time every effort should be made to broadcast the Teachings at this time, and correlate them to the plight of humanity and the plans for its future. (On behalf of Shoghi Effendi, letter dated 29 March 1945, to the National Spiritual Assembly of the United States, in *Bahá'í News*, no. 175, p. 3)

The champion builders of Bahá'u'lláh's rising World Order must scale nobler heights of heroism as humanity plunges into greater depths of despair, degradation, dissension and distress. Let them forge ahead into the future serenely confident that the hour of their mightiest exertions and the supreme opportunity for their greatest exploits must coincide with the apocalyptic upheaval marking the lowest ebb in mankind's fast-declining fortunes. (Shoghi Effendi, *Citadel of Faith*, p. 58)

Bahá'ís . . . know the goal they are working towards and know what they must do, step by step, to attain it. Their whole energy is directed towards the building of the good, a good which has such a positive strength that in the face of it the multitude of evils—which are in essence negative—will fade away and be no more. To enter into the quixotic tournament of demolishing one by one the evils in the world is, to a Bahá'í a vain waste of time and effort. His whole life is directed towards proclaiming the Message of Bahá'u'lláh, reviving the spiritual life of his fellow-men, uniting them in a Divinely-created World Order, and then, as that Order grows in strength and influence, he will see the power of that Message transforming the whole of human society and progressively solving the problems and removing the injustice which have so long bedeviled the world. (The Universal House of Justice, letter dated 19 November 1974, to the National Spiritual Assembly of Italy)

We are told by Shoghi Effendi that two great processes are at work in the world: the great Plan of God, tumultuous in its progress, working through mankind as a whole, tearing down barriers to world unity and forging humankind into a unified body in the fires of suffering and experience. This process will produce, in God's due time, the Lesser Peace, the political unification of the world. Mankind at that time can be likened to a body that is unified but without life. The second process, the task of breathing life into this unified body—of creating true unity and spirituality culminating in the Most Great Peace—is that of the Bahá'ís, who are laboring consciously, with detailed instructions and continuing Divine guidance, to erect the fabric of the Kingdom of God on earth, into which they call their fellowmen, thus conferring upon them eternal life.

The working out of God's Major Plan proceeds mysteriously in ways directed by Him alone, but the Minor Plan that He has given us to execute, as our part in His grand design for the redemption of mankind, is clearly delineated. It is to this work that we must devote all our energies, for there is no one else to do it. So vital is this function of the Bahá'ís that Bahá'u'lláh has written: "O friends! Be not careless of the virtues with which ye have been endowed, neither be neglectful of your high destiny. Suffer not your labors to be wasted through the vain imaginations which certain hearts have devised. Ye are the stars of the heaven of understanding, the breeze that stirreth at the break of day, the soft-flowing waters upon which must depend the very life of all men, the letters inscribed upon His sacred scroll. With the utmost unity, and in a spirit of perfect fellowship, exert yourselves, that ye may be enabled to achieve that which beseemeth this Day of God." (The Universal House of Justice, letter dated 8 December 1967, to an individual believer, *Wellspring of Guidance, Messages 1963–1968*, p. 133)

Paradoxical as it may seem, the prospects toward the breakthrough you anticipate in the teaching field are conspicuous in the current, distressing state of society. You must realize that the worse conditions become, the more plentiful are the opportunities to teach the Cause, the greater the degree of receptivity to the Divine Message. Bahá'u'lláh certainly gave ample foreknowledge about the radical, worldwide disturbance which His Revelation is creating as a part of the transition toward the unity and peace that are the ultimate goal of His Faith. . . .

Painful as may be the decadent scene, deep as is your sympathy for those who suffer from the terrible decline of society, you must see the possibilities which are thus provided for augmenting the healing forces of an emerging World Order. Shoghi Effendi advised the North American community plainly in this regard. "The opportunities which the turmoil of the present age presents, with all the sorrows which it evokes, the fears which it excites, the disillusionment which it produces, the perplexities which it creates, the indignation which it arouses, the revolt which it provokes, the grievances it engenders, the spirit of restless search which it awakens, must," he asserted, "be exploited for the purpose of spreading far and wide the knowledge of the redemptive power of the Faith of Bahá'u'lláh, and for enlisting fresh recruits in the ever-swelling army of His followers."

Commenting further on the global spectacle of upheavals, cataclysms and tribulations which the worsening affairs of humanity evoke at the impending approach of the Kingdom of God on earth, Shoghi Effendi addressed these words of insight and encouragement to the North American friends: "Far from yielding in their resolve, far from growing oblivious of their task, they should, at no time, however much buffeted by circumstances, forget that the synchronization of such world-shaking crises with the progressive unfoldment and fruition of their divinely appointed task is itself the work of Providence, the design of an inscrutable Wisdom, and the purpose of an all-compelling Will, a Will that directs and controls, in its own mysterious way, both the fortunes of the Faith and the destinies of men. Such simultaneous processes of rise and of fall, of integration and of disintegration, of order and chaos, with their continuous and reciprocal reactions on each other, are but aspects of a greater Plan, one and indivisible, whose Source is God, whose author is Bahá'u'lláh, the theatre of whose operations is the entire planet, and whose ultimate objectives are the unity of the human race and the peace of all mankind."

Moreover, the beloved Guardian felt that: "Reflections such as these should steel the resolve of the entire Bahá'í community, should dissipate their forebodings, and arouse them to rededicate themselves to every single provision of that Divine Charter whose outline has been delineated for them by the pen of 'Abdu'l-Bahá." By being attuned to this divine perspective, your Assembly will be able to assist the friends to see that they will not merely be able to cope with the alarming incidents of social decline they are daily witnessing, but even better than that, they will be inspired to arise with renewed vision to recruit to Bahá'í membership an increasing number of men and women whose minds and hearts are ready to respond to the Divine Message and who will join them in dispelling the bewilderment and despair gripping their fellow citizens and undermining the structure of their country.

It is also vital for your Assembly to keep in mind that the mental anguish which the prevailing situation induces can and must be overcome through prayer and a conscious attention to teaching the Cause and living the Bahá'í life with a world embracing vision. Certainly, the members of such a well established community as yours, one enjoying the special favours providentially conferred upon it by the Tablets of the Divine Plan, do realize the urgency and seriousness of their task. Surely they see with what patient endurance the dear friends in the Cradle of the Faith are meeting their God-given challenges even to the extent of sacrificing their life's blood so that the world may become a better place. Undoubtedly, the highly esteemed American believers, who bear the designation "spiritual descendants of the Dawn-breakers," know quite well that they must now seize their chance at this critical time to prove their own capacity to endure that living sacrifice which, as Shoghi Effendi said, in contrast to dying, is required of them in the scriptures of our Faith. May they be granted the celestial strength to pass, over and over again, the mental tests which 'Abdu'l-Bahá promised He would send to them to purify them, thus enabling them to achieve their divinely conferred potential as a force for change in the world. (The Universal House of Justice, letter dated 19 May 1994, in response to the National Spiritual Assembly of the United States)

Bahá'ís are encouraged to see in the revolutionary changes taking place in every sphere of life the interaction of two fundamental processes. One is destructive in nature, while the other is integrative; both serve to carry humanity, each in its own way, along the path leading towards its full maturity. The operation of the former is everywhere apparent—in the vicissitudes that have afflicted time-honoured institutions, in the impotence of leaders at all levels to mend the fractures appearing in the structure of society, in the dismantling of social norms that have long held in check unseemly passions, and in the despondency and indifference exhibited not only by individuals but also by entire societies that have lost any vital sense of purpose. Though devastating in their effects, the forces of disintegration tend to sweep away barriers that block humanity's progress, opening space for the process of integration to draw diverse groups together and disclosing new opportunities for cooperation and collaboration. Bahá'ís, of course, strive to align themselves, individually and collectively, with forces associated with the process of integration, which, they are confident, will continue to gain in strength, no matter how bleak the immediate horizons. Human affairs will be utterly reorganized, and an era of universal peace inaugurated.

Such is the view of history that underlies every endeavour pursued by the Bahá'í community.

As you know from your study of the Bahá'í writings, the principle that is to infuse all facets of organized life on the planet is the oneness of humankind, the hallmark of the age of maturity. That humanity constitutes a single people is a truth that, once viewed with scepticism, claims widespread acceptance today. The rejection of deeply ingrained prejudices and a growing sense of world citizenship are among the signs of this heightened awareness. Yet, however promising the rise in collective consciousness may be, it should be seen as only the first step of a process that will take decades—nay, centuries—to unfold. For the principle of the oneness of humankind, as proclaimed by Bahá'u'lláh, asks not merely for cooperation among people and nations. It calls for a complete reconceptualization of the relationships that sustain society. The deepening environmental crisis, driven by a system that condones the pillage of natural resources to satisfy an insatiable thirst for more, suggests how entirely inadequate is the present conception of humanity's relationship with nature; the deterioration of the home environment, with the accompanying rise in the systematic exploitation of women and children worldwide, makes clear how pervasive are the misbegotten notions that define relations within the family unit; the persistence of despotism, on the one hand, and the increasing disregard for authority, on the other, reveal how unsatisfactory to a maturing humanity is the current relationship between the individual and the institutions of society; the concentration of material wealth in the hands of a minority of the world's population gives an indication of how fundamentally ill-conceived are relationships among the many sectors of what is now an emerging global community. The principle of the oneness of humankind implies, then, an organic change in the very structure of society.

What should be stated plainly here is that Bahá'ís do not believe the transformation thus envisioned will come about exclusively through their own efforts. Nor are they trying to create a movement that would seek to impose on society their vision of the future. Every nation and every group—indeed, every individual—will, to a greater or lesser degree, contribute to the emergence of the world civilization towards which humanity is irresistibly moving. Unity will progressively be achieved, as foreshadowed by 'Abdu'l-Bahá, in different realms of social existence, for instance, "unity in the political realm," "unity of thought in world undertakings," "unity of races," and the "unity of nations." As these come to be realized, the structures of a politically united world, which respects the full diversity of culture and provides channels for the expression of dignity and honour, will gradually take shape.

The question that occupies the worldwide Bahá'í community, then, is how it can best contribute to the civilization-building process as its resources increase. It sees two dimensions to its contribution. The first is related to its own growth and development, and the second to its involvement in society at large.

Regarding the first, Bahá'ís across the globe, in the most unassuming settings, are striving to establish a pattern of activity and the corresponding administrative structures that embody the principle of the oneness of humankind and the convictions underpinning it, only a few of which are mentioned here as a means of illustration: that the rational soul has no gender, race, ethnicity or class, a fact that renders intolerable all forms of prejudice, not the least of which are those that prevent women from fulfilling their potential and engaging in various fields of endeavour shoulder to shoulder with men; that the root cause of prejudice is ignorance, which can be erased through educational processes that make knowledge accessible to the entire human race, ensuring it does not become the property of a privileged few; that science and religion are two complementary systems of knowledge and practice by which human beings come to understand the world around them and through which civilization advances; that religion without science soon degenerates into superstition and fanaticism, while science without religion becomes the tool of crude materialism; that true prosperity, the fruit of a dynamic coherence between the material and spiritual requirements of life, will recede further and further out of reach as long as consumerism continues to act as opium to the human soul; that justice, as a faculty of the soul, enables the individual to distinguish truth from falsehood and guides the investigation of reality, so essential if superstitious beliefs and outworn traditions that impede unity are to be eliminated; that, when appropriately brought to bear on social issues, justice is the single most important instrument for the establishment of unity; that work performed in the spirit of service to one's fellow human beings is a form of prayer, a means of worshipping God. Translating ideals such as these into reality, effecting a transformation at the level of the individual and laying the foundations of suitable social structures, is no small task, to be sure. Yet the Bahá'í community is dedicated to the long-term process of learning that this task entails, an enterprise in which increasing numbers from all walks of life, from every human group, are invited to take part. (The Universal House of Justice, letter dated 2 March 2013, to the Bahá'ís of Iran)

SYSTEMATIC ACTION IN COMMUNITY BUILDING, SOCIAL ACTION, AND DISCOURSE

Thousands upon thousands, embracing the diversity of the entire human family, are engaged in systematic study of the Creative Word in an environment that is at once serious and uplifting. As they strive to apply through a process of action, reflection and consultation the insights thus gained, they see their capacity to serve the Cause rise to new levels. Responding to the inmost longing of every heart to commune with its Maker, they carry out acts of collective worship in diverse settings, uniting with others in prayer, awakening spiritual susceptibilities, and shaping a pattern of life distinguished for its devotional character. As they call on one another in their homes and pay visits to families, friends and acquaintances, they enter into purposeful discussion on themes of spiritual import, deepen their knowledge of the Faith, share Bahá'u'lláh's message, and welcome increasing numbers to join them in a mighty spiritual enterprise. Aware of the aspirations of the children of the world and their need for spiritual education, they extend their efforts widely to involve ever-growing contingents of participants in classes that become centres of attraction for the young and strengthen the roots of the Faith in society. They assist junior youth to navigate through a crucial stage of their lives and to become empowered to direct their energies toward the advancement of civilization. And with the advantage of a greater abundance of human resources, an increasing number of them are able to express their faith through a rising tide of endeavours that address the needs of humanity in both their spiritual and material dimensions. . . .

Within the sphere of these enhanced interactions, individual initiative is becoming increasingly effective. In previous messages we have referred to the impetus that the institute process imparts to the exercise of initiative by the individual believer. The friends in every continent are engaged in study of the Writings for the explicit purpose of learning to apply the teachings to the growth of the Faith. Remarkable numbers are now shouldering responsibility for the spiritual vitality of their communities; energetically, they are carrying out those acts of service befitting a healthy pattern of growth. As they have persevered in the field of service to the Cause, maintaining a humble posture of learning, their courage and wisdom, zeal and acuity, fervour and circumspection, determination and trust in God have combined all the more to reinforce one another. In their presentation of the message of Bahá'u'lláh and the exposition of its verities, they have taken to heart the words of Shoghi Effendi that they must neither "hesitate" nor "falter," neither "overstress" nor "whittle down" the truth which they champion. Neither are they "fanatical" nor "excessively liberal." Through their constancy in teaching, they have increased their ability to determine whether the receptivity of their listener requires them to be "wary" or "bold," to "act swiftly" or to "mark time," to be "direct" or "indirect" in the methods they employ.

What we continue to find encouraging is how well disciplined is this individual initiative. Communities everywhere are gradually internalizing the lessons being learned from systematization, and the framework defined by the current series of Plans lends consistency and flexibility to the endeavours of the friends. Far from restricting them, this framework enables them to seize opportunities, to build relationships, and to translate into reality a vision of systematic growth. In a word, it gives shape to their collective powers. . . .

Every follower of Bahá'u'lláh conscious of the forces of integration and disintegration operating in society today sees the relationship between the rise in receptivity to the Faith in all parts of the globe and the failings of the world's systems. That such receptivity will increase as the agonies of humanity deepen is certain. Let there be no mistake: The capacity building that has been set in motion to respond to mounting receptivity is still in its earliest stages. The magnitude of the demands of a world in disarray will test this capacity to its limits in the years ahead. Humanity is battered by forces of oppression, whether generated from the depths of religious prejudice or the pinnacles of rampant materialism. Bahá'ís are able to discern the causes of this affliction. "What 'oppression' is more grievous," Bahá'u'lláh asks, "than that a soul seeking the truth, and wishing to attain unto the knowledge of God, should know not where to go for it and from whom to seek it?" There is no time to lose. Continued progress must be achieved in the activity and development of the three participants in the Plan.

'Abdu'l-Bahá has extolled "two calls" to "success and prosperity" that can be heard from the "heights of the happiness of mankind." One is the call of "civilization," of "progress of the material world." It comprises the "laws," "regulations," "arts and sciences" through which humanity develops. The other is the "soul-stirring call of God," on which depends the eternal happiness of humanity. "This second call," the Master has explained, "is founded upon the instructions and exhortations of the Lord and the admonitions and altruistic emotions belonging to the realm of morality which, like unto a brilliant light, brighten and illumine the lamp of the realities of mankind. Its penetrative power is the Word of God." As you continue to labour in your clusters, you will be drawn further and further into the life of the society around you and will be challenged to extend the process of systematic learning in which you are engaged to encompass a growing range of human endeavours. In the approaches you take, the methods you adopt, and the instruments you employ, you will need to achieve the same degree of coherence that characterizes the pattern of growth presently under way.

Sustaining growth in cluster after cluster will depend on the qualities that distinguish your service to the peoples of the world. So free must be your thoughts and actions of any trace of prejudice—racial, religious, economic, national, tribal, class, or cultural—that even the stranger sees in you loving friends. So high must be your standard of excellence and so pure and chaste your lives that the moral influence you exert penetrates the consciousness of the wider community. Only if you demonstrate the rectitude of conduct to which the writings of the Faith call every soul will you be able to struggle against the myriad forms of corruption, overt and subtle, eating at the vitals of society. Only if you perceive honour and nobility in every human being—this independent of wealth or poverty—will you be able to champion the cause of justice. And to the extent that administrative processes of your institutions are governed by the principles of Bahá'í consultation will the great masses of humanity be able to take refuge in the Bahá'í community. (The Universal House of Justice, letter dated Riḍván 2008, addressed to the Bahá'ís of the World)

In your letter, you raise various questions relating to teaching, with reference to different opinions held by members of the Bahá'í community. As mentioned in the 2008 Riḍván message, the friends everywhere are learning how best to apply a range of approaches and methods in sharing Bahá'u'lláh's Revelation, in keeping with the receptivity of their listeners. In this context, the House of Justice has been pleased to see that two developments are occurring in all parts of the globe, irrespective of the nature of the society in question.

First, the practice of discussing the principles and precepts of the Faith in a general way, which has resulted in a great many admirers of the Cause but few enrolments, is being complemented by an increasingly direct approach to sharing Bahá'u'lláh's Message. More often than not, the friends have found the presentation of the Faith outlined in Book 6 of the Ruhi Institute most useful in this respect. It is clear, however, that those making such a presentation need to avoid the trap of reducing it merely to a series of points of information that are enumerated for the listener. Results worldwide leave little doubt that the heart of the listener is touched when the teacher understands the logic underlying the presentation and is prepared to offer it in its fullness. That so many believers who have been taught the Faith in this way have, through study of the courses of the institute, become active supporters of the Cause in their communities stands as ample testimony to the validity of the method. This development represents an important milestone, indeed, in the progress of the Faith.

Second, the habit of conversing with friends and acquaintances on matters of spiritual import, now engrained in the community, is being brought to bear increasingly on interactions with people who could otherwise be regarded as strangers. This tendency is manifesting itself in a number of ways, depending on the circumstances. Not infrequently, outreach to the wider community takes the form of a visit to a home, sometimes after prior arrangements have been made with the residents, although not always. What should be understood in this respect is that such visits are not isolated acts. A visit to a home should be seen as one element of a coherent pattern of action that seeks to enable specific populations to contribute to the construction of the society envisioned by Bahá'u'lláh. At the heart of the matter, then, is how a campaign of teaching the Faith by visiting homes relates to the other activities being undertaken in a neighbourhood or village—how it relates to the efforts to hold meetings that strengthen the devotional character of the wider community, to offer classes that foster the spiritual development of children, to form groups that channel the energies of junior youth, to establish study circles, open to all, that enable people of varied backgrounds to advance together and explore the application of the Bahá'í teachings to their individual and collective lives.

In this connection, the friends sometimes raise questions concerning a passage taken from a letter dated 20 October 1956 written on behalf of the Guardian to a National Spiritual Assembly. The letter states that "to distribute Bahá'í pamphlets from door to door . . . is undignified and might create a bad impression of the Faith," adding that the Guardian "does not think the best interests of the Cause are served by such a method." This statement, which refers to a particular approach to the distribution of Bahá'í literature, does not constitute a general prohibition on visiting people in their homes with the intention of presenting the Faith to them. It is, however, a reminder of the importance of dignity in whatever method of teaching one chooses to employ. Cultures differ, and what may be considered dignified in one locality may not be so in another. Nevertheless, within the context of a pattern of action such as the one described earlier, it would often be quite appropriate for Bahá'ís to visit people in their homes to explain the nature of the core activities of the Five Year Plan and invite them or their children to take part. In many cases, a visit to the home of someone to see whether he or she is interested in learning about the Faith would also be highly fruitful.

As you continue to reflect on this subject, you should remain ever conscious of the nature of the mode of learning that characterizes the worldwide enterprise in which the believers and their institutions are engaged. Methods of teaching cannot be governed by hard and fast rules. Clearly those who do not feel comfortable employing a specific direct teaching method should not be obliged to do so. Yet it is equally important that the inhibitions of individual believers, though rooted in the prevalent culture, and undoubtedly the result of a sincere desire to safeguard the interests of the Faith, do not prevent others from learning how to approach people directly and offer them the Message for which their hearts so desperately yearn. So strong should be the bonds which unite the friends that the diversity of their temperaments and backgrounds serves to open before them new vistas for the growth of the Faith, while at the same time protecting it from extremes. (On behalf of the Universal House of Justice, letter dated 26 April 2009, to an individual believer)

Like so many communities worldwide, then, yours will find itself being drawn further and further into the life of society in the years ahead as a natural consequence of its continued expansion and consolidation. The greater the clarity of thought you maintain about the nature of this challenge, already showing signs of the pressing demands it brings, the more effective will be the response of your community in meeting it. At this stage in your development, the House of Justice encourages you to begin to examine the work of your community in terms of three broad areas of action, which, though distinct from one another, each with its own methods and instruments, must achieve a high degree of coherence between them, if they are to reinforce one another and lend substantial impetus to the movement of the Australian people towards the spiritually and materially prosperous civilization envisioned in the writings of the Faith. What will ensure this coherence is the process of systematic learning that characterizes them all.

The expansion and consolidation of the Bahá'í community itself can be regarded as one area of action, the approach, methods and instruments of which are now well understood. Social action can be considered another. This term is being employed increasingly in consultations among Bahá'ís, as a result of heightened consciousness and enhanced capacity at the cluster level. It is to be expected that a desire to undertake social action will accompany the collective change which begins to occur in a village or neighbourhood as acts of communal worship and home visits are woven together with activities for the spiritual education of its population to create a rich pattern of community life. Social action can, of course, range from the most informal efforts of limited duration to social and economic development programs of a high level of complexity and sophistication promoted by Bahá'í-inspired non-governmental organizations—all concerned with the application of the teachings to some need identified in such fields as health, education, agriculture and the environment. In this case, too, there is a vast amount of experience worldwide, fostered and correlated by the Office of Social and Economic Development, that has given rise to effective approaches, which can be exploited at the level of the cluster as soon as the processes of expansion and consolidation have advanced to the degree necessary.

Efforts to participate in the discourses of society constitute a third area of action in which the friends are engaged. Such participation can occur at all levels of society, from the local to the international, through various types of interactions—from informal discussions on Internet forums and attendance at seminars, to the dissemination of statements and contact with government officials. What is important is for Bahá'ís to be present in the many social spaces in which thinking and policies evolve on any one of a number of issues—on governance, the environment, climate change, the equality of men and women, human rights, to mention a few—so that they can, as occasions permit, offer generously, unconditionally and with utmost humility the teachings of the Faith and their experience in applying them as a contribution to the betterment of society. Of course, care should be exercised that the friends involved in this area of activity avoid overstating the Bahá'í experience and drawing attention to fledging efforts of the Bahá'í community which are best left to come to maturity without interference, such as the junior youth spiritual empowerment program. The development of instruments, methods and approaches for this area of activity is a chief concern of the Institute for Studies in Global Prosperity, based here at the Bahá'í World Centre.

The House of Justice wishes us to emphasize that the above scheme should be regarded as merely one way of conceptualizing the work of the Bahá'í community, one that avoids fragmentation and facilitates sound planning. It does not encompass the entirety of Bahá'í endeavour, the defense work being a case in point. Nor should it assume the status of a definition, as reflected in statements such as "There are three areas of Bahá'í activity." Further, in no way should the friends feel there is a division of labour, in which one group participates in the work of expansion and consolidation, and another group in each of the other two areas. All Bahá'ís should engage in efforts to expand and consolidate the Faith. They also participate, to some extent, in social action and the discourses of society. In the case of the latter two, however, where the work takes on different degrees of formality, the nature of the tasks to be carried out can become quite complex and sometimes delicate, requiring specialized training and preparation. (On behalf of the Universal House of Justice, letter dated 4 January 2009, to the National Spiritual Assembly of Australia)

Bahá'u'lláh's Revelation is vast. It calls for profound change not only at the level of the individual but also in the structure of society. "Is not the object of every Revelation," He Himself proclaims, "to effect a transformation in the whole character of mankind, a transformation that shall manifest itself, both outwardly and inwardly, that shall affect both its inner life and external conditions?" The work advancing in every corner of the globe today represents the latest stage of the ongoing Bahá'í endeavour to create the nucleus of the glorious civilization enshrined in His teachings, the building of which is an enterprise of infinite complexity and scale, one that will demand centuries of exertion by humanity to bring to fruition. There are no shortcuts, no formulas. Only as effort is made to draw on insights from His Revelation, to tap into the accumulating knowledge of the human race, to apply His teachings intelligently to the life of humanity, and to consult on the questions that arise will the necessary learning occur and capacity be developed.

In this long-term process of capacity building, the Bahá'í community has devoted nearly a decade and a half to systematizing its experience in the teaching field, learning to open certain activities to more and more people and to sustain its expansion and consolidation. All are welcome to enter the community's warm embrace and receive sustenance from Bahá'u'lláh's life-giving message. No greater joy is there, to be sure, than for a soul, yearning for the Truth, to find shelter in the stronghold of the Cause and draw strength from the unifying power of the Covenant. Yet every human being and every group of individuals, irrespective of whether they are counted among His followers, can take inspiration from His teachings, benefiting from whatever gems of wisdom and knowledge will aid them in addressing the challenges they face. Indeed, the civilization that beckons humanity will not be attained through the efforts of the Bahá'í community alone. Numerous groups and organizations, animated by the spirit of world solidarity that is an indirect manifestation of Bahá'u'lláh's conception of the principle of the oneness of humankind, will contribute to the civilization destined to emerge out of the welter and chaos of present-day society. It should be clear to everyone that the capacity created in the Bahá'í community over successive global Plans renders it increasingly able to lend assistance in the manifold and diverse dimensions of civilization building, opening to it new frontiers of learning.

In our Riḍván 2008 message we indicated that, as the friends continued to labour at the level of the cluster, they would find themselves drawn further and further into the life of society and would be challenged to extend the process of systematic learning in which they are engaged to encompass a widening range of human endeavours. A rich tapestry of community life begins to emerge in every cluster as acts of communal worship, interspersed with discussions undertaken in the intimate setting of the home, are woven together with activities that provide spiritual education to all members of the population—adults, youth and children. Social consciousness is heightened naturally as, for example, lively conversations proliferate among parents regarding the aspirations of their children and service projects spring up at the initiative of junior youth. Once human resources in a cluster are in sufficient abundance, and the pattern of growth firmly established, the community's engagement with society can, and indeed must, increase. At this crucial point in the unfoldment of the Plan, when so many clusters are nearing such a stage, it seems appropriate that the friends everywhere would reflect on the nature of the contributions which their growing, vibrant communities will make to the material and spiritual progress of society. In this respect, it will prove fruitful to think in terms of two interconnected, mutually reinforcing areas of activity: involvement in social action and participation in the prevalent discourses of society.

Over the decades, the Bahá'í community has gained much experience in these two areas of endeavour. There are, of course, a great many Bahá'ís who are engaged as individuals in social action and public discourse through their occupations. A number of non-governmental organizations, inspired by the teachings of the Faith and operating at the regional and national levels, are working in the field of social and economic development for the betterment of their people. Agencies of National Spiritual Assemblies are contributing through various avenues to the promotion of ideas conducive to public welfare. At the international level, agencies such as the United Nations Office of the Bahá'í International Community are performing a similar function. To the extent necessary and desirable, the friends working at the grassroots of the community will draw on this experience and capacity as they strive to address the concerns of the society around them.

188

Most appropriately conceived in terms of a spectrum, social action can range from fairly informal efforts of limited duration undertaken by individuals or small groups of friends to programmes of social and economic development with a high level of complexity and sophistication implemented by Bahá'í-inspired organizations. Irrespective of its scope and scale, all social action seeks to apply the teachings and principles of the Faith to improve some aspect of the social or economic life of a population, however modestly. Such endeavours are distinguished, then, by their stated purpose to promote the material well-being of the population, in addition to its spiritual welfare. That the world civilization now on humanity's horizon must achieve a dynamic coherence between the material and spiritual requirements of life is central to the Bahá'í teachings. Clearly this ideal has profound implications for the nature of any social action pursued by Bahá'ís, whatever its scope and range of influence. Though conditions will vary from country to country, and perhaps from cluster to cluster, eliciting from the friends a variety of endeavours, there are certain fundamental concepts that all should bear in mind. One is the centrality of knowledge to social existence. The perpetuation of ignorance is a most grievous form of oppression; it reinforces the many walls of prejudice that stand as barriers to the realization of the oneness of humankind, at once the goal and operating principle of Bahá'u'lláh's Revelation. Access to knowledge is the right of every human being, and participation in its generation, application and diffusion a responsibility that all must shoulder in the great enterprise of building a prosperous world civilization—each individual according to his or her talents and abilities. Justice demands universal participation. Thus, while social action may involve the provision of goods and services in some form, its primary concern must be to build capacity within a given population to participate in creating a better world. Social change is not a project that one group of people carries out for the benefit of another. The scope and complexity of social action must be commensurate with the human resources available in a village or neighbourhood to carry it forward. Efforts best begin, then, on a modest scale and grow organically as capacity within the population develops. Capacity rises to new levels, of course, as the protagonists of social change learn to apply with increasing effectiveness elements of Bahá'u'lláh's Revelation, together with the contents and methods of science, to their social reality. This reality they must strive to read in a manner consistent with His teachings—seeing in their fellow human beings gems of inestimable value and recognizing the effects of the dual process of integration and disintegration on both hearts and minds, as well as on social structures.

Effective social action serves to enrich participation in the discourses of society, just as the insights gained from engaging in certain discourses can help to clarify the concepts that shape social action. At the level of the cluster, involvement in public discourse can range from an act as simple as introducing Bahá'í ideas into everyday conversation to more formal activities such as the preparation of articles and attendance at gatherings, dedicated to themes of social concern—climate change and the environment, governance and human rights, to mention a few. It entails, as well, meaningful interactions with civic groups and local organizations in villages and neighbourhoods.

In this connection, we feel compelled to raise a warning: It will be important for all to recognize that the value of engaging in social action and public discourse is not to be judged by the ability to bring enrolments. Though endeavours in these two areas of activity may well effect an increase in the size of the Bahá'í community, they are not undertaken for this purpose. Sincerity in this respect is an imperative. Moreover, care should be exercised to avoid overstating the Bahá'í experience or drawing undue attention to fledging efforts, such as the junior youth spiritual empowerment programme, which are best left to mature at their own pace. The watchword in all cases is humility. While conveying enthusiasm about their beliefs, the friends should guard against projecting an air of triumphalism, hardly appropriate among themselves, much less in other circumstances.

In describing for you these new opportunities now opening at the level of the cluster, we are not asking you to alter in any way your current course. Nor should it be imagined that such opportunities represent an alternative arena of service, competing with the expansion and consolidation work for the community's limited resources and energies. Over the coming year, the institute process and the pattern of activity that it engenders should continue to be strengthened, and teaching should remain uppermost in the mind of every believer. Further involvement in the life of society should not be sought prematurely. It will proceed naturally as the friends in every cluster persevere in applying the provisions of the Plan through a process of action, reflection, consultation and study, and learn as a result. Involvement in the life of society will flourish as the capacity of the community to promote its own growth and to maintain its vitality is gradually raised. It will achieve coherence with efforts to expand and consolidate the community to the extent that it draws on elements of the conceptual framework which governs the current series of global Plans. And it will contribute to the movement of populations towards Bahá'u'lláh's vision of a prosperous and peaceful world civilization to the degree that it employs these elements creatively in new areas of learning. (The Universal House of Justice, letter dated Riḍván 2010, addressed to the Bahá'ís of the World)

The Guardian . . . addressed the subject of prejudice, stating patently that "any division or cleavage" in the ranks of the Faith "is alien to its very purpose, principles, and ideals." He made clear that the friends should manifest "complete freedom from prejudice in their dealings with peoples of a different race, class, creed, or colour." He went on to discuss at length the specific question of racial prejudice, "the corrosion of which," he indicated, had "bitten into the fibre, and attacked the whole social structure of American society" and which, he asserted at the time, "should be regarded as constituting the most vital and challenging issue confronting the Bahá'í community at the present stage of its evolution." Independent of the strengths and weaknesses of the measures taken by the American nation, and the Bahá'í community evolving within it, in addressing this particular challenge, the fact remains that prejudices of all kinds—of race, of class, of ethnicity, of gender, of religious belief—continue to hold a strong grip on humanity. While it is true that, at the level of public discourse, great strides have been taken in refuting the falsehoods that give rise to prejudice in whatever form, it still permeates the structures of society and is systematically impressed on the individual consciousness. It should be apparent to all that the process set in motion by the current series of global Plans seeks, in the approaches it takes and the methods it employs, to build capacity in every human group, with no regard for class or religious background, with no concern for ethnicity or race, irrespective of gender or social status, to arise and contribute to the advancement of civilization. We pray that, as it steadily unfolds, its potential to disable every instrument devised by humanity over the long period of its childhood for one group to oppress another may be realized.

The educational process associated with the training institute is, of course, helping to foster the spiritual conditions to which the Guardian referred in *The Advent of Divine Justice,* along with the many others mentioned in the writings that must distinguish the life of the Bahá'í community—the spirit of unity that must animate the friends, the ties of love that must bind them, the firmness in the Covenant that must sustain them, and the reliance and trust they must place on the power of divine assistance, to note but a few. That such essential attributes are developed in the context of building capacity for service, in an environment that cultivates systematic action, is particularly noteworthy. In promoting this environment, the Auxiliary Board members and their assistants need to recognize the importance of two fundamental, interlocking precepts: On the one hand, the high standard of conduct inculcated by Bahá'u'lláh's Revelation can admit no compromise; it can, in no wise, be lowered, and all must fix their gaze on its lofty heights. On the other, it must be acknowledged that, as human beings, we are far from perfect; what is expected of everyone is sincere daily effort. Self-righteousness is to be eschewed.

Apart from the spiritual requisites of a sanctified Bahá'í life, there are habits of thought that affect the unfoldment of the global Plan, and their development has to be encouraged at the level of culture. There are tendencies, as well, that need to be gradually overcome. Many of these tendencies are reinforced by approaches prevalent in society at large, which, not altogether unreasonably, enter into Bahá'í activity. The magnitude of the challenge facing the friends in this respect is not lost on us. They are called upon to become increasingly involved in the life of society, benefiting from its educational programmes, excelling in its trades and professions, learning to employ well its tools, and applying themselves to the advancement of its arts and sciences. At the same time, they are never to lose sight of the aim of the Faith to effect a transformation of society, remoulding its institutions and processes, on a scale never before witnessed. To this end, they must remain acutely aware of the inadequacies of current modes of thinking and doing—this, without feeling the least degree of superiority, without assuming an air of secrecy or aloofness, and without adopting an unnecessarily critical stance towards society. There are a few specific points we wish to mention in this connection.

It is heartening to note that the friends are approaching the study of the messages of the Universal House of Justice related to the Plan with such diligence. The level of discussion generated as they strive to put into practice the guidance received, and to learn from experience, is impressive. We cannot help noticing, however, that achievements tend to be more enduring in those regions where the friends strive to understand the totality of the vision conveyed in the messages, while difficulties often arise when phrases and sentences are taken out of context and viewed as isolated fragments. The institutions and agencies of the Faith should help the believers to analyse but not reduce, to ponder meaning but not dwell on words, to identify distinct areas of action but not compartmentalize. We realize that this is no small task. Society speaks more and more in slogans. We hope that the habits the friends are forming in study circles to work with full and complex thoughts and to achieve understanding will be extended to various spheres of activity.

Closely related to the habit of reducing an entire theme into one or two appealing phrases is the tendency to perceive dichotomies, where, in fact, there are none. It is essential that ideas forming part of a cohesive whole not be held in opposition to one another. In a letter written on his behalf, Shoghi Effendi warned: "We must take the teachings as a great, balanced whole, not seek out and oppose to each other two strong statements that have different meanings; somewhere in between, there are links uniting the two." How encouraged we have been to note that many of the misunderstandings of the past have fallen away as appreciation for the provisions of the Plan has grown.

Expansion and consolidation, individual action and collective campaigns, refinement of the inner character and consecration to selfless service—the harmonious relationship between these facets of Bahá'í life is now readily acknowledged. It brings us equal pleasure to know that the friends are on their guard, lest new false dichotomies be allowed to pervade their thinking. They are well aware that the diverse elements of a programme of growth are complementary. The tendency to see activities, and the agencies that support them, in competition with one another, a tendency so common in society at large, is being avoided by the community.

Finally, a significant advance in culture, one which we have followed with particular interest, is marked by the rise in capacity to think in terms of process. That, from the outset, the believers have been asked to be ever conscious of the broad processes that define their work is apparent from a careful reading of even the earliest communications of the Guardian related to the first national plans of the Faith. However, in a world focused increasingly on the promotion of events, or at best projects, with a mindset that derives satisfaction from the sense of expectation and excitement they generate, maintaining the level of dedication required for long-term action demands considerable effort. The expansion and consolidation of the Bahá'í community encompasses a number of interacting processes, each of which contributes its share to the movement of humanity towards Bahá'u'lláh's vision of a new World Order. The lines of action associated with any given process provide for the organization of occasional events, and from time to time, activities take the shape of a project with a clear beginning and a definite end. If, however, events are imposed on the natural unfoldment of a process, they will disrupt its sound evolution. If the projects undertaken in a cluster are not made subordinate to the explicit needs of the processes unfolding there, they will yield little fruit. . . .

Every follower of Bahá'u'lláh knows well that the purpose of His Revelation is to bring into being a new creation. No sooner had "the First Call gone forth from His lips than the whole creation was revolutionized, and all that are in the heavens and all that are on earth were stirred to the depths." The individual, the institutions, and the community—the three protagonists in the Divine Plan—are being shaped under the direct influence of His Revelation, and a new conception of each, appropriate for a humanity that has come of age, is emerging. The relationships that bind them, too, are undergoing a profound transformation, bringing into the realm of existence civilization-building powers which can only be released through conformity with His decree. At a fundamental level these relationships are characterized by cooperation and reciprocity, manifestations of the interconnectedness that governs the universe. So it is that the individual, with no regard for "personal benefits and selfish advantages," comes to see him—or herself as "one of the servants of God, the All-Possessing," whose only desire is to carry out His laws. So it is that the friends come to recognize that "wealth of sentiment, abundance of good-will and effort" are of little avail when their flow is not directed along proper channels, that "the unfettered freedom of the individual should be tempered with mutual consultation and sacrifice," and that "the spirit of initiative and enterprise should be reinforced by a deeper realization of the supreme necessity for concerted action and a fuller devotion to the common weal." And so it is that all come to discern with ease those areas of activity in which the individual can best exercise initiative and those which fall to the institutions alone. "With heart and soul," the friends follow the directives of their institutions, so that, as 'Abdu'l-Bahá explains, "things may be properly ordered and well arranged." This, of course, is not a blind obedience; it is an obedience that marks the emergence of a mature human race which grasps the implications of a system as far-reaching as Bahá'u'lláh's new World Order. (The Universal House of Justice, letter dated 28 December 2010, to the Conference of the Continental Board of Counsellors)

The Universal House of Justice appreciates your thoughtful inquiry concerning the relationship between eliminating racial prejudice and participating in activities of the Five Year Plan. . . .

In your letter, you observe that the many activities carried out in the past by the American Bahá'í community to address racial concerns, despite their obvious merit and the results achieved to date, have been limited in their effect and have not been systematic in nature. Your review of such efforts suggests a cyclical pattern, with fits and starts, in which a certain course of action is presented with fanfare by the institutions, many believers take part although others remain on the sidelines, activities reach a peak, and then, after months or perhaps years, attention wanes, and the community is drawn to other areas until some incident occurs or a new heartfelt appeal is uttered, thus beginning the cycle anew. Simply to repeat the approaches implemented in the past, then, will surely not produce a satisfactory result. The House of Justice notes that the pattern you describe was a characteristic common to many facets of community life, leading it, in 1996, to set the Bahá'í world on a new course. During the Four Year Plan, it wrote:

> Our hopes, our goals, our possibilities of moving forward can all be realized through concentrating our endeavors on the major aim of the Divine Plan at its current stage—that is, to effect a significant advance in the process of entry by troops. This challenge can be met through persistent effort patiently pursued. But also of vital importance to bringing about entry by troops is a realistic approach, systematic action. There are no shortcuts. Systematization ensures consistency of lines of action based on well-conceived plans. In a general sense, it implies an orderliness of approach in all that pertains to Bahá'í service, whether in teaching or administration, in individual or collective endeavor. While allowing for individual initiative and spontaneity, it suggests the need to be clear-headed, methodical, efficient, constant, balanced and harmonious. Systematization is a necessary mode of functioning animated by the urgency to act.

After a decade and a half of systematic effort, a coherent pattern of activity that advances the growth and development of the Bahá'í community and its greater involvement in the life of society has emerged. The current stage of progress and the challenges that lie immediately ahead are summarized in the Riḍván 2010 and 28 December 2010 messages. From this perspective, it is possible to see how the challenge of addressing racial prejudice is an integral part of three broad areas of activity in which the Bahá'í world is currently engaged: expansion and consolidation, social action, and participation in the discourses of society.

The pattern of spiritual and social life taking shape in clusters that involves study circles, children's classes, junior youth groups, devotional meetings, home visits, teaching efforts, and reflection meetings, as well as Holy Day observances, Nineteen Day Feasts, and other gatherings, provides abundant opportunities for engagement, experience, consultation, and learning that will lead to change in personal and collective understanding and action. Issues of prejudice of race, class, and color will inevitably arise as the friends reach out to diverse populations, especially in the closely knit context of neighborhoods. There, every activity can take a form most suited to the culture and interests of the population, so that new believers can be quickened and confirmed in a nurturing and familiar environment, until they are able to offer their share to the resolution of the challenges faced by a growing Bahá'í community. For this is not a process that some carry out on behalf of others who are passive recipients—the mere extension of a congregation and invitation to paternalism—but one in which an ever-increasing number of souls recognize and take responsibility for the transformation of humanity set in motion by Bahá'u'lláh. In an environment of love and trust born of common belief, practice, and mission, individuals of different races will have the intimate connection of heart and mind upon which mutual understanding and change depend. As a result of their training and deepening, a growing number of believers will draw insights from the Writings to sensitively and effectively address issues of racial prejudice that arise within their personal lives and families, among community members, and in social settings and the workplace. As programs of growth advance and the scope and intensity of activities grow, the friends will be drawn into participation in conversations and, in time, initiatives for social action at the grassroots where issues pertaining to freedom from prejudice naturally emerge, whether directly or indirectly. And, at the national level, the National Assembly will guide, through its Office of External Affairs, the engagement of the Faith with other agencies and individuals in the discourse pertaining to race unity.

You indicate that some friends wonder whether the Guardian's statement characterizing racial prejudice as "the most vital and challenging issue confronting the Bahá'í community at the present stage of its evolution" still applies to the racial situation in the United States, since it was written so long ago. The House of Justice has determined that it is not productive to approach the issue in this manner, as it gives rise to an implicit and false dichotomy that, either what the Guardian said is no longer important, or it is so important that it must be addressed before or apart from all other concerns. Yet, the situation is infinitely more complex. The American nation is much more diverse than in 1938, and the friends cannot be concerned only with relations between black and white, essential as they are. The expressions of racial prejudice have transmuted into forms that are multifaceted, less blatant and more intricate, and thus more intractable. So too, the American Bahá'í community has evolved significantly and is no longer at the same stage of its development; it faces a wider range of challenges but also possesses greater capabilities. The House of Justice stated that the principles Shoghi Effendi brought to the attention of the American believers more than seventy years ago are relevant today, and they will continue to be relevant to future generations. It is obvious, however, that the "long and thorny road, beset with pitfalls" upon which the friends must tread, will take them through an ever-changing landscape that requires that they adapt their approaches to varying circumstances.

In the 28 December message, the House of Justice explained that "A small community, whose members are united by their shared beliefs, characterized by their high ideals, proficient in managing their affairs and tending to their needs, and perhaps engaged in several humanitarian projects—a community such as this, prospering but at a comfortable distance from the reality experienced by the masses of humanity, can never hope to serve as a pattern for restructuring the whole of society." Even if such a community were to focus the entirety of its resources on the problem of racial prejudice, even if it were able to heal itself to some extent of that cancerous affliction, in the face of such a monumental social challenge the impact would be inconsequential. Therefore, the friends must effectively assess the forces at work in their society and, beginning in neighborhoods and clusters, contribute their share to the process of learning and systematization which, as their numbers, knowledge, and influence grow, will transform their lives, families, and communities. Only if the efforts to eradicate the bane of prejudice are coherent with the full range of the community's affairs, only if they arise naturally within the systematic pattern of expansion, community building, and involvement with society, will the American believers expand their capacity, year after year and decade after decade, to make their mark on their community and society and contribute to the high aim set for the Bahá'ís by 'Abdu'l-Bahá to eliminate racial prejudice from the face of the earth.

It is the ardent hope of the Universal House of Justice that the believers will appreciate the potentialities that exist within the current pattern of their organic activities for the realization of Bahá'u'lláh's highest aims for humanity and that they will seize their chance and commit their time, their resources, their energies—indeed their very lives—to these critical efforts for the betterment of the world. (On behalf of the Universal House of Justice, letter dated 10 April 2011, to an individual believer)

In its Riḍván 2010 message, the Universal House of Justice called on the Bahá'ís of the world to reflect on the contributions that their growing, vibrant communities will make to the material and spiritual progress of society. In this connection, the House of Justice made reference to the process of community building set in motion in so many clusters across the globe by the core activities associated with the current series of global Plans. . . . Later in the same message, the House of Justice defined the sphere of social action in these terms:

Most appropriately conceived in terms of a spectrum, social action can range from fairly informal efforts of limited duration undertaken by individuals or small groups of friends to programmes of social and economic development with a high level of complexity and sophistication implemented by Bahá'í-inspired organizations. Irrespective of its scope and scale, all social action seeks to apply the teachings and principles of the Faith to improve some aspect of the social or economic life of a population, however modestly. . . .

The endeavours of the worldwide Bahá'í community can be seen in terms of a number of interacting processes—the spiritual enrichment of the individual, the development of local and national communities, the maturation of administrative institutions, to mention but a few—which trace their origins back to the time of Bahá'u'lláh Himself and which gathered strength during the ministries of 'Abdu'l-Bahá and Shoghi Effendi. Under the guidance of the Universal House of Justice, these processes have continued to advance steadily: the scope of their influence has gradually been extended and new dimensions added to their operation. Social and economic development is among them. This particular process, pursued most notably through a variety of educational activities down the years, received considerable impetus in 1983, when the House of Justice, in a message dated 20 October, asked for "systematic attention" to be given to this area of activity following the rapid expansion of the Bahá'í community during the 1970s.

The 1983 message emphasized that progress in the development field would depend largely on natural stirrings at the grassroots of the community. It also announced the establishment of the Office of Social and Economic Development (OSED) at the Bahá'í World Centre to "promote and coordinate the activities of the friends" in this field.

. . . In September 1993, the document "Bahá'í Social and Economic Development: Prospects for the Future," prepared at the World Centre, was approved by the Universal House of Justice for use by OSED in orienting and guiding the work in this area. It set the stage for the next ten years of activity and beyond. Drawing on the significant body of experience that had accumulated over the preceding decade, the document elaborated several features common to all such efforts. Awareness worldwide of the nature of Bahá'í social and economic development grew significantly during this period as a result, and a highly consistent, much more systematic approach began to take shape. The vision that emerged at the time called for the promotion of development activities at different levels of complexity. Most central to this vision was the question of capacity building. That activities should start on a modest scale and only grow in complexity in keeping with available human resources was a concept that gradually came to influence development thought and practice.

In 2001, the Universal House of Justice introduced to the Bahá'í world the concept of a cluster—a geographic construct, generally defined as a group of villages or as a city with its surrounding suburbs, intended to assist in planning and implementing activities associated with community life. This step was made possible by the establishment of training institutes at the national and regional levels during the 1990s, which employed a system of distance education to reach large numbers with a sequence of courses designed to increase capacity for service. The House of Justice encouraged the Bahá'í world to extend this system progressively to more and more clusters in order to promote their steady progress, laying first the strong spiritual foundations upon which a vibrant community life is built. Efforts in a cluster were initially to focus on the multiplication of certain core activities, open to all of the inhabitants, but with a view to developing the collective capacity needed to address in due time various aspects of the social and economic life of the population as well.

. . . The mode of operation adopted in the area of social and economic development, in common with other areas of Bahá'í activity, is one of learning in action. When efforts are carried out in a learning mode—characterized by constant action, reflection, consultation, and study—visions and strategies are re-examined time and again. As tasks are accomplished, obstacles removed, resources multiplied, and lessons learned, modifications are made in goals and methods. The learning process, which is given direction through appropriate institutional arrangements, unfolds in a way that resembles the growth and differentiation of a living organism. Haphazard change is avoided, and continuity of action maintained.

. . . Among the elements most relevant to social action are statements that define the character of progress—that civilization has both a material and a spiritual dimension, that humanity is on the threshold of its collective maturity, that there are destructive and constructive forces operating in the world which serve to propel humanity along the path towards its full maturity, that the relationships necessary to sustain society must be recast in the light of Bahá'u'lláh's Revelation, that the transformation required must occur simultaneously within human consciousness and the structure of social institutions. . . .

Other elements that speak to the nature of social action are derived from a particular perspective on the role of knowledge in the development of society. The complementarity of science and religion, the imperative of spiritual and material education, the influence of values inherent to technology on the organization of society, and the relevance of appropriate technology to social progress are among the issues involved. . . .

Finally, at the heart of the conceptual framework for social action lie elements that describe beliefs about fundamental issues of existence, such as the nature of the human being, the purpose of life, the oneness of humanity, and the equality of men and women. While for Bahá'ís these touch on immutable convictions, they are not static—the way in which they are understood and find expression in various contexts evolves over time. . . .

. . . Bahá'í activity in the field of social and economic development seeks to promote the well-being of people of all walks of life, whatever their beliefs or background. It represents the efforts of the Bahá'í community to effect constructive social change, as it learns to apply the teachings of the Faith, together with knowledge accumulated in different fields of human endeavour, to social reality. Its purpose is neither to proclaim the Cause nor to serve as a vehicle for conversion. . . .

An exploration of the nature of social action, undertaken from a Bahá'í perspective, must necessarily place it in the broad context of the advancement of civilization. That a global civilization which is both materially and spiritually prosperous represents the next stage of a millennia-long process of social evolution provides a conception of history that endows every instance of social action with a particular purpose: to foster true prosperity, with its spiritual and material dimensions, among the diverse inhabitants of the planet. A concept of vital relevance, then, is the imperative to achieve a dynamic coherence between the practical and spiritual requirements of life. 'Abdu'l-Bahá states that while "material civilization is one of the means for the progress of the world of mankind," until it is "combined with Divine civilization, the desired result, which is the felicity of mankind, will not be attained." He continues:

Material civilization is like a lamp-glass. Divine civilization is the lamp itself and the glass without the light is dark. Material civilization is like the body. No matter how infinitely graceful, elegant and beautiful it may be, it is dead. Divine civilization is like the spirit, and the body gets its life from the spirit, otherwise it becomes a corpse. It has thus been made evident that the world of mankind is in need of the breaths of the Holy Spirit. Without the spirit the world of mankind is lifeless, and without this light the world of mankind is in utter darkness.

To seek coherence between the spiritual and the material does not imply that the material goals of development are to be trivialized. It does require, however, the rejection of approaches to development which define it as the transfer to all societies of the ideological convictions, the social structures, the economic practices, the models of governance—in the final analysis, the very patterns of life—prevalent in certain highly industrialized regions of the world. When the material and spiritual dimensions of the life of a community are kept in mind and due attention is given to both scientific and spiritual knowledge, the tendency to reduce development to the mere consumption of goods and services and the naive use of technological packages is avoided. Scientific knowledge, to take but one simple example, helps the members of a community to analyse the physical and social implications of a given technological proposal—say, its environmental impact—and spiritual insight gives rise to moral imperatives that uphold social harmony and that ensure technology serves the common good. Together, these two sources of knowledge tap roots of motivation in individuals and communities, so essential in breaking free from the shelter of passivity, and enable them to uncover the traps of consumerism.

Although the relevance of scientific knowledge to development efforts is readily acknowledged in the world at large, there appears to be less agreement on the part to be played by religion. Too often views about religion carry with them notions of division, strife, and repression, creating a reluctance to turn to it as a source of knowledge—even among those who question the adequacy of entirely materialistic approaches. Interestingly, the high esteem in which science is held does not necessarily imply that its practice and purpose are well understood. Its underlying meaning, too, is surrounded by misconception. Not infrequently it is conceived in terms of the application of certain techniques and formulas, which, as if by magic, lead to this or that effect. It is not surprising, then, that what is considered to be religious knowledge is not in harmony with science, and much of what is propagated in the name of science denies the spiritual capacities cultivated by religion.

Social action, of whatever size and complexity, should strive to remain free of simplistic and distorted conceptions of science and religion. To this end, an imaginary duality between reason and faith—a duality that would confine reason to the realm of empirical evidence and logical argumentation and which would associate faith with superstition and irrational thought—must be avoided. The process of development has to be rational and systematic—incorporating, for example, scientific capabilities of observing, of measuring, of rigorously testing ideas—and at the same time deeply aware of faith and spiritual convictions. In the words of 'Abdu'l-Bahá: "faith compriseth both knowledge and the performance of good works." Faith and reason can best be understood as attributes of the human soul through which insights and knowledge can be gained about the physical and the spiritual dimensions of existence. They make it possible to recognize the powers and capacities latent in individuals and in humanity as a whole and enable people to work for the realization of these potentialities.

. . . A civilization befitting a humanity which, having passed through earlier stages of social evolution, is coming of age will not emerge through the efforts exerted by a select group of nations or even a network of national and international agencies. Rather, the challenge must be faced by all of humanity. Every member of the human family has not only the right to benefit from a materially and spiritually prosperous civilization but also an obligation to contribute towards its construction. Social action should operate, then, on the principle of universal participation.

. . . What appears to be called for in any given region, microregion or cluster is the involvement of a growing number of people in a collective process of learning, one which is focused on the nature and dynamics of a path that conduces to the material and spiritual progress of their villages or neighbourhoods. Such a process would allow its participants to engage in the generation, application, and diffusion of knowledge, a most potent and indispensable force in the advancement of civilization.

In this connection, it is important to realize that the application and propagation of existing knowledge is invariably accompanied by the generation of new knowledge—much of which takes the form of insights acquired through experience. Here the systematization of learning is crucial. As a group of people working at the grassroots begins to gain experience in social action, the first lessons learned may consist of little more than occasional stories, anecdotes, and personal accounts. Over time, patterns tend to emerge which can be documented and carefully analysed. To facilitate the systematization of knowledge, appropriate structures have to be put in place at the local level, among them institutions and agencies invested with authority to safeguard the integrity of the learning process and to ensure that it is not reduced to opinion or the mere collection of various experiences—in short, to see to it that veritable knowledge is generated. In this regard, the authority invested in the institutions of the Administrative Order working at the grassroots to harmonize individual volition with collective will endows the Bahá'í community with a remarkable capacity to nurture participation.

No matter how essential, a process of learning at the local level will remain limited in its effectiveness if it is not connected to a global process concerned with the material and spiritual prosperity of humanity as a whole. Structures are required, then, at all levels, from the local to the international, to facilitate learning about development. . . .

. . . When development is seen in terms of the participation of more and more people in a collective process of learning, then the concept of capacity building assumes particular importance. Thus, while any instance of social action would naturally aim at improving some aspect of the life of a population, it cannot focus simply on the provision of goods and services—an approach to development so prevalent in the world today, one which often carries with it attitudes of paternalism and which employs methods that disempower those who should be the protagonists of change. Setting and achieving specific goals to improve conditions is a legitimate concern of social action; yet, far more essential is the accompanying rise in the capacity of the participants in an endeavour to contribute to progress. Of course, the imperative to build capacity is not only relevant to the individual, important though that may be; it is equally applicable to institutions and the community, the other two protagonists in the advancement of civilization.

At the level of the individual, the influence of the training institute is vital. As it helps to equip individuals with the spiritual insights and knowledge, the qualities and attitudes, and the skills and abilities needed to carry out acts of service integral to Bahá'í community life, the institute creates a pool of human resources that makes it possible for endeavours of social and economic development to flourish. The participants in such endeavours are able to acquire, in turn, knowledge and skills pertinent to the specific areas of action in which they are engaged—health, agricultural production, and education, to name but a few—while continuing to strengthen those capacities already cultivated by the institute, for instance, fostering unity in diversity, promoting justice, participating effectively in consultation, and accompanying others in their efforts to serve humanity.

Similarly, the question of institutional capacity requires due attention. As the institutions of the Faith gain experience, particularly in the context of their efforts to ensure that the provisions of the global Plans are met, they become increasingly adept at offering assistance, resources, encouragement, and loving guidance to appropriate initiatives; at consulting freely and harmoniously among themselves and with people they serve; and at channelling individual and collective energies towards the transformation of society. So, too, must every effort pursued in the sphere of social action consider the question of institutional capacity. After all, even the smallest group of individuals labouring at the grassroots must be able to maintain a consultative environment characterized by qualities of honesty, fairness, patience, tolerance, and courtesy. At a higher level of complexity, an organization dedicated to social action needs to develop the capacity to read society and identify the forces operating within it, to translate a vision of progress into projects and distinct, interconnected lines of action, to manage financial resources, and to interact with both governmental and non-governmental agencies.

The building of capacity in individuals and institutions goes hand in hand with the development of communities. In villages and neighbourhoods throughout the world, Bahá'ís are engaged in activities that enrich the devotional character of their communities, that tend to the spiritual education of children, that enhance the spiritual perception of junior youth and strengthen their powers of expression, and that enable increasing numbers to explore the application of the teachings of the Faith to their individual and collective lives. A process of community development, however, needs to reach beyond the level of activity and concern itself with those modes of expression and patterns of thought and behaviour that are to characterize a humanity which has come of age. In short, it must enter into the realm of culture. Viewed in this light, social action can become an occasion to raise collective consciousness of such vital principles as oneness, justice, and the equality of women and men; to promote an environment distinguished by traits such as truthfulness, equity, trustworthiness, and generosity; to enhance the ability of a community to resist the influence of destructive social forces; to demonstrate the value of cooperation as an organizing principle for activity; to fortify collective volition; and to infuse practice with insight from the teachings. For, in the final analysis, many of the questions most central to the emergence of a prosperous global civilization are to be addressed at the level of culture.

. . . Social action can range from fairly informal efforts of limited duration undertaken by small groups of individuals to programmes of social and economic development with some level of complexity and sophistication implemented by Bahá'í-inspired organizations. Experience makes clear that the interplay of processes that give rise to social action does not lend itself to a single formulaic description. Irrespective of circumstances, however, the scope and complexity of social action at any given moment must be commensurate with the human resources available in a community to carry it forward. What is more, ownership of the undertaking rests with the community itself, which suggests the existence of a certain degree of collective will.

Efforts, whatever their specific nature, generally begin on a modest scale. Often, in a locality where the educational activities of the training institute are firmly established and a pronounced sense of community exists, the first stirrings of heightened social awareness can be observed in the emergence of a small group which, addressing a particular social and economic reality, initiates a simple set of appropriate actions. While some efforts of this kind will naturally come to a close when their objectives have been met, others will continue. Insistence on perpetuating or even expanding every initiative, whether in terms of number of participants, expenditure, geographical coverage or complexity of work, is counterproductive. Yet there may be circumstances in which efforts will, through a continuous process of consultation, action, and reflection, give rise to an endeavour of a more sustained nature. What is important in such cases is that those involved be allowed to increase the range of their activities in an organic fashion, without undue pressure from opinions that are often based solely on theoretical considerations. The process moves forward in a flexible way as they reflect on the results of experience. The Local Spiritual Assembly, of course, serves as the voice of moral authority to make certain that, as small groups of individuals strive to improve conditions, the integrity of their endeavours is not compromised. It also remains ever vigilant, ensuring that efforts do not run counter to the overall direction in which the community is moving.

At some point, members of the community may also be able to take advantage of educational programmes promoted by a Bahá'í-inspired organization operating in the region, supported by OSED. The steady expansion of such a programme in the community will serve to increase its human resources and to reinforce organizational structures that sustain ongoing work. Eventually many of those who benefit from such programmes will, in turn, bend their energies towards the implementation of the kind of grassroots social action mentioned above. Yet, here again, whatever the ultimate vision, care is taken to begin work in a single area of action and to expand activities gradually over time. A community school, for example, can in principle become a centre for activities such as agricultural production, health education, and family counselling. But, in most cases, it is advisable for it to start simply as a school, focusing all of its resources on the children it proposes to serve.

. . . "Social change," the Universal House of Justice made clear in its Rid-ván 2010 message, "is not a project that one group of people carries out for the benefit of another," and in general Bahá'ís from one area do not establish development projects for others. The movement of individuals from community to community, and across borders, does occur however, and here every Bahá'í is guided by the words of Bahá'u'lláh: "Shut your eyes to estrangement, then fix your gaze upon unity." When Bahá'ís move residence or travel to another place in the context of some work, they form part of the collectivity of their new local communities, and all the others also see them as such. They now come under the guidance of local institutions, which are responsible for facilitating the flow of knowledge and for channelling the energies of every member of their communities; the idea of an expert from outside being allowed to impose his or her professional aspirations on the local population is thus avoided.

In the efforts of Bahá'ís everywhere, then, can be seen the emergence of a global community which, connected through its institutions, is striving to establish a pattern of activity that gives due respect to local autonomy without creating a sense of isolation from the whole, that attaches importance to material means without allowing them to become instruments of control, that provides for the flow of knowledge without introducing paternalistic attitudes, that strengthens capacity in individuals without any regard for their economic background. While vigorously engaged in activities to improve their immediate surroundings, Bahá'ís feel part of a process of development that is global in scope and influence.

. . . Social action, it has been suggested in this paper, is to be carried out in the context of a much larger enterprise—namely, the advancement of a civilization that ensures the material and spiritual prosperity of the entire human race. The fundamental teachings of the Faith that will inspire this civilization, some of which have been mentioned in these pages, need to find expression in the sphere of social action. Clearly, the application of the requisite principles to the social and material progress of communities involves a vast process of learning.

In general, a challenge for any instance of social action is to ensure consistency—among the explicit and implicit convictions which underpin an initiative, the values promoted by it, the attitudes adopted by its participants, the methods they employ, and the ends they seek. Achieving consistency between belief and practice is no small task: a deep-seated recognition of the oneness of humanity should prevent all efforts from fostering disunity, isolation, separateness or competition; an unshakeable conviction in the nobility of human beings, capable of subduing their lower passions and evincing heavenly qualities, should serve to protect against prejudice and paternalism, both of which violate the dignity of people; an immutable belief in justice should guide an endeavour to allocate resources according to the real needs and aspirations of the community rather than the whims and wishes of a privileged few; the principle of the equality of women and men should open the way not only for women to assume their role as protagonists of development and benefit from its fruits but also for the experience of that half of the world's population to be given more and more emphasis in development thought. These few examples illustrate how closely spiritual principles are to guide development practice.

If contradictions are to be avoided, the participants in an endeavour need to become increasingly aware of the environment within which their work advances. On the one hand, they are to freely draw insights from the range of philosophies, academic theories, community programmes and social movements within that environment and to keep current with the technological trends that influence progress. On the other hand, they should remain watchful lest they allow the teachings to be bent into conformity with this or that ideology, intellectual fad or fashionable practice. In this connection, the capacity to measure the value of prevalent approaches, ideas, attitudes, and methods in the balance of the Faith is vital. This capacity enables one, for example, to uncover the aggrandizement of self so often lying behind initiatives that are nominally concerned with empowerment, to discern the tendency of certain development efforts to foist upon the poor an entirely materialistic worldview, to perceive the subtle ways in which competitiveness and greed can be promoted in the name of justice and prosperity, and ultimately to abandon the notion that one or another theory or movement which may fleetingly acquire some prominence in the wider society can provide a shortcut to meaningful change. . . . (Prepared by the Office of Social and Economic Development at the Bahá'í World Center on the subject of social action, on behalf of the Universal House of Justice, letter dated 26 November 2012, to all National Spiritual Assemblies)

As you are no doubt well aware, in discussing the principle of non-involvement in politics, Shoghi Effendi wrote that Bahá'ís are to "refrain from associating themselves, whether by word or by deed, with the political pursuits of their respective nations, with the policies of their governments and the schemes and programs of parties and factions." In political controversies, they "should assign no blame, take no side, further no design, and identify themselves with no system prejudicial to the best interests" of their "world-wide Fellowship." They are called to "avoid the entanglements and bickerings inseparable from the pursuits of the politician." And they are to "rise above all particularism and partisanship, above the vain disputes, the petty calculations, the transient passions that agitate the face, and engage the attention, of a changing world." Bahá'ís and Bahá'í institutions should not take positions on the political decisions of governments, including disputes among governments of different nations; should refrain from becoming involved in debates surrounding any political controversy; and should not react, orally or otherwise, in a manner that could be taken as evidence of support for a partisan political stance. It is not for a Bahá'í, in offering social commentary, to vilify specific individuals, organizations, or governments or to make attacks on them. Indeed, the Guardian specifically cautioned the friends against referring to political figures in their public remarks, whether in criticism or support.

Furthermore, Bahá'u'lláh and 'Abdu'l-Bahá enjoined Bahá'ís to be obedient to the government of their land. Unity, order, and cooperation are the basis for sound and lasting change. Even civil disobedience, in the form of a conscious decision to violate the law to effect social change, is not acceptable for Bahá'ís—whatever merit it appears to have had in particular political settings. Ultimately, obedience to government has a bearing on the unity of the Bahá'í community itself. In a letter written on his behalf, Shoghi Effendi stated that individual Bahá'ís should not become immersed in the "faulty systems of the world" or judge their government as "just or unjust—for each believer would be sure to hold a different viewpoint, and within our own Bahá'í fold a hotbed of dissension would spring up and destroy our unity." These considerations, however, do not imply an endorsement of the actions or policies of one's government. As Shoghi Effendi explained in another letter written on his behalf: "The principle of obedience to government does not place any Bahá'í under the obligation of identifying the teachings of his Faith with the political program enforced by the government. For such an identification, besides being erroneous and contrary to both the spirit as well as the form of the Bahá'í message, would necessarily create a conflict within the conscience of every loyal believer."

The principles of non-involvement in politics and obedience to government, far from being obstacles to social change, are aspects of an approach set forth in the Bahá'í writings to implement effective remedies for and address the root causes of the ills afflicting society. This approach includes active involvement in the life of society as well as the possibility of influencing and contributing to the social policies of government by all lawful means. Indeed, service to others and to society is a hallmark of the Bahá'í life. And Shoghi Effendi has explained that "the machinery of the Cause has been so fashioned, that whatever is deemed necessary to incorporate into it in order to keep it in the forefront of all progressive movements, can, according to the provisions made by Bahá'u'lláh, be safely embodied therein." . . .

There can be no question then that Bahá'ís are committed to efforts toward social transformation. "Much as the friends must guard against in any way ever seeming to identify themselves or the Cause with any political party," Shoghi Effendi, through his secretary, cautioned, "they must also guard against the other extreme of never taking part, with other progressive groups, in conferences or committees designed to promote some activity in entire accord with our teachings—such as, for instance, better race relations." This involvement in activities for social reform and well-being can in certain circumstances even extend to taking part in demonstrations. A letter written on the Guardian's behalf indicated that he did not see any objection to Bahá'í students taking part as Bahá'ís in a protest concerning racial prejudice on campus, since "there was nothing political about it" and "he does not see how they could remain indifferent when fellow-students were voicing our own Bahá'í attitude on such a vital issue and one we feel so strongly about." Thus, individual Bahá'ís are free to participate in those efforts and activities, such as peaceful rallies, that uphold constructive aims in consonance with the Bahá'í teachings, for example, the advancement of women, the promotion of social justice, the protection of the environment, the elimination of all forms of discrimination, and the safeguarding of human rights.

In deciding whether it would be appropriate for Bahá'ís to participate in particular public activities, a crucial distinction should be drawn between those events that have a partisan political character and those that do not. A further distinction can be drawn between those activities that are fully in keeping with the teachings and that can be supported explicitly by Bahá'í institutions and those where the situation is less clear, in which Bahá'í institutions should not participate but in which individuals can be given some latitude to make a personal decision to take part, without in any way implying that they are representing the Faith directly by their choice. If a believer harbors any doubt as to the appropriateness of involvement with a particular event or approach, guidance should be sought from the National Spiritual Assembly, which is in the best position to evaluate the specific circumstances and is responsible for making the final determination on such questions.

Beyond this clarification of basic principles, there are other important considerations. Too often political goals, even when pursued in the name of justice, are a chimera, for the fundamental partisanship in contemporary political life means policies are often implemented without building consensus and consequently seeds of discontent and continuing political struggle are sown. Conflict and contention ultimately yield more conflict and contention. Eliminating social problems, rather than merely ameliorating them to an extent, requires unity of thought as well as action, an open heart as well as an open hand—conditions which Bahá'u'lláh's Revelation is intended to bring about.

For many decades following the second great war of the twentieth century, humanity moved, with fits and starts, toward the promise of a united world. The failure to complete the project of the unification of nations, however, left gaps in relations in which supranational problems could fester and threaten the security and well-being of peoples and states, leading to a recrudescence of prejudice, of divers expressions of factionalism, and of virulent nationalism that are the very negation of Bahá'u'lláh's message of peace and oneness.

One of the current features of the process of the disintegration of the old world order manifest in the United States is the increasing polarization and fragmentation that has come to characterize so much of political and social life. There has been a hardening of viewpoints, increased incivility, an unwillingness to compromise or even entertain differing perspectives, and a tendency to automatically take sides and fight. Science and religion, two great lights that should guide human progress, are often compromised or swept aside. Matters of moral principle and questions of justice are reduced to intractable liberal or conservative viewpoints, and the country is increasingly divided along divergent lines. In this context, the friends have to hold steadfastly to the Bahá'í teachings and consultative methods and not allow their pursuit of noble aims and high aspirations to draw them into one side or the other of fruitless debates and contentious processes.

In their reflections on how to contribute to the betterment of the world, Bahá'ís will undoubtedly recognize that demonstrations are not the only, or even the most effective, means available to them. Rather, they can learn and grow in capacity over time to help their fellow citizens to frame concerns in a way that rises above fissures, to share views in a manner that transcends divisive approaches, and to create and participate in spaces to work together in the quest to enact solutions to the problems that bedevil their nation. As

Bahá'u'lláh stated: "Say: no man can attain his true station except through his justice. No power can exist except through unity. No welfare and no well-being can be attained except through consultation." In this light, justice is indeed essential to resist the vain imaginings and idle fancies of social and political machinations, to see reality with one's own eyes, and to identify the requirements for an equitable social order. But then unity is essential— forged through consultative processes, including action and reflection—to achieve the power required for positive social change.

Unfortunately, sometimes when approaching such important and deeply-felt matters, the friends can create dichotomies where none exist. Thus, for example, it is contended that one must choose between either non-involvement in politics or social action; either teaching the Faith or involvement with society; either the institute process and the community-building activities it fosters or a program for race unity; and so on. Such apparent conflicts can be greatly dissipated by keeping in mind Shoghi Effendi's advice, conveyed in a letter written on his behalf, to conceive of the teachings as one great whole with many facets. "Truth may, in covering different subjects, appear to be contradictory," the same letter indicated, "and yet it is all one if you carry the thought through to the end." A careful reading of the Bahá'í writings and the guidance of the House of Justice can clarify how two matters that appear to be in tension with one another are coherent once the concepts and principles that connect them are understood. Particular circumstances in a locality, timeliness, and the periodic need for focus also have a bearing on such issues.

In a recent letter written on its behalf, the House of Justice explained to your National Assembly that the scope of the Five Year Plan offers ample opportunities for believers to address the social concerns of their communities and society as a whole. The Plan's activities for sustained growth and community building lie at the heart of a broad scheme for social transformation. The friends are called to three simultaneous, overlapping, and coherent areas of action: community-building efforts in clusters; projects and activities for social action; and involvement in the discourses of society, whether in neighborhoods or in personal or professional associations. An assessment of the efforts of Bahá'ís across the United States will reveal that there is already an army of believers working in all strata of society to promote the Bahá'í teachings and combat the spiritual and social ills afflicting their country. As the learning process that has proven to be so effective in the expansion and consolidation work worldwide is increasingly employed in all endeavors, the capacity of individuals, communities, and institutions to apply Bahá'u'lláh's healing remedy to achieve profound and lasting change will become ever more pronounced, assisting the nation along the path of its destiny. (On behalf of the Universal House of Justice, letter dated 27 April 2017, to an individual believer)

The Bahá'í teachings unequivocally proclaim the essential oneness of God and unity of all religions. "There can be no doubt whatever," Bahá'u'lláh asserts, "that the peoples of the world, of whatever race or religion, derive their inspiration from one heavenly Source, and are the subjects of one God." He explains that the Founders of the world religions, the great universal Educators of humanity, share a common purpose to unite humanity and ensure the advancement of civilization. "They all abide in the same tabernacle, soar in the same heaven, are seated upon the same throne, utter the same speech, and proclaim the same Faith." He urges the peoples of the world to "consort with the followers of all religions in a spirit of friendliness and fellowship." And He further states:

> That the divers communions of the earth, and the manifold systems of religious belief, should never be allowed to foster the feelings of animosity among men, is, in this Day, of the essence of the Faith of God and His Religion. These principles and laws, these firmly established and mighty systems, have proceeded from one Source, and are the rays of one Light. That they differ one from another is to be attributed to the varying requirements of the ages in which they were promulgated.

At the same time, Bahá'u'lláh offers a stark warning about the pernicious effects of religious prejudice, stating that "religious fanaticism and hatred are a world-devouring fire, whose violence none can quench. The Hand of Divine power can, alone, deliver mankind from this desolating affliction." He calls upon Bahá'ís to act so that "the tumult of religious dissension and strife that agitateth the peoples of the earth may be stilled, that every trace of it may be completely obliterated."

'Abdu'l-Bahá stresses that "the divine religions must be the cause of one-ness among men, and the means of unity and love; they must promulgate universal peace, free man from every prejudice, bestow joy and gladness, exercise kindness to all men and do away with every difference and distinc-tion." He furthermore observes that "religion must be the cause of fellowship and love. If it becomes the cause of estrangement then it is not needed, for religion is like a remedy; if it aggravates the disease then it becomes unneces-sary." The purpose of true religion, then, is to produce good fruits, and if, in the name of religion, conflict, prejudice, and hatred are engendered among humanity, this is due to fallible human interpretations and impositions that can be overcome by seeking the divine truth that lies at the heart of every religion. "May fanaticism and religious bigotry be unknown," He urges, "all humanity enter the bond of brotherhood, souls consort in perfect agree-ment, the nations of earth at last hoist the banner of truth, and the religions of the world enter the divine temple of oneness, for the foundations of the heavenly religions are one reality."

Religious prejudice forms a formidable barrier to the progress and well-being of humanity. This prejudice, along with many others, permeates the structures of society and is systematically impressed on individual and col-lective consciousness. In fact, it is often deliberately fostered and exploited through manipulation and propaganda, using methods that ignore truth and promote self-serving agendas for political or other expediencies. A system of governance befitting a mature human race will, in time, abandon such ways of dividing people to obtain and consolidate power, of promoting agendas benefiting only certain groups or segments within society at the expense of others, and of directing the masses "toward that prejudice and fanaticism which subvert the very base of civilization." It will instead unite people and channel capacities and resources to promote "the peace and well-being and happiness, the knowledge, culture and industry, the dignity, value and station, of the entire human race."

The destructive consequences of religious prejudice are thus of great concern to the Bahá'í community. The oneness of humankind is, after all, the pivot around which all of the teachings of Bahá'u'lláh revolve and is at once the operating principle and ultimate goal of the Bahá'í Faith. The betterment of the world, its ultimate objective, is retarded by this affliction. Further, the Bahá'í community itself has suffered the direct consequences of religious prejudice for nearly two centuries, particularly in the land of its birth.

Yet, Bahá'ís are confident that the peoples of the world can learn over time to weaken and eventually eliminate the scourge of religious prejudice. All people have the right to freedom of conscience and belief, the right to express those beliefs, and the obligation to have due regard for these same rights for others. They can then engage each other with mutual respect and find in their common values a common purpose and unity in action that contribute to the building of a better world. The Bahá'í community, for its own part, strives to foster patterns of tolerance, cooperation, and fellowship in a number of ways.

As individuals, Bahá'ís strive daily to live according to the teachings and to embody and express the principles of the Faith in action. "So free must be your thoughts and actions of any trace of prejudice—racial, religious, economic, national, tribal, class, or cultural," the House of Justice has stated, addressing the Bahá'ís of the world, "that even the stranger sees in you loving friends." Bahá'ís are taught from the earliest age about the common foundation of all the world religions, to accept and love the Founders of all of them as their own, and to embrace those of all religions or none with friendliness and fellowship.

In the affairs of the Bahá'í community, Bahá'ís are learning to transcend traditional barriers that divide people in the wider society and exacerbate tensions among people from different religious backgrounds. Shoghi Effendi explained that "every organized community enlisted under the banner of Bahá'u'lláh should feel it to be its first and inescapable obligation to nurture, encourage, and safeguard every minority belonging to any faith, race, class, or nation within it." One example is the way in which all minorities, including those from a religious minority background, are encouraged in their participation. "If any discrimination is at all to be tolerated," Shoghi Effendi has for instance stated when discussing the corrosive effects of prejudice, "it should be a discrimination not against, but rather in favour of the minority, be it racial or otherwise." The practice of Bahá'í elections is symbolic of this commitment to encouraging minorities—when a tie vote arises and one of those involved belongs to a minority group in that society, that person is unhesitatingly accorded the priority without the necessity of another vote to break the tie.

Furthermore, Bahá'ís are engaged in cities and villages across the globe in establishing a pattern of life in which increasing numbers, irrespective of background, are invited to take part. This pattern, expressive of the dynamic coherence between the material and spiritual dimensions of life, includes classes for the spiritual education of children in which they also develop a deep appreciation for the fundamental unity of the various world religions; groups that assist young people to navigate a crucial stage of their lives and to withstand the corrosive forces that especially target them; circles of study wherein participants reflect on the spiritual nature of existence and build capacity for service to the community and society; gatherings for collective worship that strengthen the devotional character of the community; and, in time, a growing range of endeavours for social and economic development. This pattern of community life is giving rise to vibrant and purposeful new communities wherein relationships are founded on the oneness of mankind, universal participation, justice, and freedom from prejudice. All are welcome. The process which is unfolding seeks to foster collaboration and build capacity within every human group—with no regard to class or religious background, with no concern for ethnicity or race, and irrespective of gender or social status—to arise and contribute to the advancement of civilization.

Another area to which the Bahá'í community has been giving a progressively greater share of attention is participation in discourses which have a significant bearing on the well-being of humanity. Its efforts in this regard have been directed towards engaging in conversations in a widening range of spaces at the international and national levels, working shoulder to shoulder with like-minded organizations and individuals, seeking, where possible, to stimulate consultative processes and draw out underlying principles around which agreement and mutual understanding can be built. A number of these discourses, such as those on the role of religion in society, religious coexistence, and freedom of religion or belief, directly address the imperative of overcoming the challenge of religious prejudice.

In this light, the Bahá'í community has particularly been a vigorous promoter of interfaith activities since the time of their inception, working alongside others to increase understanding and cooperation among religions. The achievements of the interfaith movement were highlighted in a letter of the Universal House of Justice to the world's religious leaders in April 2002. The letter also emphasized that the efforts of the movement to date, however constructive, were not sufficient to effectively address the growing challenge posed by religious prejudice and fanaticism; more was required. "With every day that passes," the letter stated "danger grows that the rising fires of religious prejudice will ignite a worldwide conflagration the consequences of which are unthinkable," and the House of Justice urged earnest consideration of the challenge this poses for religious leadership.

Fundamentally, a great share of the Bahá'í community's efforts has been directed at addressing the root cause of religious prejudice—ignorance. "The perpetuation of ignorance," the House of Justice has stated, "is a most grievous form of oppression; it reinforces the many walls of prejudice that stand as barriers to the realization of the oneness of humankind. . . . Access to knowledge is the right of every human being, and participation in its generation, application and diffusion a responsibility that all must shoulder in the great enterprise of building a prosperous world civilization—each individual according to his or her talents and abilities." This orientation has particularly manifested itself in the Bahá'í community's focus on education, which has been a central concern since the inception of the Faith; in its efforts to foster in individuals a growing consciousness and capacity to recognize prejudice and to counter it; in its practice of using consultative processes in all its affairs; and in its commitment to and upholding of the dual knowledge systems of science and religion as being necessary for the advancement of civilization. Moreover, the development of the life of the mind and independent investigation of reality, which are highly prized in the Bahá'í writings, serve to equip individuals to distinguish truth from falsehood, which is so essential if prejudices, superstitious beliefs, and outworn traditions that impede unity are to be eliminated. 'Abdu'l-Bahá offers the assurance in this respect that "once every soul inquireth into truth, society will be freed from the darkness of continually repeating the past." (On behalf of the Universal House of Justice, letter dated 27 December 2017, to an individual believer)

The House of Justice appreciates your thoughtful comments and admires your unflagging efforts over many years to address the challenge of racism in your nation, particularly at a time of its overt resurgence in a manner that would justifiably give rise to despair even in the stoutest heart. However discouraging the present events, however outrageous the injustices laid bare, however intractable the problem appears, such fresh evidences of this pernicious blight on American society can come as no surprise to those friends well informed of 'Abdu'l-Bahá's dire warnings as well as Shoghi Effendi's trenchant analysis anticipating the ultimate eradication of this evil tendency from the lives and the hearts of their fellow citizens. How much more must people endure in the years ahead? The current polarization in American society makes constructive dialogue and action ever more elusive. Even those fair-minded individuals who long to free themselves and their society from this problem—surely a vast portion of the nation—are paralyzed and divided by their divergent views, unable to create the unity necessary to advance along the path of constructive change.

It is in this context that the friends must understand their sacred obligation and the possibilities that lie before them. As you have observed, since the time of 'Abdu'l-Bahá's visit to the United States Bahá'ís have, whether individually or collectively, by themselves or in collaboration with others, been continually involved in diverse efforts to address prejudice and racism and build bonds and practices of racial accord. Such efforts, though sincere and even sacrificial, have yet to be raised to a level of systematic endeavor necessary for profound and lasting social change. . . .

Among the important lessons garnered over the past two decades is that, by focusing on insights derived from the most advanced and successful activities rather than by focusing on shortcomings and weaknesses, the community can come to understand what constitutes effective action and learn to disseminate the knowledge gained. Another lesson is how to approach the development of human resources in a manner that can efficiently multiply efforts and empower those who were previously left on the margins, or were otherwise unengaged, to become protagonists of a process of community building and social change. Therefore, it is not necessary at this time to propagate in the community a separate program centered on addressing racial prejudice before progress is possible, nor is there a need to remove one by one all the obstacles you describe before dynamic efforts can be established in a single community or neighborhood that can, once proven to be effective, be widely replicated. Consider, for example, the development of the junior youth spiritual empowerment program. Years ago, it was a mere concept; today it reaches hundreds of thousands and is having a profound impact on the villages, neighborhoods, islands, and schools where it is being vigorously implemented. This capacity for social transformation, increasingly being realized in the most advanced clusters, encompasses not just the work of community building but also the engagement of the believers, both in the discourses of society in all accessible social spaces as well as in projects of social and economic development.

The 25 February 2017 letter of your National Assembly written following consultations held at the Bahá'í World Centre is not intended simply to express a renewed concern with the challenges of race in your society and certainly not to introduce a new set of activities. It is a commitment to a path of systematic action and learning, involving community building, social action, and participation in the discourses of society, from which the community will never withdraw until the problems of race are completely resolved, no matter how long and difficult the path may be. Already your

National Assembly is aware of the strivings of thousands of friends who, like yourself, are engaged in initiatives of varying scope and effectiveness along these lines; through systematization and learning there is every confidence that, as each year goes by, we will understand the issues involved more deeply, act more effectively, and enlarge the circle of those with whom we are engaged.

The House of Justice hopes that those friends in the United States who resolve to renew their commitment to uprooting racism and laying the basis for a society that reflects interracial harmony can draw insight and inspiration from the unwavering resolve of the Bahá'ís in Iran. The messages written to the friends there in recent years, most of which have been translated into English and are publicly available, are instructive in this regard. For almost two centuries, and particularly the last four decades of relentless oppression, the Bahá'ís in Iran have remained forward-looking, dynamic, vibrant, and committed to serving Iranian society. They have refused to allow apprehension and anxiety to take hold or let any calamity perturb their hearts. They have drawn on the highest reservoirs of solidarity and collaboration and responded to oppression with constructive resilience, eschewing despair, surrender, resentment, and hate and transcending mere survival, to transform conditions of ignorance and prejudice and win the respect and collaboration of their fair-minded countrymen. Those believers in the United States who have labored so persistently to promote race unity, especially the African American friends, should appreciate in their own efforts over the years the same expression of constructive resilience, born of their great love for Bahá'u'lláh, and see in the recent turmoil opportunity rather than obstacle. They cannot, as you know, respond to the current reality in the manner consuming most of their fellow citizens; they must, by word and by deed, elevate the existing conversation and set in motion constructive approaches that will prove ever more effective over time. Shoghi Effendi has explained that such problems as are now being witnessed are inevitable as the process of disintegration advances. "All humanity," a letter written on his behalf observes, "is disturbed and suffering and confused; we cannot expect to not be disturbed and not to suffer—but we don't have to be confused."

223

The way forward has never been clearer, particularly with the new initiative of your National Assembly to organize these matters within the proven framework for action guiding the Bahá'í world's systematic endeavors. (On behalf of The Universal House of Justice, letter dated 4 February 2018, to an individual believer)

THE PROMISE OF THE FUTURE

THE PROMISE OF LITERATURE

The Destiny of America

Man can withstand anything except that which is divinely intended and indicated for the age and its requirements. Now—praise be to God!—in all countries of the world, lovers of peace are to be found, and these principles are being spread among mankind, especially in this country. Praise be to God! This thought is prevailing, and souls are continually arising as defenders of the oneness of humanity, endeavoring to assist and establish international peace. There is no doubt that this wonderful democracy will be able to realize it, and the banner of international agreement will be unfurled here to spread onward and outward among all the nations of the world. I give thanks to God that I find you imbued with such susceptibilities and lofty aspirations, and I hope that you will be the means of spreading this light to all men. Thus may the Sun of Reality shine upon the East and West. The enveloping clouds shall pass away, and the heat of the divine rays will dispel the mist. The reality of man shall develop and come forth as the image of God, his Creator. The thoughts of man shall take such upward flight that former accomplishments shall appear as the play of children, for the ideas and beliefs of the past and the prejudices regarding race and religion have ever lowered and been destructive to human evolution. ('Abdu'l-Bahá, *The Promulgation of Universal Peace*, pp. 173–74)

The immediate future must, as a result of this steady, this gradual, and inevitable absorption in the manifold perplexities and problems afflicting humanity, be dark and oppressive for that nation. The world-shaking ordeal which Bahá'u'lláh, . . . has so graphically prophesied, may find it swept, to an unprecedented degree, into its vortex. Out of it it will probably emerge, unlike its reactions to the last world conflict, consciously determined to seize its opportunity, to bring the full weight of its influence to bear upon the gigantic problems that such an ordeal must leave in its wake, and to exorcise forever, in conjunction with its sister nations of both the East and the West, the greatest curse which, from time immemorial, has afflicted and degraded the human race.

Then, and only then, will the American nation, molded and purified in the crucible of a common war, inured to its rigors, and disciplined by its lessons, be in a position to raise its voice in the councils of the nations, itself lay the cornerstone of a universal and enduring peace, proclaim the solidarity, the unity, and maturity of mankind, and assist in the establishment of the promised reign of righteousness on earth. Then, and only then, will the American nation, while the community of the American believers within its heart is consummating its divinely appointed mission, be able to fulfill the unspeakably glorious destiny ordained for it by the Almighty, and immortally enshrined in the writings of 'Abdu'l-Bahá. Then, and only then, will the American nation accomplish "that which will adorn the pages of history," "become the envy of the world and be blest in both the East and the West." (Shoghi Effendi, *The Advent of Divine Justice*, ¶123–24)

Few, if any, I venture to assert, among these privileged framers and custodians of the constitution of the Faith of Bahá'u'lláh are even dimly aware of the preponderating role which the North American continent is destined to play in the future orientation of their world-embracing Cause. Nor does any appreciable number among them seem sufficiently conscious of the decisive influence which they already exercise in the direction and management of its affairs.

"The continent of America," wrote 'Abdu'l-Bahá in February, 1917, "is, in the eyes of the one true God, the land wherein the splendors of His light shall be revealed, where the mysteries of His Faith shall be unveiled, where the righteous will abide, and the free assemble." (Shoghi Effendi, *The World Order of Bahá'u'lláh*, p. 53)

Among some of the most momentous and thought-provoking pronouncements ever made by 'Abdu'l-Bahá, in the course of His epoch-making travels in the North American continent, are the following: "May this American Democracy be the first nation to establish the foundation of international agreement. May it be the first nation to proclaim the unity of mankind. May it be the first to unfurl the Standard of the Most Great Peace." And again: "The American people are indeed worthy of being the first to build the Tabernacle of the Great Peace, and proclaim the oneness of mankind. . . . For America hath developed powers and capacities greater and more wonderful than other nations. . . . The American nation is equipped and empowered to accomplish that which will adorn the pages of history, to become the envy of the world, and be blest in both the East and the West for the triumph of its people. . . . The American continent gives signs and evidences of very great advancement. Its future is even more promising, for its influence and illumination are far-reaching. It will lead all nations spiritually."

The creative energies, mysteriously generated by the first stirrings of the embryonic World Order of Bahá'u'lláh, have, as soon as released within a nation destined to become its cradle and champion, endowed that nation with the worthiness, and invested it with the powers and capacities, and equipped it spiritually, to play the part foreshadowed in these prophetic words. (Shoghi Effendi, *The Advent of Divine Justice*, ¶116–17)

"The hope which 'Abdu'l-Bahá cherishes for you," He thus urges them, "is that the same success which has attended your efforts in America may crown your endeavors in other parts of the world, that through you the fame of the Cause of God may be diffused throughout the East and the West and the advent of the Kingdom of the Lord of Hosts be proclaimed in all the five continents of the globe. . . . Thus far ye have been untiring in your labors. Let your exertions, henceforth, increase a thousandfold. Summon the people in these countries, capitals, islands, assemblies and churches to enter the Abhá Kingdom. The scope of your exertions must needs be extended. The wider its range, the more striking will be the evidences of Divine assistance. . . . Oh! that I could travel, even though on foot and in the utmost poverty, to these regions and, raising the call of Yá Bahá'u'l-Abhá in cities, villages, mountains, deserts and oceans, promote the Divine teachings! This, alas, I cannot do! How intensely I deplore it! Please God, ye may achieve it." And finally, as if to crown all His previous utterances, is this solemn affirmation embodying His Vision of America's spiritual destiny: "The moment this Divine Message is carried forward by the American believers from the shores of America and is propagated through the continents of Europe, of Asia, of Africa and of Australasia, and as far as the islands of the Pacific, this community will find itself securely established upon the throne of an everlasting dominion. Then will all the peoples of the world witness that this community is spiritually illumined and divinely guided. Then will the whole earth resound with the praises of its majesty and greatness."

It is in the light of these above-quoted words of 'Abdu'l-Bahá that every thoughtful and conscientious believer should ponder the significance of this momentous utterance of Bahá'u'lláh: "In the East the light of His Revelation hath broken; in the West have appeared the signs of His dominion. Ponder this in your hearts, O people, and be not of those who have turned a deaf ear to the admonitions of Him Who is the Almighty, the All-Praised . . . Should they attempt to conceal its light on the continent, it will assuredly rear its head in the midmost heart of the ocean, and, raising its voice, proclaim: 'I am the life-giver of the world!'"

Dearly-beloved friends! Can our eyes be so dim as to fail to recognize in the anguish and turmoil which, greater than in any other country and in a manner unprecedented in its history, are now afflicting the American nation, evidences of the beginnings of that spiritual renaissance which these pregnant words of 'Abdu'l-Bahá so clearly foreshadow? The throes and twinges of agony which the soul of a nation in travail is now beginning to experience abundantly proclaim it. Contrast the sad plight of the nations of the earth, and in particular this great Republic of the West, with the rising fortunes of that handful of its citizens, whose mission, if they be faithful to their trust, is to heal its wounds, restore its confidence and revive its shattered hopes. Contrast the dreadful convulsions, the internecine conflicts, the petty disputes, the outworn controversies, the interminable revolutions that agitate the masses, with the calm new light of Peace and of Truth which envelops, guides and sustains those valiant inheritors of the law and love of Bahá'u'lláh. Compare the disintegrating institutions, the discredited statesmanship, the exploded theories, the appalling degradation, the follies and furies, the shifts, shams and compromises that characterize the present age, with the steady consolidation, the holy discipline, the unity and cohesiveness, the assured conviction, the uncompromising loyalty, the heroic self-sacrifice that constitute the hallmark of these faithful stewards and harbingers of the golden age of the Faith of Bahá'u'lláh.

Small wonder that these prophetic words should have been revealed by 'Abdu'l-Bahá: "The East," He assures us, "hath verily been illumined with the light of the Kingdom. Ere long will this same light shed a still greater illumination upon the West. Then will the hearts of its people be vivified through the potency of the teachings of God and their souls be set aglow by the undying fire of His love." "The prestige of the Faith of God," He asserts, "has immensely increased. Its greatness is now manifest. The day is approaching when it will have cast a tremendous tumult in men's hearts. Rejoice, therefore, O denizens of America, rejoice with exceeding gladness!" (Shoghi Effendi, *The World Order of Bahá'u'lláh*, pp. 78–79)

Whatever the Hand of a beneficent and inscrutable Destiny has reserved for this youthful, this virile, this idealistic, this spiritually blessed and enviable nation, however severe the storms which may buffet it in the days to come in either hemisphere, however sweeping the changes which the impact of cataclysmic forces from without, and the stirrings of a Divine embryonic Order from within, will effect in its structure and life, we may, confident in the words uttered by 'Abdu'l-Bahá, feel assured that that great republic—the shell that enshrines so precious a member of the world community of the followers of His Father—will continue to evolve, undivided and undefeatable, until the sum total of its contributions to the birth, the rise and the fruition of that world civilization, the child of the Most Great Peace and hallmark of the Golden Age of the Dispensation of Bahá'u'lláh, will have been made, and its last task discharged. (Shoghi Effendi, letter dated 5 June 1947, in *Citadel of Faith*, p. 37)

In the future the Cause of God will spread throughout America; millions will be enlisted under its banner and race prejudice will finally be exorcised from the body politic. Of this have no doubt. It is inexorable, because it is the Will of Almighty God. (On behalf of the Universal House of Justice, letter dated 1 April 1996, to an individual believer)

Global Unity and Peace

By My Self! The day is approaching when We will have rolled up the world and all that is therein, and spread out a new order in its stead. He, verily, is powerful over all things. (Bahá'u'lláh, *Gleanings from the Writings of Bahá'u'lláh*, no. 143.3)

How vast is the tabernacle of the Cause of God! It hath overshadowed all the peoples and kindreds of the earth, and will, erelong, gather together the whole of mankind beneath its shelter. (Bahá'u'lláh, *Gleanings from the Writings of Bahá'u'lláh*, no. 43.1)

We desire but the good of the world and the happiness of the nations; yet they deem Us a stirrer up of strife and sedition worthy of bondage and banishment. . . . That all nations should become one in faith and all men as brothers; that the bonds of affection and unity between the sons of men should be strengthened; that diversity of religion should cease, and differences of race be annulled—what harm is there in this? . . . Yet so it shall be; these fruitless strifes, these ruinous wars shall pass away, and the 'Most Great Peace' shall come. . . . Yet do We see your kings and rulers lavishing their treasures more freely on means for the destruction of the human race than on that which would conduce to the happiness of mankind. . . . These strifes and this bloodshed and discord must cease, and all men be as one kindred and one family. . . . Let not a man glory in this, that he loves his country; let him rather glory in this, that he loves his kind. . . . (Bahá'u'lláh, words spoken to E. G. Browne, from his pen portrait of Bahá'u'lláh, *Compilation of Compilations,* vol. II, no. 1578)

With reference to your question as to the meaning of the passage of "he who loves his kind" the statement of Bahá'u'lláh does not refer to any special race or class of people. Rather it includes the entire human race, irrespective of any class, creed or colour. (On behalf of Shoghi Effendi, letter dated 11 March 1937, in *Lights of Guidance,* no. 1590)

The portals of His blessings are opened wide and His signs are published abroad and the glory of truth is blazing forth; inexhaustible are the blessings. Know ye the value of this time. Strive ye with all your hearts, raise up your voices and shout, until this dark world be filled with light, and this narrow place of shadows be widened out, and this dust heap of a fleeting moment be changed into a mirror for the eternal gardens of heaven, and this globe of earth receive its portion of celestial grace.

Then will aggression crumble away, and all that maketh for disunity be destroyed, and the structure of oneness be raised—that the Blessed Tree may cast its shade over east and west, and the Tabernacle of the singleness of man be set up on the high summits, and flags that betoken love and fellowship flutter from their staffs around the world until the sea of truth lift high its waves, and earth bring forth the roses and sweet herbs of blessings without end, and become from pole to pole the Abhá Paradise. ('Abdu'l-Bahá, *Selections from the Writings of 'Abdu'l-Bahá,* no. 17.5–6)

"The whole earth," Bahá'u'lláh, on the other hand, forecasting the bright future in store for a world now wrapt in darkness, emphatically asserts, "is now in a state of pregnancy. The day is approaching when it will have yielded its noblest fruits, when from it will have sprung forth the loftiest trees, the most enchanting blossoms, the most heavenly blessings." "The time is approaching when every created thing will have cast its burden. Glorified be God Who hath vouchsafed this grace that encompasseth all things, whether seen or unseen!" "These great oppressions," He, moreover, foreshadowing humanity's golden age, has written, "are preparing it for the advent of the Most Great Justice." This Most Great Justice is indeed the Justice upon which the structure of the Most Great Peace can alone, and must eventually, rest, while the Most Great Peace will, in turn, usher in that Most Great, that World Civilization which shall remain forever associated with Him Who beareth the Most Great Name. (Shoghi Effendi, *The Promised Day is Come*, ¶8)

The Lord of all mankind hath fashioned this human realm to be a Garden of Eden, an earthly paradise. If, as it must, it findeth the way to harmony and peace, to love and mutual trust, it will become a true abode of bliss, a place of manifold blessings and unending delights. Therein shall be revealed the excellence of humankind, therein shall the rays of the Sun of Truth shine forth on every hand. ('Abdu'l-Bahá, *Selections from the Writings of 'Abdu'l-Bahá*, no. 220)

In cycles gone by, though harmony was established, yet, owing to the absence of means, the unity of all mankind could not have been achieved. Continents remained widely divided, nay even among the peoples of one and the same continent association and interchange of thought were wellnigh impossible. Consequently intercourse, understanding and unity amongst all the peoples and kindreds of the earth were unattainable. In this day, however, means of communication have multiplied, and the five continents of the earth have virtually merged into one. And for everyone it is now easy to travel to any land, to associate and exchange views with its peoples, and to become familiar, through publications, with the conditions, the religious beliefs and the thoughts of all men. In like manner all the members of the human family, whether peoples or governments, cities or villages, have become increasingly interdependent. For none is self-sufficiency any longer possible, inasmuch as political ties unite all peoples and nations, and the bonds of trade and industry, of agriculture and education, are being strengthened every day. Hence the unity of all mankind can in this day be achieved. Verily this is none other but one of the wonders of this wondrous age, this glorious century. Of this past ages have been deprived, for this century—the century of light—hath been endowed with unique and unprecedented glory, power and illumination. Hence the miraculous unfolding of a fresh marvel every day. Eventually it will be seen how bright its candles will burn in the assemblage of man.

Behold how its light is now dawning upon the world's darkened horizon. The first candle is unity in the political realm, the early glimmerings of which can now be discerned. The second candle is unity of thought in world undertakings, the consummation of which will erelong be witnessed. The third candle is unity in freedom which will surely come to pass. The fourth candle is unity in religion which is the corner-stone of the foundation itself, and which, by the power of God, will be revealed in all its splendor. The fifth candle is the unity of nations—a unity which in this century will be securely established, causing all the peoples of the world to regard themselves as citizens of one common fatherland. The sixth candle is unity of races, making of all that dwell on earth peoples and kindreds of one race. The seventh candle is unity of language, i.e., the choice of a universal tongue in which all peoples will be instructed and converse. Each and every one of these will inevitably come to pass, inasmuch as the power of the Kingdom of God will aid and assist in their realization. ('Abdu'l-Bahá, *Selections from the Writings of 'Abdu'l-Bahá*, no. 15.6–7)

Know thou that all the powers combined have not the power to establish universal peace, nor to withstand the overmastering dominion, at every time and season, of these endless wars. Erelong, however, shall the power of heaven, the dominion of the Holy Spirit, hoist on the high summits the banners of love and peace, and there above the castles of majesty and might shall those banners wave in the rushing winds that blow out of the tender mercy of God. ('Abdu'l-Bahá, *Selections from the Writings of 'Abdu'l-Bahá*, no. 146.6)

The age has dawned when human fellowship will become a reality.

The century has come when all religions shall be unified.

The dispensation is at hand when all nations shall enjoy the blessings of international peace.

The cycle has arrived when racial prejudice will be abandoned by tribes and peoples of the world.

The epoch has begun wherein all native lands will be conjoined in one great human family.

For all mankind shall dwell in peace and security beneath the shelter of the great tabernacle of the one living God. ('Abdu'l-Bahá, *The Promulgation of Universal Peace*, pp. 522–23)

One of the great events which is to occur in the Day of the manifestation of that Incomparable Branch [Bahá'u'lláh] is the hoisting of the Standard of God among all nations. By this is meant that all nations and kindreds will be gathered together under the shadow of this Divine Banner, which is no other than the Lordly Branch itself, and will become a single nation. Religious and sectarian antagonism, the hostility of races and peoples, and differences among nations will be eliminated. All men will adhere to one religion, will have one common faith, will be blended into one race and become a single people. All will dwell in one common fatherland, which is the planet itself. Universal peace and concord will be established among all nations. That Incomparable Branch will gather together all Israel; that is, in His Dispensation Israel will be gathered in the Holy Land, and the Jewish people who are now scattered in the East and the West, the North and the South, will be assembled together.

Now, observe that these events did not take place in the Christian Dispensation, for the nations did not enlist under that single banner—that divine Branch—but in this Dispensation of the Lord of Hosts all nations and peoples will enter beneath His shadow. Likewise Israel, which had been scattered throughout the world, was not gathered together in the Holy Land in the course of the Christian Dispensation, but in the beginning of the Dispensation of Bahá'u'lláh this divine promise, which has been clearly stated in all the Books of the Prophets, has begun to materialize. ('Abdu'l-Bahá, *Some Answered Questions*, no. 12.7–8)

The long ages of infancy and childhood, through which the human race had to pass, have receded into the background. Humanity is now experiencing the commotions invariably associated with the most turbulent stage of its evolution, the stage of adolescence, when the impetuosity of youth and its vehemence reach their climax, and must gradually be superseded by the calmness, the wisdom, and the maturity that characterize the stage of manhood. Then will the human race reach that stature of ripeness which will enable it to acquire all the powers and capacities upon which its ultimate development must depend.

Unification of the whole of mankind is the hallmark of the stage which human society is now approaching. Unity of family, of tribe, of city-state, and nation have been successively attempted and fully established. World unity is the goal towards which a harassed humanity is striving. Nation-building has come to an end. The anarchy inherent in state sovereignty is moving towards a climax. A world, growing to maturity, must abandon this fetish, recognize the oneness and wholeness of human relationships, and establish once for all the machinery that can best incarnate this fundamental principle of its life. (Shoghi Effendi, *The World Order of Bahá'u'lláh*, p. 202)

The Revelation of Bahá'u'lláh, whose supreme mission is none other but the achievement of this organic and spiritual unity of the whole body of nations, should, if we be faithful to its implications, be regarded as signalizing through its advent the *coming of age of the entire human race*. It should be viewed not merely as yet another spiritual revival in the ever-changing fortunes of mankind, not only as a further stage in a chain of progressive Revelations, nor even as the culmination of one of a series of recurrent prophetic cycles, but rather as marking the last and highest stage in the stupendous evolution of man's collective life on this planet. The emergence of a world community, the consciousness of world citizenship, the founding of a world civilization and culture—all of which must synchronize with the initial stages in the unfoldment of the Golden Age of the Bahá'í Era—should, by their very nature, be regarded, as far as this planetary life is concerned, as the furthermost limits in the organization of human society, though man, as an individual, will, nay must indeed as a result of such a consummation, continue indefinitely to progress and develop. (Shoghi Effendi, *The World Order of Bahá'u'lláh*, p. 163)

The whole of mankind is groaning, is dying to be led to unity, and to terminate its age-long martyrdom. And yet it stubbornly refuses to embrace the light and acknowledge the sovereign authority of the one Power that can extricate it from its entanglements, and avert the woeful calamity that threatens to engulf it. (Shoghi Effendi, *The World Order of Bahá'u'lláh*, p. 201)

God's purpose is none other than to usher in, in ways He alone can bring about, and the full significance of which He alone can fathom, the Great, the Golden Age of a long-divided, a long-afflicted humanity. Its present state, indeed even its immediate future, is dark, distressingly dark. Its distant future, however, is radiant, gloriously radiant—so radiant that no eye can visualize it. (Shoghi Effendi, *The Promised Day is Come*, ¶286)

That the forces of a world catastrophe can alone precipitate such a new phase of human thought is, alas, becoming increasingly apparent. That nothing short of the fire of a severe ordeal, unparalleled in its intensity, can fuse and weld the discordant entities that constitute the elements of present-day civilization, into the integral components of the world commonwealth of the future, is a truth which future events will increasingly demonstrate.

The prophetic voice of Bahá'u'lláh warning, in the concluding passages of the Hidden Words, "the peoples of the world" that "an unforeseen calamity is following them and that grievous retribution awaiteth them" throws indeed a lurid light upon the immediate fortunes of sorrowing humanity. Nothing but a fiery ordeal, out of which humanity will emerge, chastened and prepared, can succeed in implanting that sense of responsibility which the leaders of a new-born age must arise to shoulder. (Shoghi Effendi, *The World Order of Bahá'u'lláh*, p. 46)

What we witness at the present time, during "this gravest crisis in the history of civilization," recalling such times in which "religions have perished and are born," is the adolescent stage in the slow and painful evolution of humanity, preparatory to the attainment of the stage of manhood, the stage of maturity, the promise of which is embedded in the teachings, and enshrined in the prophecies, of Bahá'u'lláh. The tumult of this age of transition is characteristic of the impetuosity and irrational instincts of youth, its follies, its prodigality, its pride, its self-assurance, its rebelliousness, and contempt of discipline.

The ages of its infancy and childhood are past, never again to return, while the Great Age, the consummation of all ages, which must signalize the coming of age of the entire human race, is yet to come. The convulsions of this transitional and most turbulent period in the annals of humanity are the essential prerequisites, and herald the inevitable approach, of that Age of Ages, "the time of the end," in which the folly and tumult of strife that has, since the dawn of history, blackened the annals of mankind, will have been finally transmuted into the wisdom and the tranquility of an undisturbed, a universal, and lasting peace, in which the discord and separation of the children of men will have given way to the worldwide reconciliation, and the complete unification of the divers elements that constitute human society.

This will indeed be the fitting climax of that process of integration which, starting with the family, the smallest unit in the scale of human organization, must, after having called successively into being the tribe, the city-state, and the nation, continue to operate until it culminates in the unification of the whole world, the final object and the crowning glory of human evolution on this planet. It is this stage which humanity, willingly or unwillingly, is resistlessly approaching. It is for this stage that this vast, this fiery ordeal which humanity is experiencing is mysteriously paving the way. It is with this stage that the fortunes and the purpose of the Faith of Bahá'u'lláh are indissolubly linked. It is the creative energies which His Revelation has released in the "year sixty," and later reinforced by the successive effusions of celestial power vouchsafed in the "year nine" and the "year eighty" to all mankind, that have instilled into humanity the capacity to attain this final stage in its organic and collective evolution. It is with the Golden Age of His Dispensation that the consummation of this process will be forever associated. It is the structure of His New World Order, now stirring in the womb of the administrative institutions He Himself has created, that will serve both as a pattern and a nucleus of that world commonwealth which is the sure, the inevitable destiny of the peoples and nations of the earth. (Shoghi Effendi, *The Promised Day is Come*, ¶288–90)

Then will the coming of age of the entire human race be proclaimed and celebrated by all the peoples and nations of the earth. Then will the banner of the Most Great Peace be hoisted. Then will the worldwide sovereignty of Bahá'u'lláh—the Establisher of the Kingdom of the Father foretold by the Son, and anticipated by the Prophets of God before Him and after Him—be recognized, acclaimed, and firmly established. Then will a world civilization be born, flourish, and perpetuate itself, a civilization with a fullness of life such as the world has never seen nor can as yet conceive. Then will the Everlasting Covenant be fulfilled in its completeness. Then will the promise enshrined in all the Books of God be redeemed, and all the prophecies uttered by the Prophets of old come to pass, and the vision of seers and poets be realized. Then will the planet, galvanized through the universal belief of its dwellers in one God, and their allegiance to one common Revelation, mirror, within the limitations imposed upon it, the effulgent glories of the sovereignty of Bahá'u'lláh, shining in the plenitude of its splendor in the Abhá Paradise, and be made the footstool of His Throne on high, and acclaimed as the earthly heaven, capable of fulfilling that ineffable destiny fixed for it, from time immemorial, by the love and wisdom of its Creator. (Shoghi Effendi, *The Promised Day is Come*, ¶302)

The unity of the human race, as envisaged by Bahá'u'lláh, implies the establishment of a world commonwealth in which all nations, races, creeds and classes are closely and permanently united, and in which the autonomy of its state members and the personal freedom and initiative of the individuals that compose them are definitely and completely safeguarded. This commonwealth must, as far as we can visualize it, consist of a world legislature, whose members will, as the trustees of the whole of mankind, ultimately control the entire resources of all the component nations, and will enact such laws as shall be required to regulate the life, satisfy the needs and adjust the relationships of all races and peoples. A world executive, backed by an international Force, will carry out the decisions arrived at, and apply the laws enacted by, this world legislature, and will safeguard the organic unity of the whole commonwealth. A world tribunal will adjudicate and deliver its compulsory and final verdict in all and any disputes that may arise between the various elements constituting this universal system. A mechanism of world inter-communication will be devised, embracing the whole planet, freed from national hindrances and restrictions, and functioning with marvellous swiftness and perfect regularity. A world metropolis will act as the nerve center of a world civilization, the focus towards which the unifying forces of life will converge and from which its energizing influences will radiate. A world language will either be invented or chosen from among the existing languages and will be taught in the schools of all the federated nations as an auxiliary to their mother tongue. A world script, a world literature, a uniform and universal system of currency, of weights and measures, will simplify and facilitate intercourse and understanding among the nations and races of mankind. In such a world society, science and religion, the two most potent forces in human life, will be reconciled, will cooperate, and will harmoniously develop. The press will, under such a system, while giving full scope to the expression of the diversified views and convictions of mankind, cease to be mischievously manipulated by vested interests, whether private or public, and will be liberated from the influence of contending governments and peoples. The economic resources of the world will be organized, its sources of raw materials will be tapped and fully utilized, its markets will be coordinated and developed, and the distribution of its products will be equitably regulated.

National rivalries, hatreds, and intrigues will cease, and racial animosity and prejudice will be replaced by racial amity, understanding and cooperation. The causes of religious strife will be permanently removed, economic barriers and restrictions will be completely abolished, and the inordinate distinction between classes will be obliterated. Destitution on the one hand, and gross accumulation of ownership on the other, will disappear. The enormous energy dissipated and wasted on war, whether economic or political, will be consecrated to such ends as will extend the range of human inventions and technical development, to the increase of the productivity of mankind, to the extermination of disease, to the extension of scientific research, to the raising of the standard of physical health, to the sharpening and refinement of the human brain, to the exploitation of the unused and unsuspected resources of the planet, to the prolongation of human life, and to the furtherance of any other agency that can stimulate the intellectual, the moral, and spiritual life of the entire human race.

A world federal system, ruling the whole earth and exercising unchallengeable authority over its unimaginably vast resources, blending and embodying the ideals of both the East and the West, liberated from the curse of war and its miseries, and bent on the exploitation of all the available sources of energy on the surface of the planet, a system in which Force is made the servant of Justice, whose life is sustained by its universal recognition of one God and by its allegiance to one common Revelation—such is the goal towards which humanity, impelled by the unifying forces of life, is moving.

"One of the great events," affirms 'Abdu'l-Bahá, "which is to occur in the Day of the manifestation of that incomparable Branch is the hoisting of the Standard of God among all nations. By this is meant that all nations and kindreds will be gathered together under the shadow of this Divine Banner, which is no other than the Lordly Branch itself, and will become a single nation. Religious and sectarian antagonism, the hostility of races and peoples, and differences among nations, will be eliminated. All men will adhere to one religion, will have one common faith, will be blended into one race and become a single people. All will dwell in one common fatherland, which is the planet itself." "Now, in the world of being," He has moreover explained, "the Hand of Divine power hath firmly laid the foundations of this all-highest bounty, and this wondrous gift. Whatsoever is latent in the innermost of this holy Cycle shall gradually appear and be made manifest, for now is but the beginning of its growth, and the dayspring of the revelation of its signs. Ere the close of this century and of this age, it shall be made clear and evident how wondrous was that spring-tide, and how heavenly was that gift."

No less enthralling is the vision of Isaiah, the greatest of the Hebrew Prophets, predicting, as far back as twenty five hundred years ago, the destiny which mankind must, at its stage of maturity, achieve: "And He (the Lord) shall judge among the nations, and shall rebuke many people: and they shall beat their swords into plowshares, and their spears into pruning-hooks: nation shall not lift up sword against nation, neither shall they learn war any more . . . And there shall come forth a rod out of the stem of Jesse, and a Branch shall grow out of his roots . . . And he shall smite the earth with the rod of his mouth, and with the breath of his lips shall he slay the wicked. And righteousness shall be the girdle of his loins, and faithfulness the girdle of his reins. The wolf also shall dwell with the lamb, and the leopard shall lie down with the kid; and the calf and the young lion and the fatling together . . . And the sucking child shall play on the hole of the asp, and the weaned child shall put his hand on the cockatrice's den. They shall not hurt nor destroy in all my holy mountain: for the earth shall be full of the knowledge of the Lord, as the waters cover the sea."

The writer of the Apocalypse, prefiguring the millenial glory which a redeemed, a jubilant humanity must witness, has similarly testified: "And I saw a new heaven and a new earth: for the first heaven and the first earth were passed away; and there was no more sea. And I, John, saw the holy city, new Jerusalem, coming down from God out of heaven, prepared as a bride adorned for her husband. And I heard a great voice out of heaven saying, 'Behold, the tabernacle of God is with men, and he will dwell with them, and they shall be his people, and God himself shall be with them, and be their God. And God shall wipe away all tears from their eyes; and there shall be no more death, neither sorrow, nor crying, neither shall there be any more pain: for the former things are passed away.'"

Who can doubt that such a consummation—the coming of age of the human race—must signalize, in its turn, the inauguration of a world civilization such as no mortal eye hath ever beheld or human mind conceived? Who is it that can imagine the lofty standard which such a civilization, as it unfolds itself, is destined to attain? Who can measure the heights to which human intelligence, liberated from its shackles, will soar? Who can visualize the realms which the human spirit, vitalized by the outpouring light of Bahá'u'lláh, shining in the plenitude of its glory, will discover?

What more fitting conclusion to this theme than these words of Bahá'u'lláh, written in anticipation of the golden age of His Faith—the age in which the face of the earth, from pole to pole, will mirror the ineffable splendors of the Abhá Paradise? "This is the Day whereon naught can be seen except the splendors of the Light that shineth from the face of thy Lord, the Gracious, the Most Bountiful. Verily, We have caused every soul to expire by virtue of Our irresistible and all-subduing sovereignty. We have then called into being a new creation, as a token of Our grace unto men. I am, verily, the All-Bountiful, the Ancient of Days. This is the Day whereon the unseen world crieth out: 'Great is thy blessedness, O earth, for thou hast been made the foot-stool of thy God, and been chosen as the seat of His mighty throne!' The realm of glory exclaimeth: 'Would that my life could be sacrificed for thee, for He Who is the Beloved of the All-Merciful hath established His sovereignty upon thee, through the power of His name that hath been promised unto all things, whether of the past or of the future.'" (Shoghi Effendi, *The World Order of Bahá'u'lláh*, pp. 203–6)

ADDENDUM

Letters from the National Spiritual Assembly of the Bahá'ís of the United States to the American Bahá'í Community

"This Pivotal Juncture in Our Nation's History"

For the past several months, this Assembly has been deeply engaged in reflecting on both the condition of the society in which we live and serve and the profound responsibility we all bear to present the unifying teachings of Bahá'u'lláh to our fellow-citizens. The process has affirmed both the critical nature of this moment and the necessity of bold action to address the historic opportunity it presents.

At this pivotal juncture in our nation's history, our foremost responsibility is to everywhere affirm—in the Name of Bahá'u'lláh—the truth of the oneness of humanity in a manner that will have an impact for decades to come. We must accelerate our efforts to remove the stains of prejudice and injustice from the fabric of our society. As you take up this call with courage and zeal, we ask that you keep the following concepts in mind.

The tensions, divisions, and injustices that currently beset America are symptoms of a longstanding illness. The nation is afflicted with a deep spiritual disorder, manifest in rampant materialism, widespread moral decay, and a deeply ingrained racial prejudice. As a result, millions of our fellow Americans, subject to systemic injustices in many facets of life, are prevented from making their full contributions to society and of partaking fully in its benefits. No one is immune to this disorder—we are all members of this society and to some degree suffer the effects of its maladies. That we live in a critical time can be seen in the way essential questions of identity, social vision, and global relations are being raised to a degree not seen in decades.

Increasing numbers of our fellow-citizens are actively in search of solutions both moral and practical to answer them.

The resolution to these challenges lies in recognizing and embracing the truth at the heart of Bahá'u'lláh's Revelation—the incontrovertible truth that humanity is one. Ignorance of this truth—which embodies the very spirit of the Age—is itself a form of oppression, for without it, it is impossible to build a truly just and peaceful world.

The oneness of humanity is far more than a slogan or an abstract and unattainable ideal. It has profound implications for both personal behavior and for the way society is organized—challenging many current assumptions and revolutionizing our conceptions of the relationships that should exist between the individual, society, and its institutions. Awareness of the spiritual reality of human beings carries with it the moral requirement that all be given every opportunity to fulfill their potential and to contribute to the advancement of civilization. To this end, we have a twofold mission: to develop within our own community a pattern of life that increasingly reflects the spirit of the Bahá'í teachings, and to engage with others in a deliberate and collaborative effort to eradicate the ills afflicting our nation.

The teachings of the Bahá'í Faith instruct us to work to reshape society based on principles of love, inclusiveness, and reciprocity. This requires that our means be consistent with our ends—that is, by transcending current approaches that tend to divide people into contending groups, raising consciousness in such a way as to bring them together in the earnest and honest search for solutions. The language we use and the attitudes we take, while not ignoring the harsh realities that exist in the world, should appeal to the nobler aspirations of our fellow-citizens. They should reflect assurance that the vast majority of us sincerely desire justice, and must be unifying rather than divisive. Above all, our approach must be suffused with the spirit of the sacred Word, which grants us access to immense spiritual resources. Indeed, it is the one power on earth that can transform the copper of human consciousness into the gold of spiritual perception and behavior.

We have inherited a priceless legacy of service spanning more than a century, originally set in motion by 'Abdu'l-Bahá Himself. In the past two decades especially, we have obtained important insights into how our combined and various efforts make for a coherent force for progress. The more we understand the framework of action given to us in the current Five Year Plan, the better we can appreciate that it is precisely suited to the needs of the time. We are rapidly gaining the ability to engage ever-greater numbers of individuals in the work of community building who, through a sustained and meaningful process of personal and social transformation, can join together in creating effective and lasting change. The process fosters the intellectual and spiritual capacities necessary to the complex and challenging task of creating a society founded on divine principles. Surely such a convergence of capacity and opportunity is nothing less than providential.

The task of transforming an entire society will require a many-faceted approach through which a pattern of life can emerge demonstrating the rich possibilities inherent in walking the spiritual path of love and service. The Universal House of Justice, without attempting to strictly define them, has stated that these possibilities can be considered as falling into the three broad categories of expansion and consolidation, social action, and engagement in the discourses of society. They emerge organically and coherently as a community rises from one level of advancement to the next. Experience has shown how, from the humblest beginnings, a pattern of community life that includes all three dimensions can develop. All three can be seen as mutually reinforcing elements of one process—a process that must be accelerated, for it will generate the consciousness necessary to apply in both word and deed the teachings of Bahá'u'lláh to the challenges we face, not least of them the challenge of race relations. As it gains momentum, it will embrace vast numbers of people empowered to take charge of their own social and spiritual development and contribute their full share to a new way of life.

The activities at the core of our community life are the foundation for great social change. Simple as they might appear, they are, in reality, profound and revolutionary. This becomes clear as we observe systematically applied in action some of the capacities we are building through insights derived from Bahá'u'lláh's Revelation. Among them is the ability to engage in distinctive conversations of a spiritual character. We learn to converse with others about the fundamental purpose of life, the relationship of the soul with its Creator, and the implications of Bahá'u'lláh's advent and His teachings for our spiritual and social progress. We learn to create an atmosphere of reverence and devotion to God in the community, to foster a spirit of friendship and intimacy that transcends the barriers of race and class, to provide spiritual and moral education for young people, to share the lives and teachings of the Central Figures of the Faith with confidence and with sensitivity to varying situations. We also learn to walk with others on the spiritual path, in a humble posture of learning, engaging in individual and collective service for the betterment of the world. These are but a few of many examples. All these activities must increase and grow to embrace multitudes of individuals. In an ever-enlarging number of neighborhoods, for example, we will learn how best and most effectively to work among diverse populations and about the practical dimensions of interracial fellowship. Such activity—and the genuine friendships that result—will help to weaken and eventually uproot prejudice-tainted notions underlying our present social order, and can begin to undo racism in our society.

In the realm of social action, it is possible to observe the range of projects and activities that emerge organically from our community-building work and highlight those which tackle, directly or indirectly, situations with a bearing on race relations. We anticipate the emergence of more such activities as we gain in experience and capacity, and as more people become empowered to serve. In the area of discourse, we can explore and develop a conversation with the wider society which, when added to the range of conversations already cultivated by the institute process, can assist our fellow citizens to abandon the language and practices in society that have resulted in an intractable divide, unite on the basis of commonly held ideals and principles, and work together for a social order free of prejudice and characterized by unity in diversity. Such conversations will naturally come about as we pursue the work of community building at the level of neighborhoods, as well as through a diverse array of personal contacts. We can also appreciate activities of the kind in which a host of individual Bahá'ís are engaged—whether with like-minded organizations or in their professions—encouraging more Bahá'ís to similarly take advantage of opportunities in the wider community. At every level, we have much to learn from others who are striving for the same goals and with whom we can join hands in this vital and foundational work. And, through our Office of Public Affairs, we are advancing this institution's involvement in the national discourse on race drawing on insights from the various experiences of the friends and from our own previous efforts to offer a Bahá'í perspective. A process is already underway leading to a national race unity conference under the sponsorship of this Assembly, details of which will be announced in due course.

A key component of our approach is the spirit of learning. This begins with the realization that successfully giving form to the divine principles given to us by Bahá'u'lláh will require persistent effort over time. We will progress as we build on strengths that emerge through experience. If we study carefully the ways various communities are active in each one of the three broad areas of expansion and consolidation, social action, and engagement in the discourses of society, we can identify new insights and bring them to the attention of others so they can be established in more and more places. As we move forward, we will come to an increasingly profound appreciation of the rich potential inherent in this approach.

Unity and effectiveness in our work will evolve to the extent that we see our efforts as complementary and mutually enriching. By advancing energetically in all areas, we will apply our systematic approach to learning to such effect that one can envision how, in the decades ahead, Bahá'ís will contribute in an ever more effective way to the eventual eradication of racism in our country.

We take as inspiration for our service the example of 'Abdu'l-Bahá during His visit to America more than a century ago. In clear and uncompromising terms, in private meetings and public assemblies, He raised the call of the oneness of humanity. He demonstrated fully, courageously, and consistently, whether openly in large gatherings or in the smallest personal acts, the implications of that spiritual truth, and challenged others to do the same. While acknowledging its marvelous material achievements and aspirations, He unhesitatingly warned of dire consequences to American society and to the cause of world peace if her peoples failed to live up to the truth of the oneness of humanity—especially in the relations between black and white. Above all, He stressed the central and unique role ordained for the American nation in the establishment of that universal peace anticipated by all the Prophets of past ages.

Dear friends! Let us follow His shining example with a sense of urgency and with determined focus. Let us consecrate ourselves to the creation of a world in which knowledge will be the province of all; where there are no limitations imposed upon a soul by virtue of race, gender, or creed; where the material and spiritual aspects of life are in harmony; and where all of the truths essential for human progress are held sacred. To do so will require great sacrifice, courage, and audacity. A rich tapestry of community life that increasingly reflects the sublime teachings of the Blessed Beauty will not emerge of its own accord. The evils of racism, materialism, and moral decadence will be eradicated only by a love that is translated into action—such actions as deliberately going out of our way to befriend all, appreciating the indispensable contributions of all, and joining hands with all in the creation of a new world. We believe in the fundamental goodness and decency of the masses of our fellow-citizens. We are confident that Americans yearn as we do for spirituality, that they desire genuine justice and prosperity for everyone. We are assured that America's role on the world stage, however significant it has so far been, will in the future be more distinguished and praiseworthy, not because of any inherent superiority it now possesses but to the degree that its present gloom is dispelled by the Light of Bahá'u'lláh's Revelation. Surely we can, with God's assistance, and together with our sisters and brothers throughout the land, bear whatever pain and difficulties will be necessary to create a haven for a suffering and bewildered humanity.

"Address yourselves to the promotion of the well-being and tranquillity of the children of men," is Bahá'u'lláh's call to the peoples of the world. "Bend your minds and wills to the education of the peoples and kindreds of the earth, that haply the dissensions that divide it may, through the power of the Most Great Name, be blotted out from its face, and all mankind become the upholders of one Order, and the inhabitants of one City. Illumine and hallow your hearts; let them not be profaned by the thorns of hate or the thistles of malice. Ye dwell in one world, and have been created through the operation of one Will. Blessed is he who mingleth with all men in a spirit of utmost kindliness and love." And, in another instance, He counsels: "It is incumbent upon every man of insight and understanding to strive to translate that which hath been written into reality and action. . . . That one indeed is a man who, today, dedicateth himself to the service of the entire human race. The Great Being saith: Blessed and happy is he that ariseth to promote the best interests of the peoples and kindreds of the earth. In another passage He hath proclaimed: It is not for him to pride himself who loveth his own country, but rather for him who loveth the whole world. The earth is but one country, and mankind its citizens."

He especially appeals to His followers to seize the chance to make their own vital contribution to the realization of humanity's destiny:

O friends! Be not careless of the virtues with which ye have been endowed, neither be neglectful of your high destiny. Suffer not your labors to be wasted through the vain imaginations which certain hearts have devised. Ye are the stars of the heaven of understanding, the breeze that stirreth at the break of day, the soft-flowing waters upon which must depend the very life of all men, the letters inscribed upon His sacred scroll. With the utmost unity, and in a spirit of perfect fellowship, exert yourselves, that ye may be enabled to achieve that which beseemeth this Day of God.

In future communications, we will comment further on some of the themes touched on in this letter and will also share news of local and national developments. Be assured of the constancy of our prayers on your behalf.

Our love for you is limitless, our gratitude to you is inexpressible, and our confidence in you knows no bounds. (National Spiritual Assembly of the Bahá'ís of the United States, 25 February 2017)

"THE SPIRIT OF TEACHING"

With hearts filled with admiration and deepest gratitude, we salute your efforts to joyfully and meaningfully commemorate the appearance in the world two centuries ago of Bahá'u'lláh, the One Whom posterity will acclaim as "the Judge, the Lawgiver and Redeemer of all mankind." How infinitely precious was every opportunity the Bicentenary of His Birth afforded us to celebrate—with countless friends and contacts in neighborhoods, towns, and cities across the land—the immeasurable import of His example and teachings and the incalculable impact they are destined to have on the future of life on this planet!

In the United States, the Bicentenary events were attended by some 120,000 people, nearly two-thirds of them not members of the Faith. Impressive as this is, far more moving to us were stories we received from hundreds of individuals about their personal efforts to engage in meaningful conversations about the Blessed Beauty and His teachings. These testify to the devotion of the community, the receptivity of our fellow citizens, and the confirmations that descended upon all who arose to share the divine message.

Wonderful as those days were, their ultimate success will not be judged by what we did, but by what we now do. This year by no means represented the zenith of our potential as promulgators of this Cause. Rather, it fortified us for bolder and more effective teaching efforts in the years ahead. Our ardent prayer is that the spirit of teaching will so suffuse our individual and collective lives as to make of us a continually growing and invincible force for the creation of a society founded on principles of divine justice.

The time has come for a vast increase in the number and range of individual and collective teaching initiatives. Among them, devotional gatherings—where others are invited to join us in prayer and reflection on the sacred texts—can often open hearts to elevated conversations about the life and teachings of the Blessed Beauty. Continued screenings of Light to the World, coupled with discussions relating His unifying teachings to the current state of our society, will surely generate interest on the part of countless souls. A great increase in the number of firesides—where seekers have the opportunity to learn about the Faith in an atmosphere of warm hospitality—can in the aggregate serve to introduce many thousands to Bahá'u'lláh's message. Regular home visits will strengthen bonds of loving friendship and will help us to better understand each other's hopes and aspirations. Celebrations of coming Holy Days can have the same impact as those we just experienced. And there is no limit to the potential that resides in creative use of the arts as a means of attracting receptive souls. In all these and other efforts, let us introduce the universal message of Bahá'u'lláh, study His writings, and explore with our friends and contacts their implications for the reconstruction of the world. Let us see each as a portal to service, inviting those so inclined into other efforts in which we can together join hands in applying the Bahá'í teachings to the building of a new pattern of community life.

We have made historic strides in recent years, powered primarily by skills and insights we have gained from the training institute experience. Especially noteworthy is the unprecedented involvement of friends of the Faith in the life of the Bahá'í community. Of the 40,000 people now participating in core activities nationwide, approximately a third are not enrolled members of the Faith. Further, they represent a great diversity of ages and backgrounds. The achievement is significant because it reflects the spirit of love and inclusiveness that should characterize all our community's endeavors. It also reflects an understanding that all are on a spiritual journey and all are valued contributors to the task of changing the world. In our most advanced clusters, where hundreds and more are participating, we are beginning to see the emergence of regular cycles of expansion and consolidation, engagement in social action, and contributing to social discourse—in which those who until recently were unaware of the Faith are now actively involved and increasingly taking charge of their spiritual destinies.

Such emerging patterns are both an important form of growth and the foundation for sustained expansion. Yet it is essential to understand that a steady increase in the number of avowed believers is also critical and should not be regarded as a separate matter, but a natural outcome of our efforts to foster the development of an inclusive and diverse community. We seek to create the best conditions for every soul to become engaged in our community-building work, to serve and to progress, aware that each person will have different inclinations and move at a different pace. Our approach must be characterized by wisdom—always in a spirit of loving invitation, yet teaching each person according to his or her capacities and receptivity, ultimately assisting as many as possible to recognize the coming of the Promised One of All Ages.

On a practical level, we must ensure that each person we engage feels welcome to participate according to his or her interests. Some might benefit from home visits as a prelude to further engagement. Some might attend firesides all the way to enrollment before participating in institute training. Others might be eager to begin the sequence of institute courses right away. Some might attend devotional gatherings for a considerable length of time before taking part in another activity. Some will immediately engage with us in service, while others will take more time. Some may be ready sooner, others later, to formally embrace the Faith. Some may first associate with us as children or junior youth, later to be followed by their friends and family members. In every case, we must be inviting to all yet flexible in our approach, firmly assured that the confluence of all paths ultimately makes for a coherent scheme for progress. Whether serving individually or in teams, whether in focus neighborhoods or throughout our clusters, much will depend on our capacity successfully to welcome, nurture, and walk with every soul.

Dear friends! Your achievements during the Bicentenary amply proved the current potential for teaching. Go forward, then, with faith—faith that what you are striving to accomplish is God's will for the day in which we live. That it is His will for humanity to live as one family; that it is His will for every single human being to live up to his or her full potential; that it is His will for peace and justice to fill every land and for love to reign in every heart.

Be certain of His assistance. He knows you, He watches over and protects you, and He brings you victory—because you are the soldiers in His Army of Light! (National Spiritual Assembly of the Bahá'ís of the United States, 8 December 2017)

"TEACHING AND THE QUEST FOR JUSTICE"

In our February 25 letter to you last year, we illustrated how the framework of the Five Year Plan provides the most effective means to steadily and inevitably eradicate the ills that afflict our nation—racial prejudice not least among them. In our letter of December 8, we called on the friends everywhere to build on the momentum generated by their celebrations of the bicentenary of Bahá'u'lláh's birth to achieve unprecedented levels of teaching effort. At this juncture, we wish to once again address the importance of understanding our teaching work and the quest for justice as interrelated elements of a single all-encompassing process set in motion by the Blessed Beauty, to be realized through our prosecution of the successive Plans formulated by the Universal House of Justice.

Deepening our understanding of the forces at work in our society and the nature of our response as Bahá'ís—especially as outlined in the current series of Plans—is critical to the cohesiveness, strength, and progress of our community. The Supreme Body has observed that wherever an intensity of teaching and community-building activities is maintained, it serves as a strong defense against the forces of materialism that would otherwise sap the precious energies of the friends. The American people as a whole, increasingly frustrated, alarmed, and anxious, are searching for answers and for a way forward. Seeking for truth, they are daily treated to a cacophony of competing voices which, to a greater or lesser extent, rest their respective cases on faulty foundations or bespeak outmoded habits of thought and behavior. Everywhere there is an increasing longing for an authentic and credible source to which people can turn for insight and for hope. As conditions in society grow more troubled, and the needs ever more urgent and pressing, we must strive to fully appreciate both the challenges and the opportunities of the hour.

There is a wealth of guidance in the Bahá'í writings about conditions in America, the role it is destined to play in world affairs, and the challenges we are bound to face on the road toward that destiny. We commend to the careful attention of every believer certain essential texts that will both edify us and inspire our services at this critical juncture in our history. Among them are Shoghi Effendi's seminal book-length letter to the Bahá'ís of the United States and Canada, written in 1938 and published as *The Advent of Divine Justice*—especially the sections describing the spiritual prerequisites for success in teaching, which the Universal House of Justice has correlated with the capacities the Plan's framework of action is designed to foster. Likewise essential is the collection of his letters published as The World Order of Bahá'u'lláh. These writings—complementing our daily prayer, study of the sacred texts and the messages of the House of Justice, teaching, and other efforts in service—are invaluable sources of guidance and inspiration as we boldly enter the arena of action. Our permanent and seasonal schools will be arranging special programs for the study of these and other relevant texts in connection with the teaching work, and we hope that similar efforts will be made at the local level.

We cannot explore all of the themes presented to us in this guidance within the limited span of a single letter. But we do wish to call attention to a few essential concepts. First is the importance of reaching out to specific populations mentioned numerous times by 'Abdu'l-Bahá, Shoghi Effendi, and the Universal House of Justice for the unique and vital contributions they will make to the creation of the new social order envisaged by the Blessed Beauty. Fresh and revitalized efforts must be made to reach out to American Indians and African Americans. Immigrant groups should also be included for special outreach, as they too have demonstrated heightened receptivity and vast potential. We are delighted that progress is being made in various clusters on all these fronts, particularly among younger people, and increasingly involving entire families. We hope that these efforts will accelerate. To this end, we now ask for a notable increase in the number of friends choosing to live among these populations as homefront pioneers.

Bahá'u'lláh, 'Abdu'l-Bahá, and Shoghi Effendi all outlined the qualities necessary for success as a Bahá'í teacher. Among them are genuine love for all people—a love mirroring God's own love for them—demonstrating in word and deed a sincere desire for their happiness and progress. This is shown in a spirit of humility toward all, recognition of everyone's inherent capacities, a high degree of concern for the common well-being, and behavior that manifests an unbounded sense of loving fellowship. It also entails the ability to walk together with all people on the spiritual path—a path in which insights gleaned through interaction with the Word of God and their application in service are intertwined.

These qualities, characterizing individuals, institutions, and the community as a whole, provide for growing numbers everywhere to be together imbued with the spirit of the Faith. We can through systematic action—with institute training at its heart—steadily build the capacity to form deep, loving friendships inclusive of all peoples, as we pray and socialize together as true friends, provide spiritual education to our children and junior youth, consult about the conditions in our communities and act together for our common benefit, and bring insights from the Bahá'í teachings to bear on today's most pressing issues. We can envision the emergence in every locality of a rich and dynamic pattern of life, featuring a growing nucleus of those who have fully embraced the Bahá'í revelation and are active in service; beyond them a steadily enlarging circle of friends of the Faith who are also contributing in meaningful ways to the life of the community; and beyond them, still another circle of those who, whether consciously or not, are being affected by the spiritual powers released as a direct result of these efforts. This is surely the essence of our struggle for a world founded on the principles of divine justice. As we advance, this will increasingly demonstrate to a skeptical and disillusioned world the invincible power of the Cause of God.

We cannot too strongly emphasize that the need of the hour is action. Prayer, study, and reflection are all critical, to be sure—but the transforming effect of the Bahá'í revelation on ourselves and on the world can only be fully realized in the field of service. Let us move forward deliberately and prayerfully, but also urgently, to fulfill the sacred mission with which we have been entrusted by the Lord of the Age.

We are still too few in number, and the challenges ahead can seem overwhelming. Yet everything in our experience teaches us the vast benefits of serving shoulder to shoulder, of holding to a common vision, and of offering each other loving support. We know that when we try, when we help each other, when we reflect unity of purpose, when we serve together patiently, when we are true both inwardly and outwardly to our principles growing ever stronger and more effective through both steadfastness and practical experience—we attract divine confirmations and attain victory. What is more, we know that there are multitudes of wonderful, capable people eager to create a better world; people who, if given the chance, will respond with fullness of heart to the divine message.

Let us recall the words of our beloved Master, 'Abdu'l-Bahá, reminding us of the priceless opportunity that is ours—to establish once and for all a world filled with divine love and founded on justice, where every soul finds acceptance and fulfills the true purpose of life:

The Faith of the Blessed Beauty is summoning mankind to safety and love, to amity and peace; it hath raised up its tabernacle on the heights of the earth, and directeth its call to all nations. Wherefore, O ye who are God's lovers, know ye the value of this precious Faith, obey its teachings, walk in this road that is drawn straight, and show ye this way to the people. Lift up your voices and sing out the song of the Kingdom. Spread far and wide the precepts and counsels of the loving Lord, so that this world will change into another world, and this darksome earth will be flooded with light, and the dead body of mankind will arise and live; so that every soul will ask for immortality, through the holy breaths of God. (National Spiritual Assembly of the Bahá'ís of the United States, 31 January 2018)